INDIAN RESPONSE TO SHAKESPEARE

Edited by
BASAVARAJ NAIKAR

ATLANTIC

ATLANTIC PUBLISHERS AND DISTRIBUTORS

Published by
ATLANTIC PUBLISHERS AND DISTRIBUTORS
B-2, Vishal Enclave, Opp. Rajouri Garden, New Delhi-27
Phones : 5413460, 5429987

Sales Office
4215/1, Ansari Road, Darya Ganj, New Delhi-110 002
Phones : 3273880, 3285873, 3280451
Fax : 91-11-3285873
web : www.atlanticbooks.com
e-mail : info@atlanticbooks.com

ISBN 81-269-0078-4

Typeset at
APD Computer Graphics, Delhi

Printed in India at
Mehra Offset Press, Delhi

PREFACE

The myriad minded Shakespeare has captured the hearts of readers and spectators all over the world. We enjoy Shakespeare even before we understand him, because of his direct appeal to our heart. Shakespeare has always been an interesting challenge to editors, critics, translators, directors, actors and readers all over the world. All the major countries of the world have responded to his plays in their own distinct ways. Although Shakespeare was born and bred in England, he is no longer the property of England, but belongs to the entire world, because of his universal appeal. Though Shakespeare criticism has been an intellectual industry in the world, especially in England and America, one has to recognise a sort of division labour in it according to the aptitude and ability of the readers or critics. Whereas the British critics are able to hunt the sources of Shakespeare's plays, collate different editions and emend the texts, the American critics are able to analyse the themes and techniques of his plays rigorously. Whereas the German critics are able to offer philosophical interpretations of his plays, the French critics concentrate on the imagological study of Shakespeare. Whereas the Russians can offer socialistic interpretation of his plays, the Japanese critics look at him from their own perspective of Kabuki and Noh Drama.

In England and America new schools of criticism like Structuralist, Post-Structuralist and Feminist ones have been employed for the appropriation of Shakespeare as part of intellectual adventure as well as fashion. But Indian critics aping the Western intellectual trends and fashions without their equipment, if not calibre, will simply end up in a farcical job. I believe that Indians have their own role to play in the critical world. As G. Wilson Knight has pointed out long back, the Orientals can contribute a great deal to the enrichment of Shakespeare criticism by bringing the knowledge of their own distinct philosophy, religion, mysticism, dramaturgy, poetry and folklore to bear upon the interpretation of Shakespeare. The Oriental interpretation of Shakespeare will be as valid as the Occidental one. It is high time for all the Oriental scholars to realize the need for this awakening. Comparing and contrasting Shakespeare's plays, themes, techniques, imagery and style with those of indigenous playwrights will definitely yield new facets of truth and beauty of those writers. The responsibility of the Oriental critics of Shakespeare is, indeed, very great.

In India, Shakespeare has attracted the attention of all serious scholars. Shakespeare's great tragedies and last plays have a special appeal to Indians. Shakespeare criticism in India is represented by scholars like S.C. Sen Gupta, K.R. Srinivasa Iyengar, R.C. Sharma, H.H. Anniah Gowda, R.W. Desai, Amaresh Datta, Rajiva Varma, M.V. Rama Sarma, S. Viswanathan, Sukanta Chaudhuri, Basavaraj Naikar and others. Many of these Indian critics have endeavoured to articulate the Indian critical sensibility by using the tit-bits of Rasa and Dhwani concepts of Sanskrit Poetics and dove-tailing them with Western critical concepts. But there has been no systematisation or professionalisation of Rasa, Dhwani and Aucitya school of criticism in India because of lack of academic and financial support for this 'difficult' task. Most of the Shakespeare scholars in India have been working in isolation. There has been no meeting point for the Westernised Shakespeare scholars and the indigenous Shakespeare scholars of India.

Shakespeare has been quite popular on the Indian stage also, through translations and adaptations. Many plays of Shakespeare have been translated into several Indian languages and staged successfully. But unfortunately, there has been no organised effort by Indian scholars to study the advantages and disadvantages, the beauty and deformity of translations and cross-cultural adaptations. In a multi-cultural and multi-lingual country like India, the study of translations of Shakespeare's plays into various Indian languages in their historical, theoretical and applicatory aspects will yield a rich harvest of insights.

The articles in the present anthology touch upon various aspects of Shakespeare's plays, ranging from the theatrical to the literary and from the comparative to the translational approaches. R.S. Pathak discusses how the Indian scholars have tried to absorb and appropriate the spirit of Shakespeare's plays through translations, adaptations, Indianisation, enactment and cross-cultural critiques thereby demonstrating the extraordinary flexibility of Shakespeare's vision to suit different cultures. He also shows how the tenets of Sanskrit dramaturgy may be fruitfully applied to Shakespeare's plays through a brief discussion of *Hamlet*. Shabiba Khan discusses how Habib Tanveer has translated many plays of Shakespeare into Chhattisgarhi dialect which is a mixture of Bhojpuri, Bundeli, Gondi and other North-Indian dialects, in order to appeal to the heart of ordinary man. She further points out how Habib Tanveer Indianises the characters, setting and situations in many of his translations and adaptations. Mohit K. Ray shows how Shakespeare's dramatic vision is so universal and elastic that it can be appropriated even by the Kabuki stage of Japan. He discusses how the cultural situation of the Renaissance England and that in Japan were similar. The theatrical and dramatic techniques of Shakespearean plays and those of Kabuki are similar in that both are presentational rather than representational, that both rely upon men for female characters and that both Shakespeare's Globe Theatre and Tokyo Globe are alike in their globular form, multi-dimensionality and symbolism. Mohit K. Ray shows how Shakespeare, though born in Britain, belongs to the world. Basavaraj Naikar offers a comparative picture of the figure of the Jew in Marlowe and Shakespeare and shows how Shakespeare's depiction of the

Jew is more humanistic and comprehensive than Marlowe's which is Machiavellian and partial. N. Narasimha Ramayya discusses the growth of universal entropy in *Julius Caesar* very elaborately from a philosophical perspective. Shweta Khanna analyses the planes of perception in Shakespeare from an Indian philosophical perspective. Her use of Indian philosophical and parapsychological concepts like 'gross,' 'subtle' and 'causal' bodies, physical plane and astral plane in the discussion of Shakespearean characters and situations is very interesting and points a way to the Indian scholars. Basavaraj Naikar analyses Shakespeare's Great Tragedies from a Hegelian perspective and shows how the tragic heroes get themselves negated by negating the affirmative principles of life and how the tragedies point to the epic vision of Shakespeare's later plays. Sudhir Dixit draws our attention to the fact that Fate controls free will in Shakespeare's Tragedies like in Greek Tragedy and that several omens, prophesies, oracles and references to palmistry and astrology in his plays indicate the element of predetermination in life.

B.G. Tandon shows how Shakespeare, far from following the rigid rules of onstage and offstage action laid down by theorists from Plato to Ben Jonson, followed his own method of deciding the presentation of onstage and offstage action in each play according to its individual merit and contingency thereby heightening the dramatic effect on the mind of spectators. Rama Kundu looks at Shakespeare's plays from a feminist perspective and finds out that Shakespeare has ignored the 'Mother' in his plays as a dominant role either in dramatic action or in the memory of characters, barring a few exceptions. She looks at *Othello* not only from a folkloric perspective but also from a modern feminist one. Her comparison between *Othello* and Japanese and Indian folk-tales is very interesting. She shows how Othello represents the patriarchal society consisting of possessive and jealous males and suspected and wronged females. Sahdeo Chougule discusses how Hamlet suffers from loneliness and is gradually alienated from the family, society and finally from the self thereby becoming a modern existential hero. Basavaraj Naikar shows how Kuvempu has adapted Shakespeare's *Hamlet* into a typically Indian play, namely *Raktaksi* with minor changes in the nature and number of characters and situations and yet has succeeded in conveying Shakespeare's tragic vision in spite of cultural and linguistic barriers. O.P. Budholia has tried to apply a combination of Buddhist philosophy and psychoanalysis to *King Lear* and shows how Lear attains *nirvana* after undergoing a grand disillusionment. Nivedita Mukerjee highlights the spirit of reconciliation in Shakespeare's Last Plays which holds a mirror to his synthetic vision of life. Basavaraj Naikar shows how *Pericles* contains many ingredients of epic vision thereby transcending the limits of dramatic form.

Although the present anthology is a mosaic of critical approaches to Shakespeare, the seminal ideas contained in it can be expanded into systematic theories in future by serious scholars of India.

BASAVARAJ NAIKAR
Editor

CONTENTS

1

Indian Response to Shakespeare

—R.S. Pathak

"WHO NEEDS Shakespeare?" asks Sidney Finkelstein in his book with the same title, and himself provides the answer : "We all need him." Every generation and culture has had its own reasons for liking Shakespeare. According to Dryden, "He was the man who of all modern, and perhaps ancient poets, has the largest and most comprehensive soul." Dr. Johnson, however, feels that "Perhaps it would not be easy to find any author, except Homer, who invented so much as Shakespeare." Before them, Ben Jonson, Shakespeare's formidable contemporary, honoured the great master's memory "on this side (of) idolatory." More recently, T.S. Eliot has clinched the matter by asserting that "Dante and Shakespeare divide the modern world between them; there is no third." Probably no other poet or dramatist has been read and evaluated so thoroughly as Shakespeare.

The English have all along recognised the real worth of Shakespeare. Asked whether he would give up Indian Empire or Shakespeare, Carlyle would say : "Indian Empire or no Indian Empire; we cannot do without Shakespeare! Indian Empire will go, at any rate, some day; but this Shakespeare does not go, he lasts forever with us." As a repository of a great culture Shakespeare's significance can hardly be overemphasised. But what is even more important is that on account of the wisdom born out of rich humanity, his universal humanism, he has made a permanent niche in all great literary traditions. As Coleridge observes, "he is of no age — nor I may add, of any religion, or party or profession. The body and substance of his works came out of the unfathomable depths of his own oceanic mind." Shakespeare himself has gestured more than once towards the permanent contemporaneity of his work. In *Julius Caesar* (III. i. 128-30) he writes :

> How many ages hence
> Shall this our lofty scene be acted over
> In states unborn and accents unknown.

In fact, age cannot wither nor custom stale the infinite variety of his work.

Shakespeare was introduced in India, as part of the Empire's cultural and political investment, during the age of Johnson and Garrick — to be precise, in 1775, the year of the American War of Independence. Of many things that came to India from England, few are really as important as Shakespeare. Imperialism, trade and commerce and penal law have not endured but the imperishable empire of Shakespeare will always be with us. Sri Aurobindo, who regarded Shakespeare as superior to Kalidasa and particularly valued the former's essential force, beauty and creativity, wrote in *The Future Poetry* : "More than any other poet Shakespeare has accomplished mentally the legendary feat of the imperious sage Viswamitra; his power of vision has created a Shakespearean world of his own." Sri Aurobindo perceived in Shakespeare the Hiraṇyagarbha, the primordial creative energy that was before Creation itself began and was to be the cause of all Creation. To take another example from another walk of Indian life, it is on record that Gandhi, who "cultivated prayerfully" the English language, as he himself puts it, was pleased that it contained but "three-fourths Bible and one-fourth Shakespeare." Gandhi is also said to have written an essay on *Hamlet.* The architect of modern India, Jawaharlal Nehru, with the best possible English education, must have known Shakespeare more intimately. He culled the epigraph for *The*

Discovery of India from Shakespeare's well-known sonnet, "When to the sessions of sweet silent thought I summon up remembrance of things past."

Shakespeare became considerably popular right from the time of his introduction in India. While the English playhouses by their production of English, specially Shakespeare's, plays created an appetite for theatrical performances, the foundation of the Hindu College in 1816, and the teaching of Shakespeare by eminent teachers like Richardson (who was also a founder of the Chowringhee Theatre) created in the minds of the students — the intelligentsia of modern Bengal — a literary taste for drama as such, and taught them not only how to appreciate Shakespeare criticism, but also to recite and act scenes from his plays. This fashion spread to every academic institution. In 1837 Bengali students staged scenes from *The Merchant of Venice* in the Governor's house; in 1852 and 1853, the students of the Metropolitan Academy and David Hare Academy staged Shakespeare's plays, while the old and new students of the Oriental Academy staged.... *Othello* in 1853, *The Merchant of Venice* in 1854, and *Henry IV* in 1855. Shakespeare's dramas became an indispensable part of English education and a popular item in all cultural productions. The Bengali theatre which made its mark in the later decades was the natural outcome of this new-found passion.

India has had a powerful tradition of teaching Shakespeare. And scholarship in Shakespeare's works has been supposed to be the touchstone of competence and expertise in literature teaching. Some of the ways in which Shakespeare's influence has been felt here include : translations and adaptations, plays in Indian languages written on the model of Shakespeare's plays, and poetic language — specially imagery.

Rangeya Raghava, who produced fifteen rapid-fire translations of Shakespeare's plays into Hindi in one year, *i.e.* 1957-58, once said : "A language which does not possess translations of Shakespeare cannot be counted among the more developed languages." Indian genius, however, refused to be overwhelmed by Shakespeare and accepted him only after giving him a ceremonious, ritual purificatory bath. Some pioneering works in the area of translations and adaptations of Shakespeare's plays may be briefly mentioned. *A Midsummer Night's Dream* was translated into Sanskrit in 1892. More recently, S.D. Joshi and Vighnahari Dev of Pune adapted *Hamlet* under the title *Candrasenaḥ Durgaedeśasya Yuvarājaḥ*, giving Candrasena and Harṣānand names to Hamlet and Horatio respectively. This adaptation, as Takwale says in his Foreword, was "presented in the proper form fitting Sanskrit dramaturgy and literature."

In the Bangla adaptation of *The Merchant of Venice* by Hara Chandra Ghosh the centre of the play shifted from Antonio to Bhanumati, the Bengali counterpart of Portia, the play becoming a Romantic drama between Bhanumati and Cittavilas (Bassanio). Belmont and Venice become Ujjain and Gujarat respectively, and in place of Nerissa we have Sulocana and Sushila, the two attendants of Bhanumati. The protagonist of *Othello* in an Oriya translation is called Atala. Elsewhere, the Duke in *The Merchant of Venice* is designated as the Rajyapal, and Romeo and Juliet are named Chandrasheel and Charulata respectively. *Macbeth* in Kannada translation is entitled *Prataprudradeva.* Its main character is Malcolm, and the intended *rasas* are Raudra and Bhayanaka. Telugu translations of Shakespeare include : *The Comedy of Errors (Chamatkara Ratnavali), Romeo and Juliet (Malati Madhukaramu), Othello (Padmini Prabhakaramu), King Lear (Chitraketu Charitramu)* and *As You Like It (Vaidabhi Vilasamu)*. Moreover, P. Srinivasa Acharyulu wrote *Kanakangi* under the magic of Shakespeare. "In writing this drama," he remarked, "I had before me the best of tragedies of the immortal Shakespeare to guide me in the development of characters." This might have happened in some other languages also.

In Hindi, the year 1859 saw the publication of one of the first plays by Bhartendu Harishchandra's father, Girdhar Das.

And in 1879 appeared the first translation of a Shakespearean play into Hindi — *The Comedy of Errors* by Munshi Imdad Ali as *Bhram Jalak.* The translations of *The Winter's Tale* as *Sharad Ritu ki Kahani* (1881) and of *The Merchant of Venice* as *Venice ka Vyupari* (1881) were also brought out from the Mitra Vilas Press, Lahore. Other important translations are : *The Merchant of Venice* as *Durlabh Bandhu* (1888) by Bhartendu and as *Venice Nagar ka Vyapari* (1888) by Arya; *Romeo and Juliet* as *Prem Lila* (1889) by Gopinath Purohit; *Macbeth* as *Sahasendra* (1893) by Gadadhar Singh; and *As You Like It* as *Man Bhavana* (1896) by G. Purohit. In *Durlabh Bandhu*, again, characters and placenames have been Indianized. Antonio becomes Anant; Bassanio Vasant; Salerio Saral; Portia Pursri; and Venice Vanshanagar. The conflict between Christians and Jews has been shown in it as that between Hindus and Jains, and the Casket Episode is replaced by Swayamvara. Among other translators of Shakespeare's plays into Hindi a special mention may be made of Harivansh Rai Bachchan, Amrit Rai and Raghuveer Sahay. Rangeya Raghava translated fifteen plays including *Othello, Hamlet, Julius Caesar, The Merchant of Venice, Twelfth Night, Macbeth, The Tempest* and *As You Like It.* Some Hindi playwrights went to Shakespeare for models or occasional hints. Jai Shankar Prasad, for example, seems to have taken some hints for the character of Anant Devi in *Skandgupta* from Lady Macbeth. Upendra Nath Ashq's *Chacha Beta* reminds one of *Lear* at places. Shrinivas Das's *Sanyogita Swayamvar* is based on *The Merchant of Venice,* and *Randheer aur Prem Mohini* on *Romeo and Juliet.* At times Laxmi Narayan Mishra's *Mukti ka Rahasya* (1932) reveals echoes from Shakespeare.

In 1868 a Parsi theatrical company named Oriental Theatrical Company came into existence in Bombay, which was followed by other Parsi companies in different parts of the country. Under the aegis of these companies Shakespeare's plays were adapted and translated for performance, the objectives being purely commercial. Some of the leading translators were : Radheyshyam Kathavachak, Agahasra Kashmiri, Tulsidas Shaida and Narayan Prasad Betab. Betab brought out a magazine called *Shakespeare* which published translations of Shakespeare's plays such as *Romeo and Juliet* as *Bazm-e-fani* (1890); *Cymbeline* as *Meetha Zahar* (1895); *The Winter's Tale* as *Murad-e-shoke* (1895); *Hamlet* as *Khoon-e-nahak* (1898); *Othello* as *Shahid-e-wafa* (1898); and *The Merchant of Venice* as *Dil Farosh* (1900). The Parsi companies got some more plays translated in the twentieth century, which included *King Lear* as *Haar Jeet* (1902); *Twelfth Night* as *Bhool Bhulaiyan* (1905); *Antony and Cleopatra* as *Kali Nagin* (1906); and *The Comedy of Errors* as *Gorakh Dhandha* (1912). Some new translations such as that of *Romeo and Juliet* by Chaturbhuj Audichya (1911), of *Julius Caesar* by Ganpat Krishna Gurjar (1912), and of *Othello* by Govind Prasad Ghildiyal (1915) were qualitatively better than the earlier ones. Even more distinguished were Lala Sita Ram's translations : *Much Ado About Nothing* as *Manmohan ka Jal* (1915); *The Tempest* as *Jangal men Mangal; Romeo and Juliet* as *Prem Parinam; As You Like It* as *Apani Apani Ruchi; The Winter's Tale* as *Sharad Ritu ki Kahani*; *Hamlet; King Lear* as *Raja Lear* (1914); *Othello* as *Jhootha Sandeh; Cymbeline* as *Sati Pareeksha* (1925); and *Measure for Measure* as *Bagula Bhagat* (1923). In these translations and adaptations the process of Indianization is in full swing. For example, in *As You Like It* Ameens becomes Ameechand, Jaques Jayakrishna, Touchstone Moosarchand, and the Forest of Arden Aranyak. In *Measure for Measure* Vincentio is renamed Vinayak, Angelo Arjun, Claudio Kalhansa, Thomas Ramdas and Peter Hardas. Prospero, in *The Tempest*, is Poornkam, Miranda Malini, Ferdinand Pradyumna, Ariel Baital, Caliban Kalyaban, Alonso Arinash, Sebastian Shrivatsa, Antonio Anant, Gonzalo Gunjmal and Trinculo Tinkodi. Thoughts and feelings were also readjusted to suit the Indian sensibility. The Parsi Theatre did a lot to popularize Shakespeare's plays. The Maharaja of Charkhari is said to have been so mesmarized by the charm of an actress that he bought the entire Madan Theatre. Goriantheon Theatre also employed women artistes including European ladies — something rare in India. The Parsi Theatre paved the path for the drama and cinema in India and nurtured the talents of some very competent artistes. For example, David Joseph was so talented an actor that Shohrab Modi regarded him as his teacher.

Analysis and evaluation of Shakespeare brings its own challenges and rewards. And no single approach can be prescribed in the present postmodernist ethos. In the last decade or so Shakespeare criticism has disclosed what John Drakakis calls 'Alternative Shakespeares' through sustained and diverse practices and approaches. This would be in keeping with the age-old Indian way of recognising the multiplicity of approaches which maintains : *ekaṁ sad viprāḥ vahudhā vadanti.* The scenario in respect of Shakespeare studies has markedly changed in the last two decades. Although we still have traditional studies of the dramatist — his life, times and stage in journals such as *Shakespeare Quarterly* and the annual *Shakespeare Survey*, we have to take cognizance of a plethora of theorizing on Shakespeare's plays ranging from structuralism to poststructuralism. In the sphere of feminist readings alone, for example, the plurality is astounding. The earliest attempts in this direction began with Leslie Fiedler's *The Stranger in Shakespeare* (1972), which was followed by an anthology *Woman's Part : Feminist Criticism of Shakespeare* (1980) edited by C. Lenz *et al.* Germaine Greer, in *Shakespeare* (1986), positively projected Shakespeare's rejection of the archetypal 'passive woman.' Coppelia Kahn (*Man's Estate,* 1981) and Marilyn French (*Shakespeare's Division of Experience,* 1982), however, took the playwright to task for the ethos of male chauvinism dominant in his works. Lisa Jardine (*Still Harping on Daughters*, 1983) and Kathleen McLuskie (*The Patriarchal Bard*, 1985) have also contested the image of Shakespeare as a benign egalitarian, highlighting his phallocentrism and sexual *difference.* A new anthology

Women Reading Shakespeare, 1660-1900 edited by Ann Thompson and Sasha Roberts (1997) raises issues of female education, the role of women in society, family life, social relations and so on. Attempts to strategically position the marginalised voices have led to the emergence of gay and lesbian Renaissance studies like *Sodometrics : Renaissance Texts, Modern Sexualities* (1992) and *Queering the Renaissance* (1994) edited by Jonathan Goldberg. Similar efforts have been made in the realm of other literary theories also.

Times are changing very fast, and no one can afford to swear by old gods. A.C. Bradley and Dover Wilson have suffered in the hands of Terence Hawkes *(That Shakespearian Rag,* 1986). So have Frank Kermode and Marilyn French in Malcolm Evans' *Signifying Nothing* (1986). As Chris Baldick sums up, "Shakespeare criticism has...transmuted from textual study to the cultural history of representations." No serious student of Shakespeare can remain oblivious of the 'contemporary critical quarrels' (as Brian Vickers subtitles his work *Approaching Shakespeare,* 1993) or the 'paradigm shift' claimed by some postmodernists which, they think, is comparable to the Copernican Revolution. He may nevertheless ask in what way the recent works on Shakespeare have really enriched our understanding of his plays. Various theoretical models have generally failed to provide an authentic insight into Shakespeare's tragic vision or a general theory of his comedies. A sensible way out of the present critical chaos seems to be to situate Shakespeare's works within their cultural and social milieu and to evaluate them in terms of our own poetics.

In a seminal paper entitled "*Hamlet* in the Light of Indian Poetics" S.C. Sen Gupta maintains that Indian poetics — specially the *rasa-dhvani* theory — may be "profitably applied" to European literature, particularly to Shakespeare. "As an experiment," he says, "it may be tested with reference to *Hamlet,* the most complex as also the most controversial of all Shakespeare's plays." There has been no end of writing on *Hamlet.* In fact, the extant *Hamlet* criticism is so enormous that "a man", as F.P. Wilson avers, "who set out to read all the books about *Hamlet,* would have time to read nothing else, not (even) *Hamlet*". After a detailed analysis of *Hamlet* on the basis of the *rasa* theory Sen Gupta concludes : "*Hamlet* is not a play about a mission delayed and never executed in the proper sense of the term. Even the portrait of a great character is only a means to an end. The play really envisages a complex and profound state of the soul in which Aversion is compounded with many states. It is the penetrating vision of life with its sweetness and bitterness, heroism and villainy, love and hatred, laughter and sorrow, idealism and cynicism that accounts for its enduring poetic appeal."

This kind of analysis will enable us to appreciate the qualities of *Hamlet* in a better way. It will also obviate the need of calling it "an artistic failure" as T.S. Eliot does.

To my mind, the predominant *rasa* in *Hamlet* is *Śānta* (Quietistic) resulting in introspective contemplation. Hamlet is a seeker after Truth — a prince among philosophers who believes that "There are more things in heaven and earth — than are dreamt of in...philosophy" (I.iv), and that "There's nothing either good or bad but thinking makes it so" (II.ii). Hamlet's disillusionment and disgust result in his world-weariness (*vairāgya*). He turns away from all worldly action : "How weary, stale, flat and unprofitable / Seem to me all the uses of this world" (I.ii). The dominant emotion (*sthāyibhāva*) is self-enquiry and introspection engendering *Śānta rasa* and others like *Śṛṅgāra* — specially *Vipralaṁbha* — which may be seen in Hamlet's relationship with Ophelia; *Hāsya* as seen in Hamlet's encounter with Polonius and Osiric; *Karuṇa* evoked in the scenes connected with Ophelia — her madness and her songs; *Raudra* seen in Hamlet's wrath for Claudius, whom he condemns as "a cutpurse of the empire" (III.iv) and "A murderer and a villain, a slave, a vice of a king"; *Vīra* as found in Hamlet's duel with Laertes; *Bhayānaka* as experienced by Gertrude on account of Hamlet's anger in the Closet Scene; *Bībhatsa* which Hamlet has from his mother — the "seeming-virtuous queen," making him jump to the generalisation that "Frailty, thy name is woman!" (I.ii); and *Adbhuta*, the wonder and astonishment that Hamlet has on hearing about his father's ghost. The other *rasas* serve as ancillaries to the main *rasa, i.e. Śānta*, and their use is in accordance with the dramaturgical principles laid down by Bharata (VII. 126-29). The use of insights and paradigms from Indian poetics will help unearth hitherto hidden qualities of Shakespeare's plays. Even if the success is limited it is worth giving a try, for, as T.S. Eliot says, "About anyone so great as Shakespeare it is probable that we can never be right; and if we can never be right, it is better that we should from time to time change our way of being wrong."

We will continue to read Shakespeare even in the present age of growing materialism, and Shakespeare will prove to be a sensitive guide to us in all our crises. As Ben Jonson admitted, "A man so various he seems to be that he is mankind's epitome." His profound insight helped him create several immortal characters. "Of his characters," says Walter Raleigh, "we pass judgment freely; as we grow familiar with them, we seem to belong to their world." Such is the 'negative capability' of their creator that we can easily empathise with them. Characters like Hamlet represent the predicament of a human being, whatever age or country he may belong to. Hazlitt, whose evaluation of Shakespeare's characters is not different from Coleridge's in this regard, comments : "Hamlet is a name; his real? They are as real as our own thoughts. Their reality is in the reader's mind. It is we who are Hamlet." Shakespeare is undoubtedly the greatest creator of characters.

What would impress Indian mind even more is the philosophical wisdom enshrined in Shakespeare's plays. We can easily intuit what he wants to convey through lines like the following ones from *The Tempest* (IV.i) :

We are such stuff
As dreams are made on, and our little life
Is rounded with a sleep.

Talking about *Macbeth* Wilson Knight remarks in his powerful book *The Imperial Theme* that "the whole play may be written down as the wrestling of destruction with creation." In fact, the dramatist has had to grapple with the vexed problem of Evil in all his mature plays. After a decade of romantic comedies and history plays, at about his thirty-eighth year, he abandoned the sunny uplands of laughter and gaiety and plunged into the dark world of passion and temptation, crime and punishment, terror and madness. As Karamazov says in Dostoevsky's novel, one cannot perpetually live in rebellion, and by the time Shakespeare wrote his last play, *The Tempest,* he realised that love, compassion and forgiveness, loyalty and courage in the heart of man can provide solution to the problems of Evil :

...the rarer action is
In virtue than in vengeance; they being penitent,
The sole drift of my purpose doth extend
Not a frown further (V.i. 27-30).

The vision of life presented by Shakespeare may not be always rosy but it contains essential promises of hope and regeneration. In his most intense tragedy, *King Lear,* he declares,

Men must endure
Their going hence, even as their coming hither;
Ripeness is all (V.i. 9-11).

A meaningful response to Shakespeare would be a spirited journey from 'readiness' to 'ripeness', for, as Adi Śaṅkarācharya declares, "There is no other road to Truth but knowledge."

2

Literary Communication of Shakespeare and its Influence on the Ordinary Man in India — Habib Tanveer

—Mrs. Shabiba Khan

SHAKESPEAREAN LITERATURE has crossed the Space and Time dimensions and has been ruling the Indian literary circles for centuries now. The targeted group for which the literature was produced and the environment of the Sixteenth century England was also quite different from today. In India Shakespearean literature has remained a constant and never ending source of thinking, meeting, writing and referring to for solutions. This literature also forms a part of the curriculum for teaching, training, research and extension in universities, colleges and schools. Shakespeare's poems are recited, the dramas enacted and stories told in spite of the classical Elizabethan English, archaic words, traditional diction and kingly characters that abound in his works. Some of the Indian writers of the English language have openly acknowledged that Shakespeare has inspired them in their writings. Whether this base of English Literature in India is a "Reflected Glory" of this great writer is a query worth probing.

Other Propositions which need probing include :

1. Is Shakespeare's impact on Indian Literature in English visible due to his literary universality?

2. English language has flourished as an international medium of communication, but English language and Shakespeare are not synonyms and he is bound to reach a point of decline or not?
3. How his poems and plays can be interpreted in different ways and specially in the Indian context?
4. There is a common notion that Shakespeare's literature indicates only problems, it does not give solutions. How far is this true?
5. How far has Shakespeare's plays influenced the Indian regional dramatic scene?

The researcher has tried to look into these and many related aspects of the Indian literature and language scene in relation to Shakespeare and answer these questions. The research used surveys and personal interviews to reach the conclusion that "we cannot appreciate Shakespeare as an 'inkblot' into which everything can be read."

In India the needs and objectives of drama presentation in all three stages have been different be it Sanskrit Natak, Parsi theatre or present-day drama. It is an accepted fact that present drama should fulfil today's needs, otherwise it will lose its motive and spirit. Consequently, it is our constant attempt to link our problems with and find the relevance of theatre and *vice versa*, more so in the case of Sanskrit Nataks. According to need and situation this reference to context changes as well. Parsi theatre proved to be the initiatory in adopting foreign plays and specially of Shakespeare. Later these plays went on to be translated in all the major languages in India. Bengali, Gujarati and Marathi were the first ones to provide the platform to these translations. The process still continues in Hindi. An interesting point to note here is that some of the translations were so weak that it was impossible to distinguish Shakespeare in them due to the changes brought about by language and difference in presentation. Habib Tanveer's translations of Shakespearean works continues to have the same spirit but with the tang of a different language.

Ordinary Man

Habib Tanveer, who hails from Chattisgarh has translated and performed Shakespeare's plays in Chattisgarhi, a dialect which is a mixture of Bhojpuri, Bundeli, Gondi and other North Indian dialects. A common man, he has spent more than 50 years as a drama writer, director, producer and performer. When he had covered much of the ground of Indian theatre, he received a scholarship to join RADA in England. Having polished his skills further, he completed his studies in a year, visited several European Institutes of the Performing Arts, and met theatrical personalities. Paris, Vienna and Berlin featured significantly on his destination list. In England, he was greatly influenced and moved by Braikht's approach to drama and his impressions which were in force and everlasting. A German, Braikht took the colours of several cultures to paint his dramas including East, West and Africa, but in his heart he remained a German throughout. Tanveer returned to India and chose Chattisgarh to be his work land and preferred his mother tongue as the language of the plays. He also combined Urdu to a great extent with it as instrument of communication.

Romeo and Juliet

Tanveer was very clear about the spirit of Shakespearean plays and the message conveyed by them and its effectiveness as well. Everyone accepts Shakespeare to be his own and flaunts his authority over it. Tanveer on the other hand has adopted the same style, poetry, blank verse and prose at their apt places but did not take "to the letter" translations. And the reference to context and impact was not the same as well. Romeo and Juliet was translated as West Side story in America, which had a Black American background and highlighted the problems of this community. A theme which was treated in its socio-cultural context by Tanveer, was taken as that of communalism and religious discord by N.K. Sharma in his acculturation of the play. He presented it under the banner of "Act One Group" at Delhi.

Comedy

Tanveer translated *A Midsummer Night's Dream* as *Kam Dev ka Apna Basant Ritu ka Sapna.* His style was unclouded and presented a beautiful ensemble of situation-based verse, blank verse, and prose. A few lines are as follows :

मैं हूँ वन की रानी की सेवक भी परी भी
छिड़कों रानी की आंखें में शबनम ठंडी ठंडी
आगे पीछे रानी के एक साफ निकले गेंदे की
मेरे लाल गुलाल से गाल लाल यमन की सुर्ख़ी

The important feature of this play is the language of the courtesans which is Urdu, and the commoners speak in Chattisgarhi. Another significant aspect of the play is the demarcating cultural difference between rural and urban citizenry. The city dwellers signify a domination over others.

Communication with Nature

Tanveer's version maintains the same name and nature of the characters as given by Shakespeare but the background composed of nature's emblems plants, flowers, birds, trees and even insects and reptiles have been localized in Chattisgarhi. Earlier, Azhar Ali Azad Kakurvi had translated this play in Urdu with poetic configuration. Parsi theater's version was called "Jam-e-Ulfat." The names of the characters were changed and the plots were Lucknowi in their spirit and context.

Tanveer expressed his views on the subject as, "our interest is confined to the limits of our cultural surroundings and its limitations of socio-cultural forces which build our thinking. As regards our creation of literature and fine arts performance, it is mostly based on our values which we inherit from our parents and acquire from our culture."[1] Our literary creation and style of depiction is affected by the personality of creator and performer.

Critic's View

Many critics have pointed out that Tanveer's presentations seem as under rehearsed since he does not give well defined scripts to his performers in advance. His scripts evolve from the process of play presentation. The scope and method of presentation change with the number of performances. Additions and deductions are made to give a complete and effective shape to the script.[2]

This process of conception of plays is unique as it starts much prior to the actual initiation of the play and continues much beyond the culmination.The time devoted to these two exercises is much more than the actual performance time of the play.[3]

Shakespeare and Humour

Humour, which forms the distinct feature of Shakespeare's plays cannot be felt with the same intensity in translations due to the difference in power and picture painting capability of words. There are often changes to the actual humour in the form of additions or complete disregard in adaptations. Another aspect which needs attention is the mastery in characterisation and poetic vision which has direct vision and bearing on life. A message of "Live and Let Live." The smallest creatures of nature ants, bees, and spiders have recognition in the eyes of nature's law. The depiction of nature inculcates the spirit of cooperation, love, promotion of friendship and kindness towards others. Such narration is found only in Sanskrit dramas and literary works. Thus it becomes a catalyst. In an interview Tanveer expressed three types of effects clearly visible in his theatre, "1. The cultural aspect of targeted segment, 2. Which is being nourished mostly by Sanskrit drama and 3. The experiments done by Braikht, his techniques, tools and procedures have been adopted by me in my plays in a moulded form, maintaining the basic spirit that is the culture of the area." In other plays like, *Shatranj ke Mohre*, his choice was of dialects from Lucknow, while in *Agra Bazaar*, 'Taksali' was prominent and yet another, *Mere Baad*, a play based on Mirza Ghalib had his letters as the prime source of information.[4] Visible and distinct features of Shakespeare's dramas are their Epical form and Theatrical presentation which also exists in Sanskrit Nataks. In epical plays, Braikht had very finely carved out conflicts and their resolution by his unique techniques. This has been done by depicting conflicts in characters, situations and at times two contradicting stories in the same plot.

Outstanding Achievement with Shakespeare

Tanveer has mastered the art of presenting accomplished performances with the novices of Chattisgarh with the taste of folk music added to it. The highest acclaim came to Tanveer when he presented his play *Charandas Chor* at the "International Edinburgh Theatre Festival 1982." The performance did the top honours among 52 entries. This took the troop to an international level of recognition and repute.

REFERENCES

1. Habib Tanveer, "Hindustan ke Maujooda Theatre Par Eik Nazar", *Aaj Kal,* May 1994, p. 4.
2. Ashok Bajpayee, "Boli Main Bhi Samkaleen Hain Habeeb", *Kala Samay* August-January 99-2000.
3. *Ibid.*
4. Habib Tanveer, *op. cit.*, p. 7.

3

Shakespeare in Kabuki*

—*Mohit K. Ray*

THIS SHORT paper is the outcome of my aesthetic response to a production of *Hamlet* in kabuki that was staged in Tokyo Globe in 1991.

In order to understand the nature of the reception of Shakespeare in Japan in kabuki it is necessary to have an idea of the ancient features of kabuki. Kabuki is one of the four classical performing arts that are still very popular in Japan : Bugaku (the court dance), Noh, Bunraku (the puppet theater) and kabuki, each having its distinctive beauty. Bugaku is stately and elegant; Noh is remote and has an aura of mystery around it. Bugaku and kabuki which developed more or less around the same time and interanimated each other are too complex to be neatly summed up. However, since our main concern is kabuki it may be worthwhile to confine our discussion to kabuki only.

As history goes kabuki originated in 1603 when Okuni, "a foxy little nun" left her nunnery at Izmo Grand Shrine, went to Kyoto, and with some like-minded women started a showbiz on the river-bed of the Kamo, the only place where public performances were allowed at that time. Okuni, incidentally, belonged to that brief period of Japanese history when Japanese culture began to acquire some cosmopolitan

---

* This paper was presented in The World Shakespeare Conference, held in Calcutta in December 2000.

flavour before entering into a long phase of isolationism which was to end only in 1868 with the end of the shogunate. However, Okuni tried in her own way to incorporate the latest fads and may be described as ultra-modern for her age. The word "kabuki", in fact, is derived from the verb "kabuku" the basic meaning of which is "to tilt forward," and in common parlance came to signify the customs or behaviour that departed from the traditional or conventional norms. The art form that Okuni devised as kabuki combined ka(song), bu(dance) and ki(skill) and broke out from the conventional norms of codified morality. In an illustrated scroll, for example, which shows Okuni in the act of dancing we see her wearing the baggiest of the baggy trousers recently introduced in Japan by the Portuguese and lacquered "coolie hat" called "southern barbarian *kasa*" with a gong dangling on her breast. In 1629, however, the shogunate put a ban on the appearance of any female on the stage in all Japan, because they considered women a dangerous threat to public morals. Young boys took over from the ladies but soon they were also found to be equal threat to public morals. So, in 1653 another shogunate mandate was issued, allowing only adult men on the stage from that time onward. However, thanks to Japan's traditional respect for tradition and the introduction of serious restrictions imposed by the shogunate in an island country which for the most part of the development of kabuki was practically cut off from the rest of the world, kabuki gradually developed during the next two and half centuries into a highly stylized art form. Consequently, it called for a rigorous training on the part of the actors. The prospective actor had to learn the gestures, movements, and attitudes which were transmitted from one generation to another. The training is so rigorous and the skills to be acquired are so many that one can never become a perfect kabuki actor before attaining the age of fifty. A devoted kabuki actor spends six to eight hours a day, seven days a week on the stage and most of his waking hours are spent in the theater building. Theater, in a very real sense, is his life. Over centuries tradition led to the formulation of an aesthetic vocabulary which was understood and appreciated throughout the country. A certain type of hairdress, or costume at once revealed the complete nature of the character who wore it. Sometimes even a single gesture would evoke a time, a mood. Stylization of artistic expression concomitantly brought about a revolution in the make up which tended towards conventionalization of the face according to the standard type of roles. Unlike Noh which used masks, the face of the kabuki actor on stage is a compromise between a mask and a human face. The face is painted red and blue in a nonrealistic fashion which sharpens the muscular construction of the face, increases the height of the nose, draws down the corners of the mouth and emphasizes the eyes.

It remains an enigma how such a stylized classical form of theater can accommodate a Shakespearean play. Possibly it could not, remaining constantly under the shadow of official disapproval of anything new and all kinds of restraints imposed by the shogunate. Luckily, in 1868 the shogunate collapsed and with the restoration of the Emperor as the figure-head Japan entered the modern age and in 1872 the first modern theater was established in Tokyo, and as gradually all the restrictions were removed one by one, the original social stigma was also removed and the kabuki theater looked abroad for revitalization and modernization without destroying the essential character of kabuki. It was around that time — in 1880s — that the drama of the West began to be imported under the name of *shingani* (New Drama) which had an immediate appeal for intellectuals looking for a drama more in tune with the new age. One method to counter the tendency towards ossification was to present plays written by authors other than the true kabuki writers attached to the kabuki theaters. These plays came to be known as new kabuki. Around 1888 there appeared a theatrical movement known as *shimpa* that wanted to create new and vital contemporary theater on Western models.

Thus it was only after 1868, that is after the fall of the

shogunate, that Shakespeare appeared on the scene. The first attempt at adaptation of *Hamlet* was made in 1879 by Mokuami Kawatake (1816-1893) who was noted for introducing Senecan kind of play in kabuki. In 1885 a kabuki version of *The Merchant of Venice* was presented in Osaka, and that was Japan's first exposure to Shakespeare in kabuki. In 1886 a kabuki version of *Hamlet* was published. It was written by Robun Kanagaki and titled *Hamuretto Yamato Nishiki-E*. Beginning in 1907 Shoyo Tsubuchi (1859-1935) devoted some twenty years to translating the works of Shakespeare, and he is the first person to translate the entire works of Shakespeare into Japanese. In his translation he tried to bridge the gap between Japanese and Western cultures by using in his translation the tone and atmosphere of kabuki. Another person responsible for bringing about fresh blood to the new kabuki around 1907 is Ichikawa Sadanji II. Sadanji had gone to Europe, studied Western dramatic techniques at the Royal Academy of Dramatic Art in London, and, on his return, wrote many new kabuki plays modelled on Western drama and successfully produced them. We have on record that since 1885 (the year *The Merchant of Venice* was presented in kabuki) Shakespeare has been and continues to be staged in Japan either in translation in Western costume or in adaptation in kabuki. An interesting figure to remember in this connection is Kawakami Otojuro (1884-1911) who went abroad in 1899-1900 and appeared in kabuki plays (modernized form) in San Francisco, New York and Paris, and on his return, staged a production of *Hamlet* in which he played the leading role and in one scene entered the stage riding a bicycle. Hamlet on a bicycle did not appear incongruous to the audience of the time, because for them, at the time, Hamlet was as new and foreign as a bicycle and both were therefore logically bound together.

Now, the presentation of Shakespeare in translation and in Western costume is one thing. But the question that I touched upon earlier and am going to address now is : how to explain the success of a production of Shakespeare in kabuki which is so stylized. The secret, to my mind lies in the fact that beneath the formal differences there are many interesting points of affinity between the two. Historically kabuki had its beginning in Kyoto in 1603 when Shakespeare was very much alive and kicking. The first Quarto of *Hamlet* was published in 1603. In both the countries a new age had begun : in England, Renaissance; in Japan a period of peace following centuries of war. In Shakespeare boys played the roles of women, and in kabuki since 1629 after the ban on women, men started playing the roles of women. Both were theater of the masses and used eventful stories with themes of love, intrigue, bloodshed etc.

But the most important reason why Shakespeare could be adapted and effectively presented in kabuki is that both are primarily actor's theater. Unlike representational theater where a scene is laid out with alert attention to the minutest details in terms of setting, furniture, costume etc. to make it appear "real", in a presentational theater or actor's theater the onus is largely on the actor to create an illusion of reality and imaginatively transport the audience to the world of drama through his histrionics and acting with the minimal support of the theater props. The idea of the night, for example, can be conveyed by the kabuki actor alone through voice and gesture while in a representational theater this idea must be conveyed primarily by the lighting and only secondarily by the actor. Again, as in Shakespeare, so in kabuki, the actor uses time as he uses other elements of productions purely theatrically, suspending it, speeding it up, slowing it down as it suits his purpose. Shakespeare manages to have a night pass in less than 400 lines in *Othello*.

Since a kabuki actor, like a Shakespearean actor, does not so much impersonate as he acts; a man of eighty can play the role of a girl of sixteen because his perception of the role is not dependent upon the audience's aesthetic identification with the actor, but upon the audience's recognition of the technical artistry of the actor. The understanding that the actor has with the audience about the dramatic experience determines the significance of the illusion. It may be interesting to recall in this connection that no less a theater personality than Sir Laurence Olivier once played the role of Katherina (Kate) in *The Taming of the Shrew.*

Now coming to the point, both kabuki and Shakespeare are actor's theater, and the Elizabethan Globe, preeminently an actor's theater was designed to give the fullest support to the voices and gestures of the players. The London Globe which was built in 1599, burnt down in 1613, rebuilt in 1614 and demolished in 1644 was round ("the wooden O") and the thrust stage extended to the middle of the yard so that the front edge divided the building exactly at the diameter. It thus became a replica of the universe — a *theatrum mundi* — which expressed the structure of the thought of the Elizabethan age. The actor goes to the middle of the stage and shouts at the top of his lungs from the middle of his cosmos. It called for a great strength on the part of the actor to create a storm with naked human voice, without the mechanical aids of a microphone or modern acoustics. He must hold the attention of the audience and create a theatrical illusion. In this connection Beckerman writes : "The holding of attention is dramatic illusion. Whether that illusion is an imitation of contemporary life, or mythical life, the action and character must achieve a level of reality sufficient to involve us" (111). And again "...(the) attention of the actor had to be concentrated on telling the story, not develop the characters" (122). Consider, for example, the story element in the following speech of Othello :

"...in Aleppo once
Where a malignant and turban'd Turk
Beat a Venetian and traduc'd the state
I took by th' throat the circumcised dog,
And smote him — thus"

(Act V Scene ii II 255-399)

The actor must draw on his theatrical resources to transport the audience to Aleppo and make them witness the event. The job of the actor is to make the audience see things he is talking about by evoking the scene in its concrete individuality through his histrionics, the moderation and modulation of his voice, his gestures, expressions and movements. Similarly when Edgar describes the perilous height of the cliff to Gloucester in *King Lear* as

"How fearful
And dizzy 'tis to cast one's eyes so low!
The crows and choughs that wing the midway air
Show scarce so gross as beetles half-way down
Hangs one that gathers samphire — dreadful trade!
Methinks he seems no bigger than his head.
The fishermen that walk upon the beach
Appear like mice; and yond tall anchoring bark
Diminished to her cock; her cock, a buoy
Almost too small for her sight. The murmuring surge
That on the unnumber'd idle pebble chafes
Cannot be heard so high. I'll look no more;
Lest my brain turn, and the deficient sight
Topple down headlong

(Act IV Scene vi II 11-23)

The audience must visualize the whole situation. The visual images must throb with life and enable the audience to see them through "willing suspension of disbelief." In this regard the Globe stage provided the most suitable platform. The very sumptuousness of the stage elevated the actor to a level of grandeur, setting him off with elegance and opulence and gave him enormous scope for delivery, grace in manner and audacity in acting. James G. McManaway also subscribes to this view in his introduction to *Shakespeare's Globe Playhouse*. He writes : "The platform stage, for which Shakespeare wrote his plays is proving in use to be astonishingly flexible and enormously effective" (vii).

The Tokyo Globe where I saw the production of *Hamlet* in kabuki in 1991 is a re-creation of the London Globe. It is an attempt to create a Renaissance type of theater together with the medieval ideas of the theological hierarchy of heaven and hell and a compound of various ideas handed down to the Renaissance from the classical and medieval periods. Like the London Globe the Tokyo Globe also tells the actor to go out to the middle of the stage, feel all the organic energy, absorb and use it to change our perception of life. This kind of creative acting is a challenge to the actor and Shakespeare in kabuki meets this challenge remarkably well. The kabuki version of *Hamlet* that I saw was originally adapted by Robun Kanagaki in 1886, and titled *Hamuretto Yamato Nishiki-E*. Even as a script it was Japan's first meaningful introduction to *Hamlet*. In the 1991 production staged as *Hamlet* the stage script was written by Kohji Orita who also directed the play. The characters were given Japanese names. Hamlet became Wamura Maru and Ophelia, Mikariyahime; Claudius, Kanehisa Shiba; Gertrude, Seritonomae; Leartes, Harusada Keinojo Miyauchi; Horatio, Taranaga Iwamuro; Polonius, Muneharu Shuzen Miyauchi, and so on and so forth.

The fact that Shakespeare can be adapted, Japanized and effectively produced in kabuki which is preeminently a classical form, speaks volumes about the plasticity of the Shakespearean plays and their universality.

WORKS CITED

Beckerman, Bernard, *Shakespeare at the Globe*. N.Y. : The Macmillan Company, 1962.

Ernst, Earle, *The Kabuki Theater*. London : Secker and Warburg, 1956.

Gunji, Masakatsa, *Kabuki*. Trans. John Bester. Tokyo : Kodansha International Ltd., 1969.

Miyake, Shutaro, *Kabuki Drama*, Tokyo : Japan Travel Bureau, 1968.

Shakespeare, William, *The Complete Works*. Ed. Peter Alexander. London : ELBS and Collins, 1964.

Smith, Irwin, *Shakespeare's Globe Playhouse*. London : Peter Owen, Ltd., 1963.

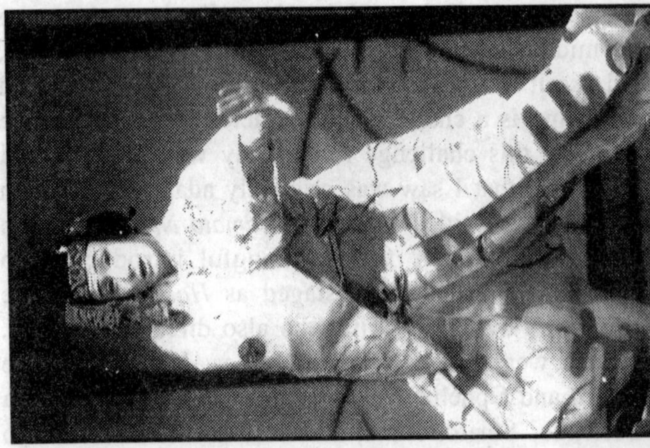

Courtesy : The Tokyo Globe

SCALE DRAWING 1 **FLOOR–PLAN AT FIRST LEVEL**

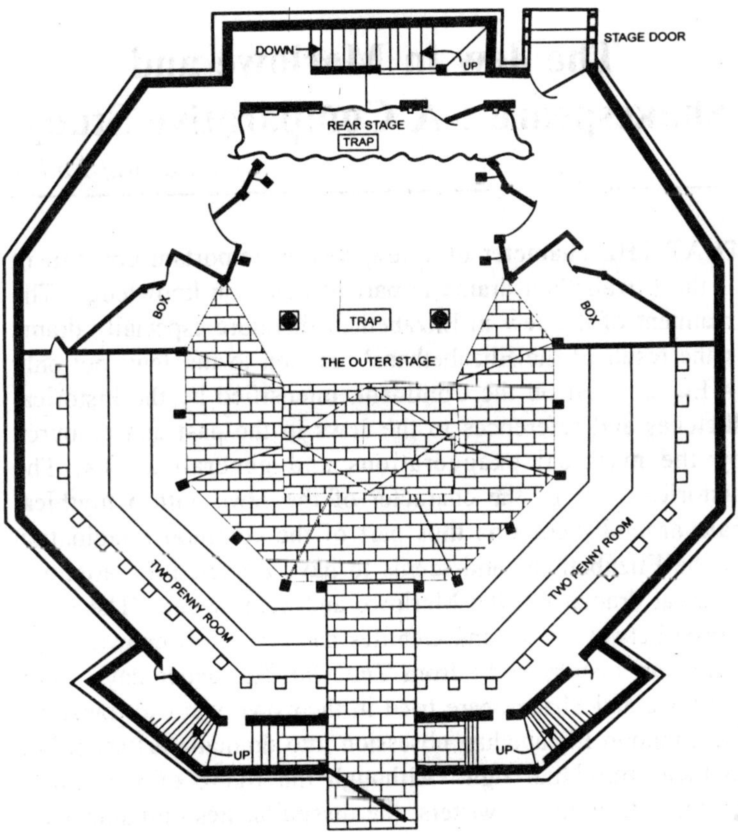

4

The Jew in Marlowe and Shakespeare : A Comparative Study

—Basavaraj Naikar

THAT THE character of a Jew was an important constituent of the Elizabethan drama is part of common knowledge. The treatment of the Jew in Elizabethan literature especially drama is the result of the Elizabethans' reaction to the Jews not only in England but on the Continent, intensified by the historical sketches and references to the Jews in the past and coloured by the mythical exaggerations and generalizations. The historical core of the character of the Jews with a mythical halo around them was thus part of the common imagination of the Elizabethans and seems to have attracted the attention of great dramatists like Marlowe and Shakespeare. The racial hatred between Jews and Gentiles has been well-known in the European history right from *The Old Testament* days. Both Marlowe and Shakespeare tried in their own ways to transform the common Elizabethan obsession into dramatic art according to their individual light. Although the figure of the Jew is common to both the writers, the dissimilarities outnumber the similarities as far as characterization, contextualization and philosophy of life are concerned.

As far as the sources of the two plays (*i.e. The Jew of Malta* and *The Merchant of Venice*) are concerned, there is no documentary evidence to pin down the characters or events upon which the dramatists have based their plays. Critics like

H.S. Bennett, therefore, opine that "We have no certain knowledge of any book or event which led Marlowe to write *The Jew of Malta,* but two important theses have been advanced to account for its appearance."[1] The first is L. Kellner's thesis that the figures of Marlowe's Barabas must have been based upon the adventurous history of a Portuguese Jew called Juan Miques of Michesius who was heard of in various countries. "The illustrious Republic of Venice, the mighty Kingdom of Spain, the conceited government of France and even the haughty papacy, all saw themselves endangered by him."[2] This Jew is said to have finally settled down in Constantinople about 1555, where he became an ally and friend of Sultan Selim II. He plotted continuously against the Christians and was made the Duke of Naxos and the Cyclades thereby assuming the name of Joseph Nassi. He was led to believe that he might become King of Cyprus and hope to establish a new Jewish State in Palestine on the sea of Tiberius.

According to the second thesis proposed by Tucker Brooke,[3] there is a greater similarity between Marlowe's Barabas and a Jew of Constantinople namely David Passi who had achieved great notoriety in Europe for half-a-dozen years and who was not only anti-Christian but also exercised his ill-will against Turks as well and set them against each other.

Although Marlowe was, thus, indirectly influenced by the historical figures of European Jews, there is no printed source to be pinned down. Professor Tucker Brooke, therefore, opines that it is unlikely that "the main theme of the tragedy was founded upon printed material."[4] He rightly points out, "I believe that from rumours and gossip, emphasized and exaggerated by contemporary feeling about Jews, that Marlowe derived his inspiration. Once again the idea of depicting a Jew, raised to power as well as to influence, we can leave Marlowe's own gifts to provide the rest. Out of a haze of surmise and unreliable report he saw clearly enough the main lines of his character. His reading and general knowledge of recent and current history gave him the rest."[5]

Similarly Shakespeare's Shylock in *The Merchant of Venice* cannot be traced to any one definite source in history or literature because of the presence of several sources. The story, for example, of the pound of flesh may be seen in the tales from Persia and India. In the West, the Roman Laws of Twelve Tables are said to have given a legal basis for several tales and ballads. The first known English version of a story about a Jew as creditor is found in the *Cursor Mundi* which dates from the end of the thirteenth century. As pointed out by John Russell Brown[6] the printed source closest to *The Merchant of Venice* is the first story of the fourth day in Ser Giovanni's *II Pecorone,* though Shakespeare has departed from it in my details. Shakespeare is also said to have been influenced by Marlowe's *The Jew of Malta.* As usual, Shakespeare transmutes all the diverse sources into his own gold and gives it a distinct stamp and colour of his own. But it should be remembered that there was no contemporary reason for Shakespeare to write about the mutual hatred between Jews and Christians. It is said that the Jews who had officially been expelled from England since the reign of Edward I, could live peaceably in London if they conformed outwardly to Christianity. There is said to be no acute hatred between Jews and Christians in the Elizabethan England. But what Shakespeare does is to offer a dramatic metaphor for the mythical-historical hatred between the two races right from the days of *The Old Testament.*

The brief examination of the sources and their transformation into dramatic art by Marlowe and Shakespeare testifies to the fact that both the dramatists were influenced by the mythical story in *The Old Testament* of the racial hatred between Jews and Gentiles and by the historical and literary sources about the Jewish life. The mythical, historical and literary sources were harmonised and transformed into art in their own distinct styles.

Although the figure of a Jew is at the heart of these two plays of Marlowe and Shakespeare, the settings are strikingly different from each other. While *The Merchant of Venice* is set in Venice and Belmont, *The Jew of Malta* has a wider and exotic setting of the island of Malta and Turkish empire. Comparatively speaking, Shakespeare's Italy appears to be more familiar than Marlowe's Spain. Whereas Shakespeare concentrates on the commercial and legal aspect of Jewish life, Marlowe includes not only the commercial, but the social and the political aspects also involving their interrelationship. Thus Marlowe's world appears to be larger than Shakespeare's geographically as well as thematically.

There is a remarkable difference between Marlowe's play and Shakespeare's as far as their characterization of the Jew and the consequent contextualization is concerned. Whereas Shakespeare's Shylock is preoccupied with his anti-Christian feeling, Marlowe's Barabas is obsessed with anti-Christian and anti-Turkish feeling almost bordering on the misanthropic.

The general racial hatred between Jews and Christians acts as a backdrop for the plots of both the plays. This hatred is, perhaps, caused by the contradictory values taught by the two cultures *i.e.* Judaism and Christianity. Whereas the Jewish values are in tune with materialistic attitude of Machiavellism, those of Christianity with their spiritualistic orientation run counter to the Jewish ones. In spite of the difference of settings and contexts between the two plays, there are certain features of Jewish sensibility common to both the protagonists. Both Barabas and Shylock are rich merchants capable of lending money to people at an exorbitant rate of interest. But they, at the same time suffer from a consciousness that they are disliked and even hated by the Christians and consequently have developed a vindictive attitude towards Christians. Both Barabas and Shylock share this trait of personality with each other. The main action of the plays is triggered off by the same reason *i.e.* ill-treatment by the Christians (either in the past or in the present). Shylock, for example, was humiliated and insulted by the rich Antonio in the past :

> Signior Antonio, many a time and oft
> In the Rialto you have rated me

About my money and my usances :
(For suff'rance is the badge of all our tribe)
You call me misbeliever, cut-throat dog,
And spet upon my Jewish gaberdine,
And all for use of that which is mine own.
Well then, it now appears you need my help :
Go to then, you came to me, and you say,
"Shylock, we would have moneys" you say so :
You that did void your rheum upon my beard,
And foot me as you spurn a stranger cur
Over your threshold, moneys is your suit.
What should I say to you? Should I not say
"Hath a dog money? Is it possible
A cur can lend three thousand ducats?" or
Shall I bend low, and in a bondman's key
With bated breath, and wisp'ring humbleness
Say this :
"Fair sir, you spet on me on Wednesday last,
You spurn'd me such a day, another time
You call'd me dog; and for these courtesies
I'll lend you thus much moneys?[7]

Whereas Shylock was insulted in the past as well as is in the present, Barabas is caught in a comparatively greater dilemma in the present. The vengeance between Shylock and Antonio is triggered off by purely economic necessity on the part of Antonio, the hatred between Barabas and Ferneze is basically occasioned by political emergency involving partial or total loss of property by Barabas. When the Turkish Emperor sends Selim Calymath to the Governor of Malta urging for the clearance of tribute pending for the last ten years, Ferneze orders that the tribute money must be paid out of Barabas' wealth. Ferneze makes no bones about the Christian hatred for the Jews :

No, Jew, like infidels;
For through our sufferance of your hateful lives,
Who stand accursed in the sight of heaven,

These taxes and afflictions are befallen,
And therefore thus we are determined.[8]

He orders that the tribute-money of the Turks should be levied among the Jews and that each one of them has to pay one-half of his estate. He further orders that he who refuses to pay, should become a Christian and that he who refuses to become a Christian should lose his entire wealth. The open hostility of Christians towards the Jews exasperates Barabas beyond measure who, therefore, interrogates as follows :

What, bring you Scripture to confirm your wrongs?
Preach me not out of my possessions.
Some Jews are wicked, as all Christians are;
But say the tribe that I descended of
Were all in general cast away for sin,
Shall I be tried for their transgression?[9]

Thus the mutual hatred between Christians and Jews happens to be the general cause for the ill-will between Shylock and Antonio and between Barabas and Ferneze, the Governor of Malta, although the immediate contexts sparking off the racial hatred are local and contingent. They, therefore, decide to have recourse to revenge which is, in Bacon's opinion, a wild form of justice. Vengeance, thus, becomes the common denominator of their behaviour.

Shylock in *The Merchant of Venice* wants to take revenge upon Antonio by lending him three thousand ducats against the security of a bond which states that he can cut off a pound of flesh from Antonio's person in case Antonio fails to return the money at the end of three months' time. Antonio who is badly in need of money accepts the conditions of the bond and takes the loan only to give it to Bassanio thereby enabling him to make a trip to Belmont for courting his would-be wife Portia. Similarly revenge happens to be a means for Barabas in *The Jew of Malta* of redressing the wrong done to him by Ferneze, the Governor of Malta. When forced by the Governor, Barabas loses his entire property. His house being converted into a nunnery, he grows desperate and, therefore, hitches many a Machiavellian plan to avenge himself upon the Christians. Barabas who used to boast of his riches and call himself richer then even the Biblical Job, feels now utterly humiliated. Although his property has been confiscated, Barabas wants to salvage at least some gold and jewellery that he has hidden in his mansion. He, therefore, employs a cunning method of sending his daughter Abigail in the guise of a nun to the nunnery and getting the hidden gold and jewels for his livelihood.

Although vengeance happens to be a common feature of these two Jews, there is a marked difference between the two in the execution of their plans. Whereas the Jew in *The Merchant of Venice* is more legalistic, the Jew in *The Jew of Malta* is more opportunistic. Whereas Shakespeare's Jew is more sober and sophisticated, Marlowe's Jew is more scheming and action-oriented. Shylock remains passively vindictive until the expiry of three months period for Antonio's forfeiture of bond, but Barabas works busily like an activist marshalling all the means of vengeance. He, for example, knows that Mathias and Lodowick are in love with his daughter. But he is so callous that he sets the two lovers against each other and succeeds in getting them killed mutually in a treacherous manner. He hires a Turkish slave called Ithamore and sends poisoned rice-porridge to the nunnery and causes the death of all the nuns including his own daughter. He is so callous that he does not mind killing his own daughter Abigail who had changed her affection for him on account of his treacherous murder of her real lover Mathias. Abigail reveals the secret of her father's treachery to Friar Barnardine in her last confession to him. Barabas is happy under the illusion that nobody knows about his treachery. But when Friar Barnardine and Friar Jacomo go to his house and accuse him of the treacherous murder of all the nuns in the nunnery, he is shocked to learn that he is betrayed by his own daughter. Now Barabas hits upon another callous plan of wriggling out of the crisis. He, therefore, orders his slave Ithamore to strangle

Friar Barnardine and shift the blame of murder on to Friar Jacomo thereby dragging him to the court of justice. Later when betrayed by his own slave to Bellamira, the courtesan, Barabas poisons Bellamira and Pilia-Borza by offering them poisoned flowers. Finally when Barabas is imprisoned by the Governor after the revelation of the formers crimes, he takes a narcotic drug which induces sleepiness in him. The Governor mistakes the sleeping Barabas for dead and orders his body to be thrown out of the city-walls for providing a feast for vultures. But Barabas recovers his senses after a few hours and helps Selim Calymath to destroy the city of Malta by betraying the Governor and becoming himself the Governor of Malta. Thus Barabas' Machiavellian career continues unchecked. He employs all the Machivellian tactics like cunningness, callousness, opportunism, betrayal and turning tables etc., to wriggle out of the crises and to achieve his malicious ends. The play, therefore, degenerates from tragedy to farce, as T.S. Eliot has pointed out.[10] Barabas' career of evil deeds is a hectically busy one, whereas Shylock's is one of eager and quiet waiting for the moment of legal judgement. Comparatively speaking, Shylock appears to be a greater gentleman than Barabas.

Another common feature of these two Jews is that both of them have a daughter each who falls in love with a Christian youngman. But again there is a striking difference between their contexts. There is a remarkable difference between the two fathers' behaviour towards their daughters and their irritating and insulting love affairs.

Although Shylock's daughter falls in love with the Christian youngman called Lorenzo, he never goes to the extent of punishing his daughter or his son-in-law. All that he does is to complain about it to the public and remain helpless. His anti-Christian feeling never goads him to take any drastic steps to prevent the love affair. But Barabas, as his very name phonetically suggests, behaves in a barbaric and unscrupulous fashion in killing the two lovers of his daughter first and his own daughter later. In the process of wreaking vengeance against his enemies in a Machiavellian manner, he loses his very humanity. He, thus, becomes an incarnation of pure evil without an iota of good in him. That is why David M. Bevington[11] compares him to 'Vice' of Morality Drama. But Shylock impresses us as basically a human being in spite of his hatred of Christians on account of his willingness to understand the sophistries of legal argument and judgement and gentlemanly acceptance of his final defeat. Shylock, thus, emerges as a rounded character whereas Barabas strikes us as an incarnation of pure or mere evil. Whereas Shylock is more reasonable in his behaviour, Barabas is simply unscrupulous and shameless. Barabas does not care for whether the means employed for the achievement of his ends are fair or foul. All that he is bothered about is the achievement of his ends no matter what the means is. In this sense he becomes a complete embodiment of the Machiavellian philosophy of life. But comparatively speaking, Shylock appears to be more gentlemanly as he is ready to admit his folly and the inadequacy of his legal argument when the judge *i.e.* Balthazar asks him to cut off his pound of flesh from Antonio's body without shedding even a single drop of blood or an ounce less or more of flesh than his share of one pound. When he is asked by the judge to sign a bond to the effect that he is ready to gift away half of his property to his daughter and her Christian husband, he agrees to oblige them simply because he has to respect the Law and its sanctity. Although he knows that the letter of the Law is on his side, he is convinced by the judge's sophisticated argument that the spirit of Law is not on his side.[12] He is sharp enough to realize the limitation of his claim and therefore, accepts the judgement unconditionally.

But Barabas does not respect any law whether it is legal or moral and goes on betraying everyone treacherously until the moment he is himself betrayed by Ferneze and trapped into death. In a way Barabas' life is an allegorical picture of the self-destructive nature of evil. The death of Barabas not only helps Ferneze to regain his State and his Governorship but enables him to capture Selim Calymath and keep him as a prisoner until the damage done to the city of Malta is amply compensated for by the Turkish Emperor.

Comparatively speaking, Shylock's fight with Christians in general and Antonio in particular is legal or juristic, but Barabas' fight with Ferneze and other Christians is financial, emotional and activistic. Whereas Shylock learns his lesson at the right moment before losing his entire wealth, Barabas does not learn his lesson until the last moment of life because of his apparent success in all the previous misadventures. "He has a plan for every emergency."[13] But finally he is defeated by the moral and metaphysical law of life. Part of the difference between the two is ascribable to the difference in their age. Whereas Barabas is a hot-blooded youth with exuberant energy in him, Shylock is an old man with a relatively more mature mind than Barabas'. Part of the difference between the two is attributable to the density of their evil philosophy. Shylock's hatred, for example, is directed against Christians only but Barabas' hatred goes beyond Christians to Turks and even others and makes no discrimination between daughter and servant; or nuns and friars. All the callousness is perhaps caused by his philosophy which recognizes no sin in the world. The spirit of Machiavelli behind says :

> I count religion but a childish toy
> And hold there is no sin but ignorance.[14]

His Machiavellianism is expressed in his clear-cut advice to his newly bought Turkish slave, Ithamore :

> First, be thou void of these affections,
> Compassion, love, vain hope, and heartless fear;
> Be mov'd at nothing, see thou pity none,
> But to myself smile when the Christians moan.[15]

All these details of behaviour testify to the fact that he is a callous opportunist and sadist who delights in evil for its own sake. His description of his youthful career marked by a multitude of evil deeds indicates his demoniac quality :

As for myself, I walk abroad a — nights,
And kill sick people groaning under walls,
Sometimes I go about and poison wells;
And now and then, to cherish Christian thieves,
I am content to lose some of my crowns,
That I may, walking in my gallery,
See 'em go pinion'd along by my door.
Being young, I studied physic, and began
To practise first upon the Italian;
There I enrich'd the priests with burials,
And always kept the sexton's arms in use
With digging graves and ringing deadmen's knells.
And after that, was I an engineer,
And in the wars 'twixt France and Germany,
Under the pretence of helping Charles the Fifth,
Slew friend and enemy with my stratagems :
Then after that was I an usurer,
And with extorting, cozening, forfeiting,
And tricks belonging unto brokery,
I fill'd the gaols with bankrupts in a year,
And with young orphans planted hospitals;
And every moon made some or other mad,
And now and then one hangs himself for grief,
Pinning upon his breast a long great scroll,
How I with interest tormented him.
But mark how I am blest for plaguing them.
I have as much coin as will buy the town.[16]

As Barabas' confession clearly indicates, he is a whole-hearted devotee of evil who does not differentiate between good and evil. He appears to be a true descendant of Satan and takes delight in immoral activities. His motiveless malignity inspires him to trouble or murder even the innocent beings including priests, orphans and women.

Barabas is not only extraordinarily able to exercise his destructive powers, but is lucky enough to have the services of equally efficient Turkish slave Ithamore who is a vehement hater of Christians. Ithamore describes his own special ability as follows :

> Faith master.
> In setting Christian villages on fire,
> Chaining of eunuchs, binding galley slaves.
> One time I was an hostler in an inn,
> And in the night time secretly would I steal
> To travelers' chambers, and there cut their throats.
> Once at Jerusalem, where the pilgrims kneel'd,
> I strewed powder on the marble stones,
> And therewithal their knees would rankle so,
> That I have laugh'd a good to see the cripples
> Go limping home to Christendom on stilts.[17]

There is, thus, a good deal of similarity between Barabas and Ithamore as far as their evil nature is concerned. Both of them are united in their hatred of Christians and both of them can do anything or everything. Qualitatively speaking there is no difference between them. But there is only one difference between the two *i.e.* financially they are not equal. Hence the master-slave relationship between them. In addition to utilizing the services of Ithamore, Barabas takes the active help of his daughter also for his machinations. Compared to Barabas, Shylock is a very simple, straightforward and honourable person who does not have a rich history of evil deeds and who has no efficient slave like Ithamore and whose daughter does not offer any help to him. All his struggle with Antonio is only legal. Whereas Barabas' evil is complex and multidimensional, Shylock's evil happens to be one-dimensional.

In both the plays there is mutual accusation between Jews and Christians about the values of their religions. In *The Jew of Malta* Barabas' hatred of Christians is motivated by his jealousy for the political power enjoyed by the Christians who become kings by the law of inheritance. Likewise the Christians have their own complaints against the Jews. Ferneze, the Governor of Malta, for example, explains the reasons for his special ill-treatment of Barabas by attributing it to his covetousness which is a sin according to Christianity :

> Out, wretched Barabas :
> Sham's thou not thus to justify thyself,
> As if we knew not thy profession?
> If thou rely upon thy righteousness,
> Be patient, and thy riches will increase;
> And covetousness, O, 'tis a monstrous sin![18]

Similarly Shylock in *The Merchant of Venice* gives vent to his hatred of Christians by pointing out how the Christian vindictiveness masquerades as humility. Likewise the Christians have their own complaints against the Jews. Antonio, for example, comments upon Shylock :

> Mark you this Bassanio,
> The devil can cite Scripture for his purpose, —
> An evil soul producing holy witness
> Is like a villain with a smiling cheek,
> A goodly apple rotten at the heart.
> O what a goodly outside falsehood hath![19]

The complaints against the inimical race is mutual. Each party tries to justify the values of its own religion by laughing at or denigrating those of the other.

In *The Merchant of Venice,* the judge tries to change the heart of Shylock by asking him to exercise the divine-like mercy :

> The quality of mercy is not strain'd,
> It droppeth as the gentle rain from heaven
> Upon The Place beneath : ...
> It is an attitude to God himself;
> And earthly power doth then show likest God's
> When mercy seasons justice : therefore Jew,
> Though justice be thy plea, consider this,
> That in the course of justice, none of us

Should see salvation : we do pray for mercy,
And that some prayer doth teach us all to render
The deeds of mercy.[20]

The judge, thus, tries to highlight the value of mercy which is an important value of Christian faith. But when Shylock refuses to exercise such a divine mercy, he is defeated in his own coin of strict justice thereby made to lose half of his property.

Barabas is proud of his race and his wealth. He is out and out materialistic and hates not only the Christian spirituality but the internal contradictions of Christianity :

Who hateth me but for my happiness?
Or who is honour'd now but his wealth?
Rather had I, a Jew, be hated thus,
Than pities in a Christian poverty;
For I can see no fruits in all their faith,
But malice, falsehood, and excessive pride,
Which methinks fits not their profession.
Haply some hapless man hath conscience,
And for his conscience lives in beggary.[21]

There is a deep seated jealousy in Barabas against the Christian establishment, but he has the satisfaction of belonging to a wealthy community :

They say we are a scattered nation :
I cannot tell; but we have scambled up
More wealth by far than those that brag of faith.
There's kirriash Jairim, the great Jew of Greece,
Obed in Bairseth, Nones in Portugal,
Myself in Malta, some in Italy,
Many in France, and wealthy everyone;
Ay, wealthier far than any Christian.
I must confess we come not to be Kings;
That's not our fault : alas, our number is few,
And crowns come either by succession
Or urg'd by force; and nothing violent,

Oft have I heard tell, can be permanent.
Gives us a peaceful rule; make Christian kings,
That thirst so much for principality.[22]

In addition to accusing the inimical faiths, both Barabas and Shylock quote the Scripture in support of their financial achievements. Whereas Shylock cites the Biblical example of how Jacob increased his wealth by exercizing his commercial cleverness (*MV*, I, iii, 65-85), Barabas refers to Job's loss of wealth when his own property is confiscated by the Governor of Malta (*JM*, I, 185-202). Thus both of them are conversant with the Biblical details which are relevant to their personal contexts.

Both the plays of Marlowe and Shakespeare are dramatic metaphors of the authorial vision or philosophy of life. There appears to be a remarkable difference between Marlowe and Shakespeare as far as their philosophies of life are concerned. Marlowe's Jew is a Machiavellian and an incarnation of pure evil or 'Vice' figure of Morality Drama. His evil nature is multi-dimensional and he is more enthusiastic and energetic than Shylock. He has a plan to get out of every emergency. He can take the guise of a fiddler and offer poisoned flowers to Bellamira etc. He is successful all through his evil career until finally he is defeated almost by chance. Thus there is no growth in the character of Barabas although he is quite lively in his misadventures. David M. Bevington rightly points out, "...there is no development of motivation at all. Each variation on the theme of vice casts additional light on the nature and operation of evil. The process does not logically unfold, but elaborates and intensifies by repeated example."[23] All these details of characterization prove beyond any doubt that Marlowe's philosophy is rather negative or at best "Morally neutral."[24] In spite of all the fullblooded liveliness of the character of Barabas, he is an embodiment of pure evil who, therefore, represents only half the truth of life without the other half of good forces of life. Thus Marlowe's vision of life appears to be amoral if not immoral and partial, as compared to Shakespeare's vision which recognizes both the evil and good elements in life by showing the defeat of evil and triumph of good in the life of Shylock. No critic has failed to notice the essential 'humanity' of Shylock in spite of his anti-Christian feeling. Shakespeare shows the growth in Shylock's personality by depicting his realization of folly and acceptance of the court judgement in a gentlemanly fashion. Shakespeare's vision is positive, humanistic and comprehensive.

REFERENCES

1. H.S. Bennett, ed., Introduction, *The Jew of Malta* and *The Massacre at Paris*, (London : Methuen & Co., 1931), p. 9.
2. *Ibid.*, p. 9.
3. *Ibid.*, p. 9.
4. *Ibid.*, p. 9.
5. *Ibid.*, p. 9.
6. John Russell Brown, Introduction, *The Merchant of Venice,* The Arden edition (London : Methuen & Co., 1971), p. xxviii.
7. Christopher Marlowe, *The Jew of Malta,* in *The Complete Plays,* ed., J.B. Steane. Harmondsworth : Penguin Books, 1971, I, iii, 101-124.
8. *Ibid.*, I, ii, 65-70.
9. *Ibid.*, 114-19.
10. T.S. Eliot, *The Sacred Wood,* (London : Methuen & Co., 1948), p. 92.
11. David M. Bevington, "The Jew of Malta," *Marlowe : A Collection of Critical Essays,* ed. Clifford Leech, (New Delhi : Prentice-Hall of India, 1979), p. 150.
12. E.F.J. Tucker, "The Letter of the Law in "The Merchant of Venice," *Shakespeare Survey* : 29, ed. Kenneth Muir, (Cambridge University Press, 1976), pp 99-100.
13. David M. Bevington, p. 150.
14. Christopher Marlowe, *The Jew of Malta,* Prologue, 14-15.
15. *Ibid.*, II, iii, 174-77.
16. Christopher Marlowe, *The Jew of Malta,* II, iii, 179-206.
17. *Ibid.*, I, ii, 207-217.
18. *Ibid.*, 122-28.
19. Shakespeare, *The Merchant of Venice,* I, iii, 93-97.

20. *Ibid.*, IV, I, 180-98.
21. Christopher Marlowe, *The Jew of Malta*, I, I, 114-22.
22. *Ibid.*, I, I, 123-37.
23. David M. Bevington, p. 155.
24. *Ibid.*, p. 157.

5

The Growth of Universal Entropy in *Julius Caesar*

—N. Narasimha Ramayya

I

CAESAR'S WILL

JULIUS CAESAR gives a superman concept to the world and it is not acceptable to his own followers. Perceptions and contaminations defy the authority of his will. There was no tendentious scope though the people suspected his bonafides of thought. Caesar is a pathfinder making his headway into the chaotic world of Rome and it is a replica of the world full of uncertainty, indiscipline and stultification. *Julius Caesar* has to be studied under three perspectives : emotional, intellectual and political. Perhaps the chauvinistic tendency of Caesar is to be condemned by one and all.

There is an individualistic approach to the collectivist study of the chaotic world in this play. "...Heideggar clearly claims that beings are and are what they are even if there are no people."[1] The whole acclamation is uncertainty like a minority cell of ideas. The inexactness of relationship is $\Delta p \ \Delta q = h$ and there has been a fusion of vitalist antiromantic and mystical philosophies. "Their fundamentally antiscientific and antirationalistic attempts continue to this day."[2] Perhaps the uncertainty principle and the notion of causality go hand in hand and sometimes with a challenge to each other. Deterministic theory of probabilities is nothing but an ever operating quantum mechanics. Acausal laws are both probabilities and predictions yielding the fruits of epistemology. This is enunciated in Kantian epistemology or Schrodinger equation of indeterminism or macroscopic world of preeminence. Of course, complacency leads to conclusion. The whole Caesar's will is subjection or sublimation of :

> "the astronomical constitution of the cosmos or macrocosm, and the anatanital physiological and psychological structure of man, the microcosm."[3]

Again he writes :

> "Thus the primordial matter of the principle of death and dissolution is held in subjection."[4]

May be this is called a holistic approach by the latter philosophers.

Kinetic energy is a mobile force of a moving body as in the society and the potential energy is in the constant body like the sun. The earth, therefore, carries kinetic energy to any extent including Caesar's will in this play. The idea of consecration was a symbolic preservation of the Roman culture dogmatically attached to the enhancement or extension of the old feudal values.

Invigorating improvisation of thought often leads to stultification and venality, and *Julius Caesar* is no exception to them. Our concern is with creation, mutation and demise as a part of the intellectual quest. Anti monopolist subtleties entered many walks of life including that of political arena.

"He (Ponnelly) also wrote a novel, *Caesar's Column*, in which he seemed to predict that the lower classes, driven desperate by the ills from which they suffered would join a great Brotherhood of *Destruction* that eventually would bring down civilization."[5] (Italics mine) It seems Bacon wrote Shakespeare and may have inspired and influenced him. Nature restricts her bestowal of power on everybody and sooner or later takes it back when the person nears his end. This has been true also in the case of Julius Caesar.

Energy is a sacred action of power that colludes with persons in a given society just like in a diatomic or polyatomic gas. "When two of its molecules collide they will, in general tend to rotate, as well as to deflect each other."[6] It may be a translation to rotation or *vice versa* and all the assumption is an emission of the internal energy. This parallelism is an incidious affair as a social drama on par with the physical reactions in the world.

The cosmic element in a Shakespearean play is laudable since it suggests the human struggle against some mysterious force and the characters meet their doom in the hands of some malignant power. Raghukula Tilak writes :

> "Universality is achieved by connecting the Dramatic personae with the universe at large. His works thus acquire cosmic significance, and his personages become the symbol of mankind struggling against the forces of evil."[7]

All the odds, therefore, may be an outcome of man's own errors. Sense of motivation is derived from the tragic flaw and serious convulsions of fate. Dowden says : "Tragedy as conceived by Shakespeare is concerned with ruin or restoration of the soul and of the life of man. In other words, its subject is the struggle of good and evil in the world."[8]

Shakespeare displays his acute disappointment in *Julius Caesar*. Cazamian notes :

> "The choice in this very year of the subject of *Julius Caesar,* and the glorification, at Caesar's expense, of Brutus the conspirator, can best be explained by political events and by the poets increasing pessimism."[9]

May be it is nothing but the court machinations of Essex and others in the court of Elizabeth I and Southampton was a key accomplice. The whole apotheosis undergoes a change of *Katharsis* (Catharsis) towards an anathema of change.

The conspiracy has been monitored and masterminded by

Cassius and there is nobody to avert it on Caesar's side in his camp. Above all Caesar's own adamant nature seems to have brought about his own destruction. For instance, while refusing freedom for Publius Cimber, he says in Act III Scene I :

> "I could be well moved, if I were as you;
> If I could pray to move, prayers would move me :
> But I am constant as the northern star"[10]

People speak of principles because they are not principled yet. Actually *Julius Caesar* reminds us of the *Animal Farm* and the commandment thereon. George Orwell writes :

> "There was nothing there now except a single commandment. It ran all animals are equal. But some animals are more equal than others."[11]

It is almost satire on totalitarian state and the state-craft in *Julius Caesar*. We can conclude the play as the *Animal Farm* :

> "Twelve voices were shouting in anger, and they were all alike. No question, now, what had happened.... The creatures outside looked from pig to man, and from man to pig, and from pig to man again, but already it was impossible to say which was which."[12]

It is a beautiful caricature of the human nature personified and embodied in each allegorical face of man is equal to animal snout. The resumption of excitement is a suicidal attempt at every stage full of vehemence and resentment. Sagacity and equanimity fail in the face of fate in *Julius Caesar*. It is stated :

> "Possibly, Elizabethan audiences attached a little more importance to the fact that one was a king and the other a prince; perhaps they were readier to credit that Julius Caesar was a colossus and not as some modern directors have tried to persuade us, a mere Massolini."[13]

The Roman society is heterogeneous and envy is common in such society and the superman, as such, cannot please one and all. A critic could say :

> "Shakespeare's world is... a panorama in which the immense variety of life is brought before us, and some moods, some moments, some experiences are quite as dark as anything in ancient tragedy — but the world is not."[14]

Indeed this is a strange phenomenon of a Shakespearean tragedy.

Mark Antony's oration is pathetic and powerfully inciting and solemnizing *pari passu.* When he thinks fully convinced that the citizens are well incited he narrates how the stabbing occurred one by one that the traitors proved their insurgency. He says, "O, what a fall there my countrymen!"[15] And then again he says without a pause :

> "O, now you weep, and I perceive you feel
> The dint of pity : there are gracious drops"[16]

The whole play seems to have began with Caesar's will and ends with the death of Brutus and Cassius as a climax of melancholy born of the universal entropy. When the 2nd triumvirate is formed with Octavius, Mark Antony and Lepidus they are very much interested to see the will of Julius Caesar perhaps only to veer the serenity and modesty of their departed leader.

Caesar's ghost is all prevalent throughout the play invisibly watching the situation combined with stoic virtues. The ghost appears when Brutus is alone in his tent pondering over the future plans of the battle at Phillippi. It is almost a caution to Brutus : "Beware, Phillippi" and he would meet him there in a short course of action.

We may call Caesar's will is an antidote to his psycho-neurosis of inept supermanship. No one can fulminate him aloud nor can anyone defy him; hence the fabrication of conspiracy by disgruntled politicians who end their "psychic motif" in a polarization. They wrongly interpret his will to be lurid only to insinuate Caesar. May be Caesar is a victim to an inexpressible megalomania that desires no accompaniment at all. Force is equal to power in politics and the same "force = inertial mass × acceleration where the inertial mass is a characteristic constant of accelerated body."[17] This can be elaborately stated as :

$$\text{acceleration} = \frac{\text{gravitational mass}}{\text{(inertial mass)}} \times \text{(intensity of the gravitational field)}^{18}$$

In that case it is a mass or jerk that jeopardises the human nature and the solemnity of luck spontaneously growing towards entropy.

Conclusively we can estimate that man is a plethora of dreams and a delirium of havoc. Psychological importance is more valid than the anathema in Caesar's will. However, the complacent attitude of man is a typical caricature of the human pleasure for a selfish motive and there is no wonder even in the case of Caesar's own personality. Joseph L. Henderson notes :

> "In war time for instance, one finds increased interest in the works of Homer, Shakespeare, or Tolstoy, and we read with a new understanding those passages that gives war its enduring (or archetypal) meaning."[19]

We try to seek symbolic meaning for a mythological background in *Julius Caesar* for his lostness and cognition.

Julius Caesar's regime is a significant period of epoch-making Roman History that had shone as Hesperus and disappeared. Joseph L. Henderson further comments :

> "There godlike figures are in fact symbolic representatives of the whole psyche, the larger and more comprehensive identity that supplies the strength that the essential ego lacks."[20]

Yet man does not understand his own lacuna that ends in ultimate chaos and doom.

II

TRIBUTES OF ANTONY

Multiplicity of ideas and idealisms as simple isolated entities are irreducible to a single unit called monism. Thus pluralism has worked no authenticity in anybody as such. *Julius Caesar* is a drama dialectics : a contradiction of genres and species as a tributary of metaphysical thinking. May be it is a compromise of syllogism and transcendentalism, a truce of sinecures and the workaday world. May be it is an identical rebellion against a feudal society embedded in the thought of Caesar. Herbert L. Dreyfus thinks :

> "The only cosmology we can affirm with the certainty Plato recommended is our own (communal or individual) world picture, our own way of setting things up for manipulation the way dictated by desires."[21]

Uncertainty is, therefore, indeterminacy or imprecision that runs into infinity.

$$\Delta p \, \Delta q \geq h | 2\pi$$
$$\Delta E \, \Delta t \geq h | 2\pi$$

This may be cited from Heisenburg's "anauschalich" unfriendly perceptual. The heuristic approach of Shakespeare, likewise, involves holism and finally confusion well accepted universality. It is a movement between "reality and self-consciousness."

Antony is a nice man because he has been trained up in warfare and not in politics. There is no deliverance for a sick society much less for a mental case. Norman J.G. Pounds writes :

> "About 575 B.C. this archaic Rome merged into early classical Rome. There must have been some kind of synoecism...close to Hellenic style."[22]

Incorrigible people can never be reformed. There is some depravity in Antony's speech in spite of its flamboyance and revenge motive or as a victim to some motiveless malignity.

There was no dearth of prophets and philosophers in the Roman culture. Soothsayer and Cinna are living examples reminding the platonic life of the early Greek culture. Caesar, whereas, is a multifaceted personality as a product of the Roman history. Though he is not a pedantic bore he is never in dilemma even in a pensive mood of his times. Everything in distructible and Caesar does not know this philosophic aphorism and Antony too does not remind him of this. Walter Kaufmann comments :

> "One must insist on the tragic nature of conflicts and solutions only where this is necessary to vindicate a superior view."[23]

The name of the flaw that is detrimental to the human society is ambition. In that respect a Shakespearean play is on par with the Sophocles' bifocal themes. A Shakespearean tragedy such as *Julius Caesar* is a living example as a contribution of hypersensitivity and hamartia.

There are as many types of elements as points of interaction to connote the celebrities of life such as infirmity, sickness, ambition, dissatisfaction, sorrow and other passions. Walter Kaufmann observes :

> "One might have expected Schopenhauer to realize all this, such he stressed the universality of suffering more than any previous philosopher."[24]

The universal suffering is an indication of the Buddhist feeling and the fourfold path.[25]

Antony has a great regard for Caesar and his nobility and he doles out the eulogy and words of panegyric for Caesar. On the contrary, Brutus has a sarcastic and a doubtful eye upon Caesar. Brutus murmurs by the end of the Second scene :

"Brutus (aside) : That every like in not the same,
O Caesar,
The heart of Brutus yearns to think upon!"[26]

We don't know whether he really mourns for his yearning.

Apparently the play reaches its climax with the speech of Antony at the forum in honour of Julius Caesar who is no more nor his ambitious plan of enriching Rome. Turning tables is the art of Antony's speech and especially to maintain his upright character as a loyal citizen of Rome when he pleads for equity and justice. He uses all touching sentences without any malice as in :

"I come to bury Caesar, not to praise him
The evil that men do lives after them,
The good if often interred with their bones,
So let it be with Caesar."[27]

He can create irony through his speech and that proves fatal to Brutus and others in the end.

"For Brutus is an honourable man,
So are they all, all honourable men."[28]

The word of honour is embedded deep in tinge of allegory that can provoke citizens and prick the conspirators. For some the glamour is in conspiracy and for some others in exposing it. Antony is the second type who can debunk the misdeeds of treachery in the play. He cleverly manages to speak :

"I speak not to disprove what Brutus spoke,
But here I am to speak what I do know."[29]

This is a remarkable artistry as embodied in the personality of Antony and every line of his speech is an outstanding peroration to inspire the virtuosity among the citizens and countrymen. He speaks eloquently and pauses with a little interruption of citizens in whom the wisdom is to dawn yet before they take to cudgels against the conspirators. He says :

"My heart is in the coffin there with Caesar
And I must pause till it came back to me."[30]

On each of the words there is impressive effect of punning, quibbling and ambiguity which can evoke nostalgia in any listener. Antony is a skillful virtuoso full of language, valour and determination. The tragic element depends upon determinism too to recall the philosophical pioneers : Aristotle, Hume, Schopenhauer, Nietzsche and Kant with his "constructive conditions" or in other words stoic "tragic itself."

Shakespeare's dramaturgy is deeply safe in the lines of Mark Antony's speech and he can invite the citizens to any extent. The command of the language and craftsmanship are in his hands now and if time permitted he could have been a great statesman too. All the citizens at the forum are fully prepared for revenge against the conspirators. They utter :

"Revenge ! About ! Seek ! Burn ! Fire ! Kill !
Stay ! Let not traitors live."[31]

Their mental agony is fully prepared psychologically to fight the injustice and treachery. Antony's words are ironic as well as sarcastic with a purpose of didactic mutiny. He says again, "I am not orator, as Brutus is."[32]

He has every quality of wit and wisdom and on the contrary, Brutus is a victim to mental aberration. Blunder, splendour, and etiquette are the characteristics of a Shakespearean tragedy. Brutus fails to deal with the mob psychology whereas Antony is successful in the ablazed status of mutineers now. The language of the citizens is very significant and it acts simply as an antidote for all the earlier rancour against Caesar inculcated by Brutus and his followers. The citizens say "noble Caesar," "royal Caesar" and the melee is so intense that we cannot differentiate distinctively who is who. Added to it Antony's clever and balanced language gives a tinge. "Here was a Caesar! when comes such another?"[33] While declaring the properties bequeathed Caesar for the nation — arbors, new planted orchards, and promenades and so on and thus Caesar is a nationalist misunderstood by his own countrymen including Brutus.

At last Antony heaves a breath of sigh that his project has worked wonderfully through his provocative speech. He says :

> "Now let it work. *Mischief*, thou art afoot,
> Take thou what course thou wilt."[34]

Perhaps he foresees this is the starting point of general chaos and entropy. Temerity is no end at any case and the human mind cannot eschew dynamism since propriety is a different matter. May be it is a data based structure of computerised feelings in the guise of a drama.

Brutus and Cassius are the most aggrieved parties when they are closeted in camera meeting at Sardis and their mental agony is their own grief. Of course, the hotchpotch adjustment is an intense contention based on the factionalism and conspiracy that ought to have culminated in a calumny and bitter fight against the enemies. The badblood is inherent in Brutus and Cassius as a part of their living entropy in their structural energy of their minds. The potentialities decide the stature of the human beings in this play of havoc and histrionic disillusionment.

We can bring in Newton's third law of Motion to recognise the chaotic condition that denote. It is almost a circuit critical of denouement that will end in a crisis at last. "To every action there is always an equal and opposite reaction."[35]

The moon is attracting the earth with a certain force (action). The earth also attracts the moon with an equal and opposite force (reaction).[36] The whole universe is subjective to this type of phenomenon including the life of Antony too. On the contrary, Brutus is a peculiar combination of sordid melancholy, less wisdom and more knowledge unaware of the consequences whatsoever. It is a clear cut example of motiveless malignity. People condescend as though they were born for the emancipation of mankind and if it were really a case they should conduct themselves properly in life.

Some people are very cranky and we have to deal with them cleverly. Antony is an intelligent warrior and he outlives the eventful history of his times. He can manage with Octavius who is a crank as a young politician. In Act V when they meet in the plains of Phillippi we are not sure whether these two generals are really at loggerheads. Octavius replies him ultimately "I do not cross you, but I will do so"[37] as a remarkable showiness of his princely status as a crowned prince. When Antony charges Brutus and Cassius for their vileness he uses animal imagery that befits their bestial nature. He says :

> "You show'd upon teeth like apes and fawn'd like
> hounds,
> And bow'd like bondmen, kissing Ceasar's feet;
> While damned Casca, like a cur behind
> Struck Caesar on the neck, O you flatterers!"[38]

There are a number of charges and countercharges on each other so that the vendetta may be intensified.

In every part of the battlefield at Phillippi there is confusion and disorder as though it were not confined geographically to a single place. Cato declares that is the son of Marcus Cato. Lucilius tempts the first soldier with money. He says :

> [offering money] There is so much
> thou will me straight;
> Kill Brutus, and be honour'd his death"[39]

When these confabulations are going on Mark Antony appears on the stage. In fact, he likes Brutus so much that he wants to spare the life of the latter and it is an indication of Mark Antony's nobility. He orders Lucilius or rather urges him;

> "Go on,
> And see whether Brutus be alive or dead

> And bring us wold in to Octavius' tent
> How everything is chanced."[40]

In that case there is nothing wrong if Brutus is renamed as the hero of *Julius Caesar* whether right or wrong. The ambivalence is in the eyes of the observer as in Cato's tastes or Brutus' temperaments. May be Brutus is priggish or uppish or even brutal for the reason that he is prepared to emancipate the Roman world from the so called tyranny.

In a primordial society the interaction is as confusing as adiabatic or isothermal calculation of the universal entropy on par with the hydrodynamics, thermodynamics, electrodynamics. Now we may call in this play of *Julius Caesar* it is nothing but politic dynamics significantly achieving political machinations right from Aristotle to Shakespeare.

The play is so artistically framed that Antony pays his glowing tributes to Brutus in his final speech. One has to accept the greatness of one enemy's too and that is called goodness.

> "His life was gentle, and the elements
> So mix'd in him that Nature might stand up
> And say to all the world "this was a man!"[41]

Octavius too supports the views of Antony as a way of requiem in honour of Brutus. Octavius says taking this opportunity :

> "According to his virtue let us use him,
> With all respect and rites of burial."[42]

There would be a common condolence to his memory by one and all, and thus his speech is a memorial service. He has been given a VIP treatment on his death though he was almost a sinecure in his lifetime.

In the terrestrial phenomenon the worldly magnetism is predominantly functioning similar to the transformation taking place in a given society of a country. Likewise as in thermodynamics under the exigencies of time we can borrow the terms adiabatic process and isothermal process to maintain the natural balances of man in the society. Man as a visionary could estimate the changes to muffle up his own ventriloquism. We are sure that :

> "The first law of thermodynamics states that the amount of heat given to a system is equal to the sum of increase in the internal energy of the system and the external work done."[43]

Similarly the society is also a heat producing body fit for confrontations and confabulations.

Duplicity of personality or self (split personality) is an invidious malady inherent in every human being and Antony is no exception. He wants to pay his glowing tributes as a faithful follower of Caesar, but he also wants to be an important supremo as a great warrior. His valour is evidently not able to sustain only after the extinction of his mentor, Julius Caesar and, in the company of the other triumvirs and subsequently in *Antony and Cleopatra*. May be sometimes he is carried away by his own "subliminal effect of psyche" as a dreamy statesman with an introvert tinge. If that were the case he lingers between consciousness and ambitions motifs and ambitions like his master, Julius Caesar. The whole Roman history would have taken a chaotic turn but for his shrewdness as an archetypal symbol of statesmanship. As a matter of fact, many Roman heroes deserve a psychiatric treatment since they suffer from obsessions and emotional dreams, which they want to translate into realities through strife and strategems. It is asserted :

> "The archetype is a tendency to form such representations of a motif representations that can vary a great deal in detail without losing their basic pattern."[44]

The world is full of heroes and hero makers who want to poise the historical perspective and psychological meaning if not a fantastic absurdity and Antony is the latter instance. There could have been voluminous hazards to project such people as pragmatists monitoring some unusual cause.

Antony could have been a heroic trickster playing the major role of a historic figure through his ego consciousness. His personality resolves around supplication — application of strength, while dealing with the statecraft of his age succinctly. We may describe that everything is in relatively motion including the human mind. Though it is nebulous :

> "Every general law of nature must be constructed that it is transformed in to a law of exactly the same from when instead of space time variables x, y, z, t of the original coordinate system k, we introduce new space time variables, x′, y′, 3′, t′ of a coordinate system k′"[45]

Thus it is the universe of entropy and relativity is a farcical phase of it that creates an illusory human mind of reality in a mirage of feelings.

The inconceivable is conceivable world of entropy and one wants to hoodwink the other. Hoodwinking is in human nature that is hypocritically hidden in an individual capacity. So far as Antony is concerned he is a noble soul and exceptionally too good to live in a world of stratagems. We come across his end in *Antony and Cleopatra* (40 B.C.?) as he meets his death through a suicide. On the whole the whole Roman history seems to be full of turmoil at every level.

III

THE ROLE OF CONSPIRATORS

Universal connection of phenomenology is the central idea of *Julius Caesar* in contract with the Utopian idealism of self-possessed by Caesar himself. It is felt that :

> "The universal interaction of bodies determines the existence of concrete material objects and all their specific features."[46]

Without this concept of universal phenomena the world would be a chaos. Every objective law has its own say in the body of phenomena and entropy as if it were a Herculean task.

Concatenation of events is the watchword of entropy as we find in the portrayal of these characters represented by all the conspirators. Brutus is the stupid character (Keith Wilson personal interview) and he connects his so-called patriotism with his enviable affections to that of Caesar whereas Caesar is gullible to believe him.

As it appears as in Heideggar it is a controversy of pragmatism and dogmatism in a Shakespearean drama too. Valour is confused with trauma or rather one with the other. Heideggar states :

> "This valour is not a heroism of action, but a disposition of thought with respect to the history of being."[47]

Valour cancels the joy and leads to melancholy as in the case of conspirators conspicuously notorious impostors. It is something like a link between veracity and vacuity. Presentiment is an arbitrary focus of the mind. We can deduce imperatively and quote :

> "The second law of thermodynamics says that natural processes have a tendency to increase in entropy, or disorder, and most physicists viewed this as a statistical law."[48]

Witch-hunting is a common weakness of every society and the whole problem is with the quislings and every one behaves as a raving lunatic according to his own penchant. Smattering is not a grave offence whatsoever in the political field of knowledge.

There were no canons of heresy and the conspirators wanted to establish a new system that degenerated into a diffusion of disorder constantly a variable of entropy in the universe. The histrionics and the choreography cannot take care of the human psychology. Hence this realistic study of these characters deeply committed to conspiracies. There was no "harmony of interests" and as such there was no attempt for a corporate state to link up the plebians and publicans. If the conspirators were striving to establish the dictatorship of proletariat, if any, the attempt was in vain. The age of Julius Caesar seems to have been an age of travails and turmoils, historically or politically speaking as a period of polemical dynamism which would involve intrigue, and intricacies. Every careerist is a mean fellow and all the conspirators are careerists reflecting the worldly wisdom. They are more or less lowborn fellows and their genes determine the character and philosophy of life in a permissive society. The empirical unsystematic disturbance of the Roman society is something like the collision of photons and mesons of cosmic rays. The same fusion of fission in a historic society may result in explosion or radiation of inhuman behaviour.

History makes a correlative record of physics and sociology. The zeal is in its veneration, right or wrong. All the conspirators are demagogues including Brutus himself much concerned with the physical world. All bumptious fellows turn to perversity at the end and that is a Shakespearean tragedy. Conspicuously it is an amalgamation of the human weaknesses with the universal melancholy. Mark Van Doren comments :

> "Caesar is not a noble Roman, not one of Plutarch's men. He is that rarity in the play an Elizabethan personality, he is one of Shakespeare's men."[49]

The whole play is a record of sound and fury with a few moral undertones that end up in juxtaposition of the good and evil.

If there are evilsome conspirators like elfin prodigies, there are also honest fellows such as Mark Antony and Lepidus on the other hand. Nauseating ill-will is expurgated mostly and the horror and malice remain as absurdities unmollified. May we call the feeling a prodigious melancholy of the mind. Everywhere every one projects the bitterness, disgust and helplessness since most of the people misappropriate the feeling of gratitude. Scathing words are always calculated to impress the other party and Antony could do wonders by virtue of his oratory.

The terminology of Brutus' speech is muffled up in calculated offensive words of crafty criminology and apparently Shakespeare was highly competent also in jurisprudence. The negative approach of the words is worth mentioning here such as censure, judge, ambitions, dearth, offended, vile, offences and so on. He speaks the word offend four times diligently and emphatically as a peroration. With all said and done Brutus may be a noble man who has acted meanly, and some people have kind tongue to hide their cruel heart. He may not be a powerful orator as Antony is, who brings about the whole destruction of the conspirators. In the lesser mortals, auguries may change to vagaries and they bring no redemption in their lifetime, and tragic impressions might create cosmic changes in nature. Julius Caesar may have been an ethical hero who wanted to emulate himself as an emancipatör and misunderstood by his own senators and plebians. Perceptions fail as impossible and implausible transformations because of the quislings in any society. Tribulations for a purpose metamorphosise the woman soul to the worst as in Sophocles, Ayscheles, Euripides and lastly Shakespeare.

Caesar's observation about Cassius as said to Antony is noteworthy. He says :

> "Yond Cassius has a lean and hungry look,
> He thinks too much : such men are dangerous."[50]

Cassius is lanky and crafty unlike Brutus. Thomas Carter further states :

> "Very simple when it suited, but always subtle and deceptive, watchful, envious, ambitious, jealous sarcastic and bitter. He was a close observer and could weigh men with unfailing accuracy."[51]

He appears as if he is feverish and suffering from unknown malaise of vendetta as the most lean and dangerous conspirator of all. Full of recrimination the end of Cassius and Brutus is pathetic. Thomas Carter further notes in his book :

> "Great flocks of ravens, crows, and kites overshadowed the armies and wheeled in circles above the heads of Cassius and Brutus."[52]

The solemnity is realised only through the homage of Octavius and Antony to the memory of Brutus befitting a soldier. In a primordial society the vortex feelings of uncommon conjectures is a common affair of conspiracy because of the selfish human minds. In spite of Plotinus and his neoplatonic approach to life on a mystic combination of the spirit and the matter there has been no social revolution to amplify or extenuate human weaknesses. At the outset there is a cordial welcome to Julius Caesar despite the clandestine conspiracy against him. The assassination is a turning point undoubtedly in the Roman politics and the human history.

The dastardly action of the conspirators is exposed sooner or later in a hectic manner bringing about their own end in Act IV. Brutus and Cassius have no option at the end but to die. The mortality of a human being is in his own decision guided by fate.

There is no consternation or remorse in Cassius even on the battlefield and he is still pungent while he accuses Octavius :

> "A peevish school boy, worthless of such honour
> Join'd with a masker and a reveler!"[53]

Cassius reminds us more or less of Edmund and his villainy. Nevertheless, the storm is within and without gathering its momentum. "The momentum of a body is the product of its mass and its velocity as in $M = m \times v$." Here the mass is the mass of sin, crime and guilt raised out of the murder of Julius Caesar that shall wrest the mental peace of Cassius and Brutus with full velocity towards destruction in the high drama of conspiracy. *Sarvam sithilayathe.* Every thing in destructable, and wreck is a toxic phenomenon in *Julius Caesar*.

The philosophy of life varies according to the growing age and there is no wonder even if Brutus could speak philosophy. His words are more or less confession when he nears his death. He speaks out his remorse when he runs over the sword of Strato.

> "Fare well, good Strato. (Runs on his sword)
> Caesar, now be still :
> I kill'd not thee with half so good a will"
> (Dies)[54]

May be it is a sort of poetic justice whatever be the version of his friends and foes alike. The words of a Roman soldier are like that of a cricket player in a winning match spoken so sportively even in the end.

Law of nature is phenomenal law of physical and metaphysical world, wherein the society revolves in variegated colours of cosmic and tragic flaws for which the good and evil are responsible. Even if there is a mushroom growth of evils, Nature can check them for her own purpose and we can put it as $E = Mc^2$ = Brahman.

Any disgruntled politician would become a nationalist philosopher be it Brutus or Antony or anybody else. The dichotomy is between realism and idealism similar to that of materialism and spiritualism. The individualist philosophy is suppressed and nullified when the socialist values desist the former. No humanist has the barriers of race or nation or religion and so is Shakespeare like Thomas Woolsey, Garibaldi, Kamal Pasha Ataturk and Khediev. May be the obscurity is because of man's oblivion and so is the case with almost all the characters in the play at different satisfaction. (But the Indians are the most silent spectators and they can visualise stoicism in anywalk of life and the dreamy world unlike the Romans.) There is always a confrontation of the old values and the new values when the valueless world is entering the arena of entropy. Or sometimes they may indulge in dubbing the truth, and life is only a chance. Since the universal entropy is immeasurable it is conjectural like the conversation of Achilles and a tortoise. Stigma is also a symbol developing into unconsciousness so as to prick the heart unawares. Nobody can save a nation which indulges in delinquency and stultification. With all-round grief of mortification and with no emancipation this elemental body would decay and die into space and dissolve into five elements of the universe. Soul is nothing but a relinquishment of the realities of life. The present restitution of delirium of mind is the ordeal of life; yet so prime ordeal of the early times.

Contentment is the best source of inspiration and unfortunately no conspirator has contentment, and there arises the trouble failing their sagacity towards the wrong illusory directions. Almost all the conspirators are jubilant temporarily caught in euphoria as though they are convalescent from a stroke of melancholia. Frankly speaking they have no refinement whatsoever. The principle of inexplicability tends to explain uncertainty and that is a failure attempt to reach a stage beyond imagination.[55]

IV

SHAKESPEAREAN WOMEN

"Shakespeare has only heroines and no heroes" says Sir Walter Raleigh. If that is the case both Calpurnia and Portia are the noble souls in *Julius Caesar* without any feminine ruses. Shakespeare seems to have ignored the portrayal of termagant women to denote exemptions from trepidations. May be this is also a part simulation by an artist.

Lack of receptivity added to nihilism is well grounded in the lostness of a Being and that creates the mortality on the ontological basis sacrosanct from mental illness. The feeling may have originated in Julius Caesar either in search of identity or to attain the traits of masculine vigour. Shakespearean women are in the quest of vigour (Life Force) in a vital vacuity.

All the miraculous events are spectacular events whatsoever. If Shakespearean women lost something by way of love they gained something by virtue of their marriage. He compensates by ennobling their status as human beings and it is all warranted at any level to fill in the gap left over by the sacrificial women. They would depreciate any sense of treachery or human misbehaviour though they themselves suffer from the sense of belonging. Had we adopted the bilingual method also in social reforms the Roman history would have been entirely different and for that matter any history in the world. But the human mind is not that developed at any case to subsume the entropy of the universe.

Sometimes even the graceful action degenerates into a bigger turmoil because that is a way of the universal life. We can notice :

> "The universal connection of phenomena is infinite in its manifestations. The connections between objects and phenomena may be mediate or immediate, permanent or temporary, essential or unessential necessary or accidental, functional or non-functional...."[56]

Any grace may change to disgraceful chaos at any time because Nature plays havoc with the human life.

Shakespearean women are immortal and superb even in death because of their infinite variety and if that were the case the living examples are Calpurnia, Portia and Cleopatra — all are royal in their tastes, temperaments and behaviour. Though the human weakness culminates only in death they became immortalized because of their virtuous life. It appears all the while that Portia has been the first victim to villainy of Brutus since the latter hides his cruel heart every time from her. Women can manage anything deftly but here they are so noble that they forget their crafty skills. Perhaps this is the reason why Walter Kaufmann comments :

> "...it is plain that Hegel had a lively appreciation of Shakespeare's tragic art...."[57]

The credit goes to the intensity of feeling that arises from the heart of woman.

Premonition is the watchword of the Roman womanhood and Calpurnia is a living example of this type. In the very beginning of the 2nd scene of Act II she warns Caesar "you shall not stir out your house today."[58] But Caesar is equally adamant and thrillingly determined not to be afraid of anything on the earth. He utters :

> "Caesar shall forth : the things that threatened me
> Ne'er look'd but on my back; when they shall see
> the face of Caesar, they are vanished."[59]

According to Calpurnia the whole nature is disturbed. Yet Caesar says like a pontiff :

> "Cowards die many times before their death;
> The valiant never taste of death but once,
> ....
> Will come when it will come."[60]

He philosophizes the inevitability of death. Caesar is noble and he would not speak lies whereas the conspirators are mean. The primary conspirator is Decius Brutus to play the mischievous role whereas fortitude is the pleasure of Caesar's will power and Calpurnia's humour. Caesar may not give vent to cowardice since it is not in his nature. Factionalism has been in the Roman culture and for that matter it is in the human culture as a part of the history. Any greatman is an idealist and so is Caesar, who has been misunderstood by his companions and confidants. The restoration of his stature by way of compensation is only an eyewash of the history, and, as such, all the triumvirates failed thereafter.

Portia is a noble lady; she is very much worried about the future, Caesar and the fate of Rome. In Act II she makes Lucius run to Senate to know the things befallen or perhaps overtures. She is also very much agitated about the vagaries of her own husband a bondman to moods and vicious deeds. Young blood, out of frenzy, is in search of bloody cruelty and this feeling subjects with the growth of age. Blurting and flirting are common weaknesses of mankind or rather of womankind. But unusually Shakespearean women are away from capricious and coquettish strands of life. They never brag unlike their counterparts, men and heroes. "When beggars die, there are no comets seen, the heavens themselves blaze forth the death of princes"[61] tells Calpurnia as a warning to Caesar. On the contrary, Caesar accosts :

> "Cowards die many times before their death;
> The valiant never taste of death but once."[62]

Caesar is not afraid of death because death "will come when it will come" as inevitability.

It is a traumatic experience when the windy night is blowing on Rome and the beggars and lions are let loose. We don't know whether the ghost of Caesar is awaited in future.

Shakespearean women are not conscious of power struggles lest they should lose their domestic chastity and womanhood unlike the modern world of political awakening. Entropy is an ever widening process and there is no end to its dimensions. May be this is called as therapeutic idealism born as male-female symbolism latent in the human mind. But this is a gross material developing or rather degenerating into anarchy.

The human society contains three types : extraverts, introverts and archetypes unfamished and bewildering sometimes. If studied under the impact of Jungian symbols it is nothing but a premonition that what Calpurnia's dream foreshadows. "As a general rule, the unconscious aspect of any event is revealed to us in dreams, where it appears not as a rational thought but a *symbolist* image. As a matter of history, it was the study of dreams that first enabled psychologists to investigate the unconscious aspect of conscious psychic events."[63] (Italics mine). If that were the case our study is a transcendence from the unconscious to a conscious level.

Woman's consciousness is a study of her psychological lust provoking the dreams of phenomena, sights and sounds. May be it is due to her neurotic effect called sixth sense.

Reveries are mental reactions → fan fantasies → manifestations → psychic ultimately tragic dreams symbolically the evils that are ahead piousness is a mental euphoria and it can be covered the rough wit and wisdom.

The world of dreams is a field of psyche, neurosis and phenomenology, where perhaps, epistemology has no place or rather it enervates into nothingness as an illusory melancholy. According to Carl Jung :

"...that dream symbols are for the most part manifestations of a psyche that is beyond the control of the conscious mind."[64] The experience of dreams is nothing but an ambivalent and allegorical enticement of the mind.

V

LESSER CHARACTERS

Thraldom is the characteristic of disclosedness in a Shakespearean drama. The universal movements are dependent on perturbation theory. According to Heisenburg :

> "Even worse, electrons in atoms repel each other with an electrical force that is almost equal to the attraction of the nucleus."[65]

The accidental degeneracies are also frequent as in planetary motions. The atom and light are complementary to anecdotes of a Shakespearean tragedy.

All the archaic mood is only a symbolism. David C. Cassidy writes :

> "Since time and space are relative concepts, they are not the same in all moving reference systems."[66]

It is all a quantum negative energy but leading to perturbation that is infinitesimal. Ideas evaporate though they have negative or positive inkling just like the philosophical postulates. The physical world is a combination of ugliness and general chaos that affects the psychological reaction of man. The Shakespearean characters cannot live in their own world of concatenation and, on the other hand, they meander to the social world to create an interaction.

The postponement of death is called life and we are much fascinated by it. Many great people were desultory readers including Shakespeare. Lesser characters determine the fate of country just like the dacoits in India and they can pull down any great personality without the evidence of vehemence. The pliability of the kinetic energy and potential energy can transform the creative energy into a creative force or power. There is no wonder if Caesar has grown ambitious and dictatorial accordingly to attain the power of a supremo in the political field of a kingdom. People play with dogs because their wives do not allow them to play with them and yet they do not grow currish. Some people are remembered as heroes and some as villains. All the triumvirs are heroes and all the conspirators are villains.

Shakespeare has produced exemplary characters and some of them are either abnormal or subnormal. The whole atmosphere revolves around the power struggle and the periphery is barbarity of the uncultured folk. Brutus is the noblest conspirator perhaps, but he is stupid. (Personal interview with Keith Wilson M.A. Tripos from Cambridge Varsity, 10-8-1965.) No conspirator is ready to heed to the killing of Mark Antony by and large and this proves as a boomeranging fatality to them.

Premonition is a keystone of a Shakespearean drama and more so in *Julius Caesar.* Conspicuously enough Artemidorus a teacher of Rhetoric in Act II scene iii is a living example and he can foresee the things to warn Caesar. He cautions him at the outset : "Caesar beware of Brutus" and so on.[67] He is ranked with another soothsayer in the drama. But all the inclination of these people appears to be creating a sort of confusion to save the world from heeding to confusion and not to create any consternation or compunction in Caesar whatsoever. The whole turmoil is a portending doom awaiting the hero and by and large the Roman history.

The servant sent by Antony to Brutus is a connecting link to patch up trepidation and differences of both the treasury benches and the conspirators and it is an attempt for a truce. The high level diplomacy starts in Act III scene i and the servant ushers in Antony while praising Brutus. Even a servant is a worldly wise man and he says in praising perorations : "Brutus is noble, wise, valiant and honest"[68] as if Caesar was not. It is almost a struggle for a compromise of amelioration and stultification at length to hoodwink the "blindmouths" of Rome. The plebian society could easily overshadow the publicans to any extent as Brutus underestimates them. In fact the uneducated many are more dangerous than the educated few and it seems the whole play is a conflict between the elite and the laity class. All the lesser mortals are more or less the black sheep in any society to resolve the disputable points of view. In life, which is a tragicomedy Max Scheler might say :

> "We can hardly call it tragic for a good man to defeat and bring about the downfall of an evil man, nor for a noble man to the same to a peasant. Moral precludes a tragic impression here...."[69]

In this play Cassius is the mentor for all the group of conspirators. The flaw itself is a severe punishment of gods and it looks a preposterous disbelief and the lesser characters always go for a dastardly reaction. Yet it is a foolish action to rejoice their own defensive attempts as if the phenomenology has ignored humanism. May be that can be called a tragic impression full of gloomy universal entropy. Walter Kaufmann, in this connection, comments :

> "...the phenomenon of the tragic is nevertheless not derived merely from artistic presentations. The tragic is, instead, an essential element in the universe itself."[70]

In *Julius Caesar* we feel that vagaries and maladies of the human mind go side by side stimulating the perversity in the wrong direction.

The citizen appearing at the forum are credulous peasants of Rome. They are much impressed and feel elevated with the speech of Brutus, who banks upon his so-called patriotism much less than his own self-respect or dignity. They head to the placating speech of Brutus at length and to pay their last homage to the departed 'tyranny'. The citizens represent the mob psychology and they can be easily carried away by anyone's provocative speech. At first they have no individuality and secondly they belong to the proletarian class of Rome. The citizens are mostly servitors who may have been servile at least in their previous birth.

The lesser mortals are vagrant and docile but also rebellious and hostile sometimes to recall scholar's tragic implicitness. "Autheben" is a Hegelian term for tragic sublimity with a connotation of destruction.[71] We cannot rule out the sagacity of citizens too. For instance, the second citizen doles out wisdom and says to Cinna "...they are fools that marry : You'll bear me a bang for that, I fear."[72] *Julius Caesar* is a full drama with complementary accomplishment of worldly wisdom too. Yet it is an elusive psychosis of history, politics and psychology which banks upon partly fantasy and partly reality. Cinna gives perhaps a wrong dose of poetry and emulation just like that in an imperfect society as a sanctuary of human imperfection. According to Aristotle the six elements are plot, character, diction, thought spectacle, and music.[73] Drama is a visual art like painting. The conspirators are notorious careerists unlike Julius Caesar and Mark Antony but all their endeavours are fragmentary. Neoplatonism may have oriented the Roman thought as a reactionary measure and a repertoire of declining mystic emanation. It is stated philosophically :

> "Matter is only the lowest link in the hierarchy of the universe, emanation of the 'world soul' over which rises the spirit and still higher the 'prime esteem' or the 'one'."[74]

Philosophy is both the end and means of life since it deals with the insignificant and significant things at a time.

The lovable theory is the theory of social contract that is at stake because of the universal entropy and the stigma thereof. There are a number of lesser mortals appearing in Act IV who could have been venerable to Brutus and *vice versa*. In fact there are two rows some of them are the followers and some other are the servants of Brutus and Cassius. Apparently Shakespeare dumps in this Act many of them such Lucilius, Titinius, Messala, Varro, Clitus, Claudius, Lucius, Pendarus and so on. Varro and Claudius carry out the final command of Brutus who says, "Go and command me to my brother Cassius,"[75] and they say obediently, "It shall be done, my lord."[76] In the Roman culture the master is also a steward who can exonerate the crime of lesser mortals, who play infinitesimally minor role in politics. They can't help oozing favour, if any in support of their own convictions as the past commitments. May be this is called a polemical approach to life.

In Aristotlean language a tragedy is a mimesis of action containing a plot (mythos) and a fall from good fortune to misfortune. May be it is a personal reaction to the gloomy world all-around in the vicinity. In an impasse of morale and recognition the tragic flaw fails as destiny is supposed to be predominant over the chiaroscuro of a protagonist, who is a celebrity as in *Julius Caesar*. The minor characters can justify their adjustment with the ambient world but not the hero in any haphazard manner. Shakespeare writes a Greek tragedy about the Roman History to the British audience of the Elizabethan Age. The characters could have been worst among the least in *Julius Caesar* who could dish the hero and condemnation of such hero in the ultimate result.

On the foreground there is the battlefield and in the background there is compunction and in between are the lesser mortals at Phillippi to decide the fate of Rome like a hung parliament. It is perhaps sacrilege to believe the projecting words of Cassius and Brutus who are simply go-getters and traducers whatever be their pleas in self-defense.

Comely demeanour is elicited from the comely behaviour of the quislings too. But the world is full of ingratitude as a law of nature. In the field of battle there is no single deed of Cassius and Brutus without an aide or ensign and all of them are alarmed to caution their masters and Roman leaders. They are active and conscious Titinius, Pindarus and Messala and so on. Pindarus ascends the hill and Cassius perhaps in remorse :

> "This day I breathed first, time is come round,
> And where I did begin, there shall I end,
> My life is run his campass. Sirrah, what news?"[77]

People could beguile anybody else to any extent. The criminals are hypocritical and they too can speak philosophy and metaphysical onerism or onerous amplitude. The ontological background states that matter was disillusioned only as a transcendence from the scattered shape to oneness. The same feature in the long run degenerated and developed as the existential acumen of fellowmen. Cassius is imperfectly introspective rather than incorrigible strategist when he utters in the last scene of his life :

> "Come down; behold no more,
> O, coward that I am to live so long,
> To see my best friend ta'en before my face!"[78]

His last lines are pathetic evoking mercy when Pindarus stabs him. He says :

> "Caesar, that art avenged,
> Even with the sword that kill'd them (Dies)."[79]

Then Pindarus flees away to some unknown land, perhaps to antipodes to escape the wrath of Romans. Titinius kills himself after speaking to Messala boldly and a helpless following of Cato, Messala, Lucilius, Labeo, and Falvius, and Brutus is ready to give a second and last fight.

Brutus has faithful followers and servants such as Dardanius, Clitus, Strato and Voluminius finally. Brutus can now speak also philosophy. He says to Clitus :

> "Sit thee low, Clitus; slaying in the word;
> It is a deed in fash, Hark thee Clitus."[80]

He knows that his "hour is come" and it is a premonition of his end. He has decided to run on the sword helped by his faithful Voluminius. Any land on the earth would have been a land of demons and tyrants after the fall of denosaurs. Man is a sophisticated animal.

All the lesser characters have a major and important role to play till Brutus by his own will. Messala, Strato, Lucilius, Clitus have their own version about Brutus assessed so nobly and so virtuously that Brutus becomes a noble Roman by way of catharsis. Lucilius exclaims :

> "So Brutus should be found, I thank thee,
> That thou has proved Lucilius, Brutus saying true."[81]

Adiabatic process and Isothermal process are applicable even in the case of lesser characters and their study since they are also a part of the dynamic and whirling society. We are sure :

> "If a system is perfectly conducting to the surroundings and the temperature remains constant throughout a process, it is called an isothermal process."[82]

Man can give in and give out his inner energy to safeguard himself. The system absorbs heat from the surroundings and maintains a constant temperature and that is heat energy inside as in :

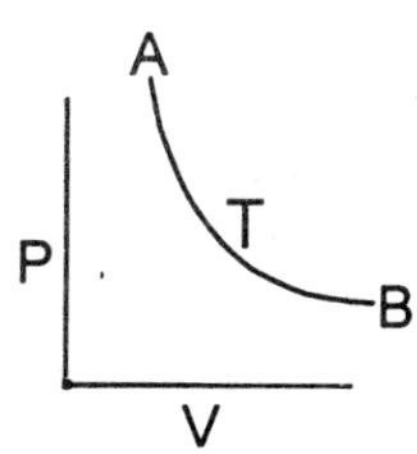

This can also be explained through adiabatic process wherein :

> "the working substance in perfectly insulated from the surrounding. The sudden bursting of a cycle tube like man's temper is an adiabatic process as in :
>
> $\delta H = D \quad \delta H = dv + \delta W$
>
> $O = dv + \delta W$."[83]

At the most there may be an impeachment of the incorrigible elements without amends or emendation of scurrilities.

The image is very essential in a social drama with a historical perspective much less in Elizabethan drama. We come across both the good and evil elements in *Julius Caesar* as in the world. John Knox, Martimer, and Thomas Cranmer could have done wonders by way of reforms and tenets of new Christianity unlike John Wycliff and Lollards. For instance Picador notes :

> "At this stage it is possible to put together the historical material (or archetypal hero images) and the data from the dreamer's personal experience in order to see how they corroborate, contradict, or qualify each other."[84]

We look for quantity and not for quality and masses go only for the former. Experiences testify that mind is a complex of hooliganism and simplicity alternatively with an intermittent hoax. Orpheus was killed by Thracian women though he could lull the trees and animals through his music.

Even the lesser characters have dreamy ideas apart from their own psychosis and psychological empathy. The whole study of life-drama is a space travel with heuristic ambivalence that leads us to temporal mutation in the process of continuum. The motion is set apart on the basis of analogy in the universe or the four-dimensional space-time to correlate with the philosophy of life. Moral values take care of themselves like the variables of universe and its study. The order of preferences is only a big confusion such as a transmission from physics to metaphysics — *a priori*. It is stated that :

> "*A priori* is used to qualify knowledge obtained prior to and independent of experience, knowledge which is inherent in consciousness from the beginning as opposed to *a posteriori* knowledge."[85]

In Kantian terminology :

> "The a priori forms of sensibility (space and time) and reason (cause, necessity etc.)."[86]

Since the sensory perception is underliably true may be this is a contrast or magnitude of the physical world compared to apperception as a Leibnitzian term. Forthwith we jump from the world of perception to the world of conception and amplitude.

VI

MELANCHOLY

The world moves on between audacity and alacrity. The causal relations are determined by the manifestations of nature herself. "Connections between phenomena are not to be reduced to the merely physical interaction of bodies."[87] These relations may be biological or social relations governing the human progress at length. This may be due to the cognitive sense of recognition lost somewhere unawares.

The early Jew culture developed into the Christian culture, superstitions and political upheavals in lieu of the inborn human weaknesses. Evidently this is in *Julius Caesar*. In a mentally sick society the temporality is pragmatism.

Virulence is the starting point of melancholy In the dichotomy of flesh and spirit the former is the root cause for the latter. The ideas flare up because of the contòrtions and distortions of the language. The quixotic effect of the minor characters too contribute a lot to the nasty weight of their misbehaviour. The 15th and the 16th century inquisition may have played its major role to ward off the proselytizing phenomena of the so-called character of heresy. Likewise, this is a common feature even in the case of the universal phenomena. Born wrote :

> "The motion of the particles follows probability laws, but the probability itself spreads out in accordance with the causal law."[88]

So also there is a contamination of politics unamenable to the law in *Julius Caesar*. Qualitatively speaking :

> "The reciprocal relations between the uncertainties in the measurements of energy and time or momentum and location — that is by Heisenburg's uncertainty relations."[89]

Studied under this conceptual thinking the whole human relations are uncertain. The probable variables are the components of Energy E and momentum P, Position Q and Time t.[90]

The spontaneous relation takes place in spontaneous dispersion of energy that has to be united in course of time with the decay of the solar energy some day. S.F. Mason states :

> "Calculations on this basis showed that the sun had been in existence for some twenty to thirty million years, and that it would last for another ten million years or so."[91]

So is the case of the earth as estimated by Kelvin and Huxley. Another scientist W.C. Dampier states :

> "The kinetic theory of gases enables us to translate into molecular terms the process by which entropy increases."[92]

It is nothing but a physical consciousness leading to entropy that contains psychologically a transformed force of matter and consciousness in the shape of "sensations, perceptions and other mental activities" put together as melancholy — a part of the universal phenomena. May be in Eddington's language it is self-knowing but not real though it is called "time's arrow." W.C. Dampier comments :

> "If in our equations, we find that entropy is diminishing and energy becoming more available we should know that we were tracing a process backward from its end towards it beginning."[93]

In this system of study it may disturb the time schedule of the past, the present and the future. It is believed that :

> "Occasionalism did not give satisfaction for long and, in fact, the mind-body problem has remained one of the main problems of Western philosophy right down to the 20th century."[94]

Man is microcosm and Godhead is macrocosm.

Schopenhaur realises the universality of suffering and it is said " — the universality of suffering is the first of the Buddha's four noble truths' — and Buddhism and tragedy represent the utterly different responses to suffering."[95]

Again he writes :

> "The demand for so-called poetic justice rests on a total failure to understand the nature of tragedy, indeed of the nature of the world."[96]

The protagonist is also a pharmakos and there can be no poetic justice in the case of sufferers. The contrastive repulsion is because of the repugnance and malice of the universalised individual nature of the human being. Spacious sorrow and the animal imagery mark the order of the day.

Destruction is implicit in naturalism and determinism which otherwise may be called "inevitability." Character is destiny in an all pervasive postulate put forward in every Shakespearean play and more so in *Julius Caesar*. Precisely it is an antidote to mesmerise dogmatism incorporated in the classical tragedy. Indictment is an undercurrent of platonic idealism in Shakespearean drama like an insidious disease that bursts out at length to involve in universal suffering.

Paradoxical illusions make philosophy just like the dogmatic postulates cannote materialism. The pity is that there is no moralism in an unscrupulous society at any stage. "The Greeks and Shakespeare were less moralistic and found tragic whatever inspired ruth and terror."[97] May be it is an outfit or spillover of Aristotle's "Hamartia." In nature tragic and pitiful are identical in contrast with horror and terror.

By the end of 3rd set everything is almost set on fire. The rebellious citizens are with cudgels against the conspirators. The first victim of the climactic scene is Cinna who is charged with the bad verse besides his participation as a conspirator. After their cross examination they shout at him with no smile but a direct torture.

> Third citizen : "Tear him, tear him! come, brands, ho!
> fire brand!!
> To Brutus', to Cassius', burn all : some to
> Decius' house, and to some Casca's, some to
> Legarius'; away, go!"[98]

Now the wheel of fire is full that accumulates no sanity. Even tribunes and heralds can create a widespread damage in a closed society and it is purely a psychological character born of inferiority complex and the idea of belonging. They can also create Nuremberg crimes since they cannot fight overtly.

How the power of Brutus is gone when he listens to the suicide of Portia who could not bear his absence for a long time :

> "And her attendants absent swalledfire."[99]

The remaining half is with the realisation of his guilt which is a sort of redemption. He says to Cassius, "Our legions are brimful, our cause is ripe."[100] He is also sure that power is dwindling in his camp too and he utters the often quoted lines very appropriately introspective.

> "There is a tide in the affairs of men
> Which taken at the flood leads on to fortune;

Omitted, all the voyage of their life
Is bound in shallows and in miseries."[101]

Currently he is sure of the poetic justice born out of pure melancholy if not self-realisation. The sonorous turmoil can destitute him of all goodwill and sympathy but the torture, agony and repentance if any. Added to the misery the ghost of Caesar appears to aggravate the apathetic solemnity.

A priori is continuum without broken relationship of the matter and uniformity in relative motion and structure. Melancholy is a global phenomenon and a state of a dilapidated mind that leads to the general destruction. There may have been some celestial fiery bodies even on the sun too and when they reach the earth with utmost velocity they may lose their heat because of the misons and other particles. This is a wonderful world wherein every organism emits heat that ends in deletion and the universe may be over within no time according to the will of nature. The passing of time is a relative term and nothing is certain in its calculation may be that is in terms of indifferent planets in different ways. We may call it grit on periodicity of time as we have divided in terms of seconds, minutes, hours, weeks, months and years leading towards infinity. The universes not finite, hence it is uncertain its length and breadth and there can be no space without time or *vice versa*.

Presumably it is an infinitesimal feeling or a mimetic status of the mind that foreshadows the amplitude in a universal suffering. There has been a struggle for hegemony in every nation and there is no wonder if it were in England or Rome, people emotionally fighting. Perseverance is the quality of zealot as in the case of Shakespearean character more so in *Julius Caesar*. The world is like a big lake full of crocodiles and other water animals full of prurience.

The self-efficacy and free will are at stake as if it were a computerised mechanism combined with symbolism. Then we call it "gravity of space" mechanized in music, mathematics and philosophy engrossed in the natural phenomenon in which the protagonist is a part. There is an unconscious unison of symbolism and conscious symbolism like dogmatic and pragmatic approaches to the study of life and religion without levity. There is no end to the ever expanding spacial universe and its entropy that includes new galaxies, quasars and farther heavenly bodies. Rechard Thompson points out :

> "In addition to pairs of galaxies with discordant redshifts, Arp points out something even stranger — it appears that quasars and galaxies can eject other quarars and galaxies.... The exploding galaxy NGC 520 has a fairly low red shift."[102]

So many nabulous ideas and so many UFO in the Universal Globe and Beyond and there is no end to them.

People are in the grip of calamities and melancholy and there is no end to them. Religious scriptures advocate various methods to overcome such shortcomings at length. Interestingly enough there is a threat of doom every time with foreshadowing thought of melancholy and its reservations ahead. It is predicted :

> "Scientists theorise that comets have collided with earth several times in the past. What happens when a comet collides with a partner? We might know in July 1994 when comet Shoemaker — Levy — a (it is named after the astronomers who discovered it) collides with the largest planet in the solar system — Jupiter."[103]

Thus there are more and more chances of destruction and we are nearer to death than to life. (The crash can stretch over a period of seven days in the latter part of July.) But perils come even to nincompoops and the brave alike.

VII

THE UNIVERSAL ENTROPY

There is nothing new in the system of happenings since the world began with a teleological concept or an endless motivation of a supernatural power where there is no beginning and no end. May be it is infinitesimal and infinite where energy projects itself as an entropy. The weakness of the human mind is in its projectile of the personality which is incomplete and imperfect.

The universal entropy is a scientific trophy or a collateral misnomer that pervades over Newtonian Mechanics, Galeleon Mechanics Lorentz transformations and Einstein's Generals Relativity. The Euclidean Geometry is an upsurge or a transcendence to the Four dimensional concept that includes x, y, z and time. The curvature has been a tenor towards immeasurable time and space or the transformation of unknown Fourteen dimensions of the flight of cosmic race from the outer space to the Earth.

Scientific cognition keeps up the spirit of knowledge called cognitional general. Marginal sciences appear :

> "Which connect formerly remote fields of knowledge (eg. biochemistry astrophysics etc.) and ultimately the laws of universe with a specific purpose to project the human personality."[104]

The universal entropy is a cosmic study of the primordial chaos or the last disorder as a degeneration of order to disorder that becomes inevitable at the end. In a drama such as *Julius Caesar* :

> "Universality is achieved by connecting the *dramatis personae* with the universe at large. His works thus acquire a cosmic significance, and his personages become the symbol of mankind struggling against the forces of evil."[105]

In Shakespeare, of course, every thing starts in conflict and ends in feuds to bring about the so-called catharsis perhaps. Destiny plays havoc with the life of man and perhaps it is a part of the cosmic energy that radiates to overpower the determinism and fatalism alike. The same type of feeling overlaps in a novel like Dostoevsky's *Crime and Punishment* too rather a transmission from overbearing puritanism to yielding despair.

Bragging is a part of villainy but it is a part of the human nature right from Julius Caesar to any lesser mortal in the play. This behaviour may be compared to a trajectory path of a bullet. Anger is a projectile of the mind like revenge. The universal growth of entropy $= \frac{\text{perturbation}}{\text{approval of anarchy}}$ which may be nil at 0° temperature and it is hypothetical to believe its occurrence. It is nothing but a catastrophe of idealism and cataclysm if any. Belligerent nations always try to fight like the incoherent individual, or the protons and neutrons where they are charged with dynamism. On the other hand, Shakespearean women do not berate openly in any drama and perhaps it is their exceptional quality of stoic virtues as human beings. They do not tend even to ponder over the gloomy ideas of negativism. "Psychic phenomena are a standard feature of human societies in all times and places...."[106]

Judged under the heading of formalism the twentieth century art is concomitant of surrealism, cubism and expressionism as a part of futurism. But it has been there from the days of Shakespeare as an abstract art that may have overlapped even the renaissance art. The fatigue of the human mind may lead to the blooming of empirical knowledge that what has happened in the case of both major and minor characters of *Julius Caesar*. The flamboyant speech of both Antony and Brutus are the examples of this kind and also of telepathy post-judged bilaterally. Vindication of paranoeia is the watchword of philosophy.

Each character seems to have suffered from paranoeia but each person dies before he gets redemption in the play. *Coup d'tat* becomes the vouchsafed philosophy in every permissive society lest the cleverness should be ignored in the political life. Universal entropy is a checkmate for both stagecraft and statecraft where there are no scruples. The supernatural foreboding of Caesar's ghost is noteworthy as the voice of a supramental force or clandestine energy. J. Walker McSpedden notes :

> "One night while Brutus is dying awake and restless in his tent, the ghost of Caesar appears and tells him 'thou shalt see me at Phillippi."[107]

When we think of attaining crisis in the middle of the play we must feel also the dramatic conflict at the very outset of *Julius Caesar.*[108] Currish ideas survive and uphold scurrilities and cunningness because they cannot eliminate them.

Caesar is a charismatic hero though he is an ambitious celebrity as an administrator. A villainous assiduity is a feverish threat to the human as extended by Cassius. Caesar observes him "such men are dangerous" and he can vitiate Brutus into a sinful action against Caesar. Whether it is Aristotle or Plato, Heisenburg's theory is a transcendence from particular to symmetry or rather asymmetrical concept of cosmos. Heisenburg writes his new equation :

$$\text{``}r\mu \frac{\delta \psi}{\delta u\mu} \pm l^2 r_\mu r_5 \psi (\psi \overline{r}_\mu r_5 \psi) = 0\text{''}$$ [109]

This is not new formula that denotes the desiccated decrepitude or assumptions.

People in the world are corrupt because they lack character irrespective of their caste, creed and status and create problems for others. "Schopenhauer may be right that Shakespeare surpasses the tragic poets of Greece as a poet of despair."[110] Admirably enough Shakespeare is a poet par excellence who would work about indictment and anger of nature against the human being.

In Sartrian language hope starts at the other side of despair *mutatis mutandis* the compensation for wrong calculations, when the human nature fails among bizarre temptations. Tendencies of the mind are always acute for the legalities of life provoking inspirations and no solution. Any fortuitous occurrence is a part of tragic flaw that lends us to negation of limbo. Nietzsche is a living example of this type that banks upon a Dionysian approach of art. There is no end to meanness in any society and more so the Roman society was more or less lackadaisical in righteousness. The luxuriant entropy is a resumption of the primordial disorder inherited through generations. The infuriated insurgency is a growing disorder that culminates only in deaths and murders. All unswerving controversy leads to an endless conflict and then to personal maladies as the social anarchy. The egregious news in the human suffering dissipated in alacrity and assiduity or daring audacity. The universal entropy is a language of "savage spectacle" exonerated for all the human feeling. The words used here in Antony's speech can denote what a havoc was created by the assassination of Julius Caesar. *e.g.* — butchers costly blow, dumb mouths, curse, limbs of men, domestic fury, dreadful objects, blood and destruction, infants quartered, revenge, Ate the goddess of mischief, havoc, dogs of war, foul deed, carrion men, burial and so on.[111]

The animal imagery is a trade balance or a sacred thread that keeps up the rapport of ethics and misbehaviour. But none can withstand the discreet words of Antony after Julius Caesar is murdered, and he contracts the servant of Octavius Caesar at first through soothing words about Caesar. Life lingers between credence and perseverance, symmetry of words and prevarication since it is full of lively deceit, fraud and exploitation every time. There is no deference accredited at any stage.

Brutus speaks defensive argument to the disturbed and agitated audience at the forum only to extenuate his guilt, and according to him the impugned article is Caesar's will or rather his ambitions. Although his plea is for the death of Caesar in full bloomed perorations and deprecation, he is only a contrast to Mark Antony and his inspiring oratory. Brutus says impressively but to no heed :

> "...not that I loved Caesar less, but that I loved Rome more."[112]

Again he speaks :

> "As Caesar loved me, I weep for him; as he was fortunate, I rejoice at it; as he was valiant, I honour him; but as he was ambitious, I slew him."[113]

No offender, as such, accept his own crime and puts forward a number of arguments. Yet the citizens understand what is what since the whole trouble in the drama is started out of envy. The biggest villain is Cassius and he is deputed to go to the other part of Rome to convince the proletarian public for staying Caesar.

In the universe it appears that the potential energy is in the wrong place of the natural phenomena. Walter Kaufmann believes :

> "The assumption is that the numinous and that the tragic are comparable to logic and mathematics in being equally irreducible to psychology."[114]

The tragic element is perhaps an irreducible idiosyncrasy that acts and reacts foolishly on the life of the innocent and the ambitious alike.

Rome is a living example of the universal entropy perhaps in microcosm as a part of the turmoiled universe. The words ambitious and honourable are in contrast with each other as if they were the superimposed structuralism. The non-appearing policy leads to a quagmire trepidation mainly borne by quislings.

Sometimes the non formal functioning of the human mind cherishes absurdity as philosophy. Antony's funeral oration is a powerful inciting speech in a phased manner the whole world is a meretricious jumble of words and euphoria as apparently the noble cause is in the non-approval of things. The way of the world in either sadistic or masochistic for no reason at all.

Cruelty is the habitat of political thought in *Julius Caesar*, which is not perhaps sacrosanct to sanity at any level. Coleridge seems to have regarded Shakespeare primarily a "philosophical teacher", and craftsman only later. Samuel Johnson comments :

> "The dramatists contemporary with Shakespeare except for Ben Johnson and Beaumont and Fletcher were almost wholly neglected from 1642...."[115]

Johnson may have been short of elementary notes on Shakespeare's *Julius Caesar* perhaps not concerned with the infallibility of the drama to the extent of emendation and the incongruity. Johnson further states : "His tragedy seems to skill, his comedy to be instant."[116] In that case Shakespeare can eschew baffling entropy through declamations and actions as antidotes to barbarity. Further Johnson criticizes :

> "To alter is more easy than to explain, and temerity is a more common quality than diligence."[117]

He is always great and nobody can dare despise or condemnation of Shakespeare. Tragedy is the handiwork of philosophy lovable and movable in texture and structure. Recrimination is easier than approval and appreciation in general.

The imperfection of the human knowledge is an impeachment of all the cohorts that entails the unassailable general accusation or chaos in a Shakespearean drama be it the swelling Cydnus, Ilium of Troy or the angry Tiber in full sweep. The angry mood of the citizens in the Forum is in contrast to that of Senators and conspirators.

> "Second citizen : Go fetch fire.
> Third citizen : Pluck down benches.
> Fourth citizen : Pluck down forms, windows, anything."[118]

Morals are rare scruples in a sick society that has no edge over the entropy.

Whether it is Lorentz transformation or relativistic theory the universal entropy cannot desist itself in nature. Albert Einstein's enunciation is :

> "The connection prevails that the experimentally assured duality of nature (corpuscular and wave

> structure) can be realized only by such a weakening of the concept of reality."[119]

It is certain that Einstein wants to explain the *dvaita* (duality) and the four dimensional nature in scientific terms against the sinister nature of man. Again he states :

> "It is due to this fact that, according to the theory of relativity the time x_4 enters natural laws in the same form as the space coordinates x_1, x_2, x_3."[120]

The outlay is stripped in the so-called culture of mankind. The four dimensional term called 'continuum' is known as the 'world' in the language of Minkowski is a continuation of events to no end at last. Spacc is Euclidean and 'existence' is the characteristic of the four dimensional word of coordinates on the rotational system.

VIII

CONCLUSION

One man's show or upmanship has been proved detrimental to the individualist himself, and Caesar is an individualist. The theory of an abandonment exists as an elixir in vacuity or indictment. Nature eliminates even the most intelligent people and Caesar is one of them. The idiocyncracies emerge as the polemics of the study oscillating betwccn presentment and instant imprecision. We believe though reluctantly :

> "And this reciprocal relationship between uncertainties in measurement also holds for other conjugate pairs of variables, such as energy and time. This, in a few words, is Heisenberg's uncertainty principle."[121]

The vindication of uncertainties is philosophy.

Vindictive capitalism must have been affected the Roman polity to adopt the principle of utilitarianism for dogmatic progress and never to implement it fully well. The entire materialistic world is a part of cosmos where there can be no teleological background perhaps and the ethical law is a temporary solution as an antidote for prepared chaos. The gravitational pull is as good as the solar system that governs the social interaction of the individuals at length. At every step, therefore, we find that the universality of hell is let loose and it requires an amendment to the apperception, a term used by Leibnitz.[122]

Shakespeare could not write an aphoristic style because he is primarily concerned with the ambivalent characteristic of the human nature. He has a common device of pruning over the words *e.g.* : — Brutus is brutal, Legarius is legate, Caesar is the 'cour de lion' or the lionhearted born under the zodiac sign of Leo.

Brutus concludes his speech when he allows Antony to speak for the dead Caesar and it is a foolish act perhaps. Brutus says conclusively :

> "With this I depart — that, as I slew my best lover for the good of Rome. I have the same dagger for myself, when it shall please my country to need my death."[123]

Brutus is overwhelmed with fear and guilt simultaneously though he acts boldly.

Julius Caesar is a Shakespearean vortex that combines sadness and equanimity plus imprecations of evilsome forces. May be that it incorporates the presentation of non-cooperation as 'serendipity' at every level till it results in the disarray of cosmic disorder. Caesar may have been a regent conscious of regality and not philosophy; otherwise, his life could have been like that of Socrates. He is neither illusioned nor disillusioned under the guise of power. People are jubilant over cruelty too, and that is the message of a revenge play.

The play moves away from equanimity towards tribulations of the suffering mind. For that matter every one is more or less alarmed though he is a scoundrel and never a simpleton.

The Second Triumvirate is only a helpless alliance with Octavius, Lepidus and Mark Antony, a political jigsaw puzzle of format. At length with covert matters they can go ahead with appropriate calculations of the future. Octavius concludes :

> "*Let us do so : for we are at the stake,*
> *And bay'd about with many enemies;*
> *And some that smile have in their hearts, I fear,*
> *Millions of mischiefs.*"[124]

Whatever be the internal bickerings they have to face the topsy-turvy Roman world full of disorder and annoyance. *Julius Caesar* is a computerised form of the human brain with so many devices, stratagems and psychological upheaval unified and let off finally.

The disgruntled fellows become either philosophers or warriors to accomplish their latent ego. But politics has been the most lucrative profession even in a bourgeois society. Brutus is a tactless man to behave stupidly while discharging his onerous duties to indoctrinate the Roman public.

The panorama of the dramatic structure in *Julius Caesar* is determined by the magnitude of occurrences and in the intensity of feelings from Lupercala to the Battle of Phillippi. Mark Antony is a greater impressario than Brutus as a mature warrior and statesman.

As in the care of thermodynamics also in an insular society the adiabatic process and isothermal process are common to maximise things of unrest or to reduce it to stand-still.

> "If winter comes, can spring be far behind?
> But then where is the winter?" — Shelley.

Now storm within and storm without as though every one is a victim of malaise. However, in a given society vegetarianism promotes cunningness and non-vegetarianism develops ferocity.

Ideas always formulate in the mind and perish as if the mind is caught with some fear or favour zealously engaged to come out of some entropy. In a primitive culture the proximity of man is with nature and God would not bolster up unwholesome culture even if we invoke him out of devotion. Roman culture is, therefore, more or less a primitive and ambivalent culture where emotions are more effective than the reasoning capabilities. Carl Jung states while mentioning a healing the split :

> "It remains quite natural for men to quarrel and to struggle for superiority over one another."[125]

Whatever be the arguments pros and cons inconsistency leads to moralisms in every society.

Recalcitrance, torpor and aegis are in the human blood *mutatis mutandis* entropy changing into energy very often. The whole system of the universe is a plethora of constant and coordinates within an encircling gloom and perversity. All Shakespearean characters are akin to a connotative and denotative meaning of life that circumvents chaos. The whole play is a long march between two extremes of entropy and energy not to distort or disprove the realities of life. Complacency and contrition are not new to an old drama of historical type. Most of the characters are mercuric and volatile being capable of machinations and stratagems. They advocate and spearhead a notorious ideology that results in nothingness to cover up and compensate some ulterior motive of clandestine adversity.

Julius Caesar is a political extravaganza with no catholicity but animosity that radiates baser elements of the human nature, a cryptogram of mind pollution as in a Revenge play. In *Julius Caesar* there is neither love nor lust although love has an ambrosian effect for the purblind eyes. In general people suffer from maeopia or paranaeia lingering between euphoria and euphemism and consequently the contingent gloom all-around. In *Triumph of Love* V.V. Kiran says :

> "In the end there is neither love nor lust
> Dear, whether you retire last or first."[126]

Sarvam sithilayaté. Every thing is destructible including the universe.

In a so-called society of intellectuals every act of stultification and delinquent life moves on with a tendentious purpose though they never admit the venality and mental corruption. Everyone is a victim to vanguard of malevolence. Among Shakespearean men and women no one feels consciously of guilt or crime whatsoever. Woman has been treated a chattel in every society including the Roman and the British societies.

The degeneration of democracy is dictatorship or *vice versa* as seen in *Julius Caesar* or in any society in the world. There is always a fear of presentiment as if Rome were a prefecture of universal doom. But it is a transcendence surrealistic feeling to eternal entropy.

NOTES

1. Heideggar, *Heideggar : Critical Reader.* USA : Blackwell Publishers. 1992, p. 92.
2. David C. Cassidy, *Uncertainty*, p. 254.
3. W.C. Dampier, *A History of Science,* p. 81.
4. *Ibid.*, p. 81.
5. John D. Hicks *et al.*, *The American Nation.* Boston : Houghton Miffin Company, 1965, p. 190.
6. Nelkon & Parker, *Advanced Level Physics.* New Delhi : Arnold Heinemann Publishers, 1982, p. 229.
7. Dr. Raghukula Tilak, *History of English Literature.* Meerut : Raj Hans Agencies, 1990, p. 166.
8. Quoted Dowden, *History of English Literature*, p. 146.
9. Louis Cazamian, *A History of English Literature.* London : J.M. Dent and Sons Ltd., 1957, p. 417.
10. *Julius Caesar*, p. 143.
11. George Orwell, *Animal Farm.* New York : New American Library, 1946, p. 123.
12. *Ibid.*, p. 128.
13. Walter Kaufmann, *Tragedy and Philosophy*, p. 377.

14. Walter Kaufmann, *Tragedy and Philosophy*, p. 374.
15. *Julius Caesar*, p. 155.
16. *Ibid.*, p. 155.
17. Albert Einstein, *Relativity*. London : Methuen & Co. Ltd., 1979, p. 65.
18. *Ibid.*, p. 65.
19. Joseph L. Henderson, *Man and his Symbols*, p. 99.
20. *Ibid.*, p. 101.
21. Herbert L. Dreyfus & Harrison Hall (ed.), *Heideggar : A Critical Reader*. USA : Blackwell Publishers, 1992, pp. 210-11.
22. Norman J.G. Pounds, *Hearth Home, A History of Material Culture*. USA : Indiana University Press, 1989, p. 62.
23. Walter Kaufmann, *Tragedy and Philosophy*, p. 335
24. *Ibid.*, p. 339.
25. *Ibid.*
26. *Julius Caesar*, p. 138.
27. *Ibid.*, p. 152.
28. *Ibid.*
29. *Ibid.*, p. 153.
30. *Ibid.*, p. 153.
31. *Ibid.*, p. 156.
32. *Ibid.*, p. 156.
33. *Ibid.*, p. 157.
34. *Ibid.*, p. 157.
35. N. Subrahmanyam & Brijlal, *Principles of Physics*. New Delhi : S. Chand & Co., 1982, p. 61.
36. *Ibid.*, p. 62.
37. *Julius Caesar*, p. 172.
38. *Ibid.*, p. 173.
39. *Ibid.*, p. 280.
40. *Ibid.*, p. 181.
41. *Ibid.*, p. 183.
42. *Ibid.*, p. 183.
43. N. Subrahmanyam et al., *Principles of Physics*. New Delhi : S. Chand & Company, 1982, p. 374.

44. Carl Jung (ed.), *Man and his Symbols,* p. 58.
45. Albert Einstein, *Relativity.* London : Methuen & Co. Ltd., 1979, p. 43.
46. *Dictionary of Philosophy.* USSR : Progress Publishers, 1984, p. 438.
47. Heideggar, *A Critical Reader.* USA : Blackwell Publishers, 1992, p. 165.
48. David C. Cassidy, *Uncertainty the Life and Science of Heisenberg.* New York : W.H. Freeman & Company, 1992, p. 224.
49. M. Van Doren, *The Tragedy of Julius Caesar* (an old script), p. 104.
50. Quoted Thomas Carter, *Stories from Shakespeare.* London : George G. Harrap & Co. Ltd., 1954, p. 182.
51. *Ibid.,* p. 180.
52. *Ibid.,* p. 201.
53. *Julius Caesar*, p. 174.
54. *Ibid.*, p. 182.
55. Richard L. Thampson, *Vedic Cosmography and Astronomy.* Los Angeles : The Bhakti-Vedanta Book Trust, 1989, p. 173.
56. *Dictionary of Philosophy.* Moscow : Progress Publishers, 1984, p. 438
57. Walter Kaufmann, *Tragedy and Philosophy.* Princeton : Doubleday & Company Inc., 1969, p. 333.
58. *Julius Caesar*, p. 135.
59. *Ibid.,* p. 135.
60. *Ibid.,* p. 135.
61. Thomas Carter, *Stories from Shakespeare*, p. 187.
62. *Ibid.*, p. 187.
63. Pictador, *Man and his Symbols Conceived and edited by Carl Jung.* London : Aldus Books Ltd., 1964, p. 5.
64. *Ibid.,* p. 53.
65. *Uncertainty, The Life and Science of Werner Heisenberg,* p. 144.
66. *Ibid.,* p. 276.
67. *Julius Caesar*, p. 138.
68. *Ibid.,* p. 145.
69. Quoted Walter Kaufmann, *Tragedy and Philosophy*, p. 351.
70. *Ibid.,* p. 352.
71. *Ibid.,* p. 355.
72. *Julius Caesar*, p. 158.

73. *Tragedy and Philosophy*, p. 60.
74. *Dictionary of Philosophy*, p. 292.
75. *Julius Caesar*, p. 172.
76. *Ibid.*, p. 172.
77. *Ibid.*, p. 177.
78. *Ibid.*, p. 177.
79. *Ibid.*, p. 177.
80. *Ibid.*, p. 181.
81. *Ibid.*, p. 183.
82. *Principles of Physics, op. cit.*, p. 374.
83. *Ibid.*, p. 375.
84. Picador, *Man and his Symbols conceived and edited by Carl Jung*. London : Aldus Books Ltd., 1964, p. 109.
85. *Dictionary of Philosophy*, p. 25.
86. *Ibid.*, p. 26.
87. *Ibid.*, p. 438.
88. *Uncertainty, The Life and Science of Werner Heisenberg*, p. 219.
89. *Ibid.*, p. 248.
90. *Ibid.*, p. 249.
91. S.F. Mason, *A History of the Science.* London : Routledge & Kegan Paul Ltd., 1953, p. 403.
92. W.C. Dampier, *A History of Science.* New Delhi : S. Chand & Comp. Ltd., 1982, p. 487.
93. *Ibid.*, p. 487.
94. A.C. Combie, *Augustine to Galileo*. London : William Heinemann Ltd., 1957, p. 395.
95. Walter Kaufmann, *Tragedy and Philosophy, op. cit.*, p. 339.
96. *Ibid.*, p. 340.
97. *Ibid.*, p. 367.
98. *Julius Caesar*, p. 159.
99. *Ibid.*, p. 167.
100. *Ibid.*, p. 169.
101. *Ibid.*, p. 169.
102. Richard L. Thomson, *Vedic Cosmography and Astronomy*. Los Angeles : The Bhakti-Vedanta Book Trust, 1984, p. 150.

103. *The Hindu*, dated 22-1-94, Supplementary, p. IV.

104. *Dictionary of Philosophy*. USSR : Progress Publishers, 1984, p. 438.

105. Dr. Raghukula Tilak, *History of English Literature*. Meerut : Raj Hans Agencies, 1990, p. 166.

106. *Vedic Cosmography and Astronomy*, *op. cit.*, p. 112.

107. J. Walker McSpedden. *The Tragedy of Julius Caesar* (a script), p. 107.

108. W.H. Hudson, *An Introduction to the Study of Literature*. London : Morrison & Gibb Ltd., 1957, p. 201.

109. David C. Cassidy, *Uncertainty, Life and Science of W. Heisenburg*. New York : W.H. Freeman & Company, 1992, p. 542.

110. *Tragedy and Philosophy*, *op. cit.*, p. 345.

111. *Julius Caesar*, p. 149.

112. *Ibid.*, p. 150.

113. *Ibid.*, p. 150.

114. Walter Kaufmann, *Tragedy and Philosophy*, p. 353.

115. S. Johnson, *The Preface to Shakespeare*. London : Macmillan, 1957, p. 99.

116. *Ibid.*, p. 39.

117. *Ibid.*, p. 62.

118. *Julius Caesar*, p. 157.

119. Albert Einstein, *Relatively*. London : Methuen & Co. Ltd., 1979, p. 157.

120. *Ibid.*, p. 122.

121. *Uncertainy the Life and Science of Werner Heisenberg*, p. 228.

122. Apperception in the dependence of every new perception on the previous experience of a man and on his psychic condition at the moment of perception". *Dictionary of Philosophy*, p. 25.

123. *Julius Caesar*, p. 151.

124. *Ibid.*, p. 160.

125. *Man and his Symbols*, *op. cit.*, p. 91.

126. V.V. Kiran, *Triumph of Love*. Hyderabad : 12-1-1956; Old Mallepally, Hyderabad, 1970, p. 29.

6

Planes of Perception in Shakespeare : An Indian View

—*Shweta Khanna*

THE PAST four centuries have witnessed innumerable attempts to find "a clue to the vast powers of Shakespeare's imagination,"[1] and a sensitive critic observes :

> "The striking peculiarity of Shakespeare's mind was its generic quality, its power of communication with other minds, so that it contained a universe of thought and feeling within itself.... He was nothing in himself; but he was all that others were, or that they could become. He not only had in himself the germs of every faculty and feeling, but he could follow them by anticipation, intuitively, into all their conceivable ramifications, through every change of fortune or conflict of passion or turn of thought. He had 'a mind reflecting ages past' and present. All corners of the earth, kings, queens and states, maids, matrons, nay the 'secrets of the grave' are hardly rid from his searching glance.... The world of spirits lay open to him, like the world of real men and women : there is the same truth in his delineations of the one as of the other."[2]

Hazlitt's observations aptly indicate the essence of Shakespeare's universal appeal, which is considerably enhanced, even at its best, by the vast and powerful dimension added to it, by what has generally been termed the 'supernatural' in his plays. The following considerations present a humble attempt to look deeper into this vital aspect of Shakespeare's work, from the perspective of Indian philosophical tenets.

> "There are more things in heaven and earth, Horatio,
> Than are dreamt of in your philosophy"
>
> (*Hamlet*, I. v. 166-67)

Prince Hamlet's memorable words to Horatio are charged with a confidence that emerges from his encounter with the ghost, indicative of the realm beyond the normal, ordinary plane of perception. The meeting-point of two apparently mutually exclusive states of existence is charged with a potential that eventually culminates in the restoration of "the royal bed of Denmark" which had become "a couch for luxury and damn'd incest" (*Hamlet*, I. v. 82-83), to its original, pure state. The "cost of this redemption is high, its result is a new creation."[3] Fredrick Turner observes, significantly :

> "Hamlet does not discover the crime in that region of consciousness in which a detective, for instance, might discover it. The crime is perceived by him in the deepest regions of his spirit, and strikes at the foundations of his being. Consequently, his attitude to it is not the same as the attitude of Fortinbras or Laertes to their father's deaths."[4]

Turner also argues that other devices, such as narration by an eye-witness could have been used to present the details of king Hamlet's murder, but Shakespeare has, with the superb insight and skill, transformed the "primitive materials" of *The Spanish Tragedy* by involving them as "a strange basis for a sophisticated play."[5]

Moreover, it must be acknowledged that the ghost is not only "an expression of something in Hamlet's mind,"[6] but is also seen by Marcellus and Bernardo for three successive nights before Hamlet is made aware of its appearance by Horatio, who has kept watch with the other two guards on the third night. Horatio's initial sceptical stand and his subsequent reactions at the sight of the ghost, not only create the proper ground for Hamlet's encounter with his father's ghost but also absorb the audience in the atmosphere of the play to the point where a *spontaneous,* not merely a *willing* "suspension of disbelief" is almost instinctively and totally affected.

It has been observed that the themes of Shakespeare's plays from "Hamlet onwards...reach below the rational, into the realm of the subconscious, into the primitive experiences which exist in the recesses of every human mind, though we are unwilling to acknowledge them. ...all these things reach down to such depths in us that often a sensitive being can hardly bear to look at what is passing on the stage."[7] *Hamlet* presents "types of conflict which consciousness normally declines to acknowledge",[8] though the total impact is felt to be "penetrating into our inmost nature";[9] hence the protagonist appears to have "a seemingly uncanny power to baffle rationalizing commentary."[10]

Critics and scholars focussing their attention on isolated plays or individual characters alone, may find themselves all the more baffled. A comprehensive study of the complete works of Shakespeare might, however, present perspectives provoking closer and deeper investigations into the depth and mystery of consciousness that Shakespeare has spontaneously unravelled in the varied and enthralling nuances of his plays, which have held audiences spell-bound in all quarters of the globe for more than four centuries!

The general view that Shakespeare merely "dramatized" the beliefs of his age, catering to common tastes, or attempted merely to please individual monarchs with special interests, appears too naïve in the context in which the creative genius of the dramatist radiates the dynamic force of total absorption at its deepest and highest plane.

Hamlet's "fate cries out" (*Hamlet*, I. iv. 82) as the ghost appears and beckons him to follow it. Breaking away with unyielding, instinctive determination from friends trying to hold him back, Hamlet follows the ghost, whose narrative totally confirms what his "prophetic soul" (*Hamlet*, I. v. 40) had instinctively known. With the same force of will, he once more summons every force to hold together his overwhelmingly shattered physical and mental state :

> "O all you host of heaven! O earth! what else?
> And shall I couple hell? O fie! Hold, hold my heart,
> And you, my sinews, grow not instant old,
> But bear me stiffly up! Remember thee!
> Ay! Thou poor ghost, while memory holds a seat
> In this distracted globe."
>
> (*Hamlet*, I. v. 92-97)

The brief re-appearance of the ghost in the closet-scene highlights certain fundamental issues vitally related to understanding Shakespeare, specially from the Indian standpoint. The reactions of Hamlet and Gertrude to the appearance of the ghost present a juxtaposition of two distinct planes of perception virtually negating each other, yet ultimately affecting a positive response and change, in Gertrude. The queen, alarmed at what she believes to be a fit of madness in Hamlet, questions : "To whom do you speak this?" and Hamlet, surprised, counter-questions : "Do you see nothing there?" The dialogue continues :

> "Queen : Nothing at all : yet all there is I see.
> Ham : Nor did you nothing hear?
> Queen : No, nothing but ourselves.
> Ham : Why, look you there! Look how it steals away!
> My father in his habit as he lived!
> Look, where he goes, even now, at the portal!"
>
> (*Hamlet,* III. iv. 133-38)

To Hamlet, the presence of the ghost is 'real' and 'immediate' : he 'sees' the ghost and desperately tries to make his mother see it too; yet though Marcellus, Bernardo and Horatio have also seen the ghost, Gertrude does not. The ghost is obviously not an illusion, but an "honest" ghost, as Hamlet puts it, yet Gertrude simply cannot see it! Her allusion to Hamlet's 'madness' makes him burst forth :

"My pulse as yours doth temperately keep time,
And makes as healthful music : it is not madness
That I have utter'd : bring me to the test,
And I the matter will re-word which madness
Would gambol from."

(*Hamlet,* III. iv. 140-44)

Gertrude's awareness is limited, as that of most ordinary individuals, to a perception of the gross, physical, material plane only. The average mind, continually exposed to sense-stimuli from the phenomenal world, can hardly be aware of, what according to the Indian view, are the 'subtle' and 'causal' bodies, which, on being activated, reveal many other planes of existence than are commonly known. Most people are, in fact, unaware of, and would even refuse to entertain the fact that "the world in which we live is powered by invisible forces of nature."[11] A few psychiatrists have, however, unhesitatingly acknowledged that "our normal waking consciousness is but one special type of consciousness, whilst all about it...lie potential forms of energy entirely different!"[12]

David Frawley, Director of the American Institute of Vedic Studies, indicates that the "astral" (Sūkshma Sharira) and the "causal" (Kārańa Sharira) bodies "function as vehicles for the inner self."[13] in fact, "they are not bodies in the physical sense",[14] but a kind of "vibratory field which encloses the underlying consciousness."[15] The 'subtle' or 'astral' body is the "energetic basis of the physical body.... Psychic ability or E.S.P. derives from the functioning of the astral organs, which are not limited like the physical organs."[16] Frawley further elaborates :

"The astral world is experienced in dream, vision and trance. After death we sojourn in the astral world, which we may experience (according to our Karma) as various positive or negative, heaven or hell-like

> states, as the subtle energies accumulated during physical life get released. Artists can access the astral realm during life...."[17]

The sensitive prince Hamlet is, therefore, aware of both the physical and the astral planes at certain crucial moments of life. Both planes exist for him together, and are simultaneously 'real' to him, but Gertrude's awareness is restricted only to the physical plane. Moreover, Hamlet lives only till the ghost's command is fulfilled, this being the only deep-rooted destined end for which he survives....

After his miraculous return from the sea, "that strange episode, which...like an active hiatus between the play's middle and last phases dramatises the forces at work",[18] Hamlet becomes aware even of the "divinity that shapes our ends/ Rough-hew them how we will." (*Hamlet*, V. ii. 10-11)

He gains a profound insight, in fact, into the 'causal' plane as the end approaches. The 'causal' body, "a kind of supermind...centred in the heart...stores the seeds or impressions of Karma that motivate us...."[19] Hamlet is aware, deep within, of what is to happen in the duel with Laertes, and tells Horatio "But thou wouldst not think how ill all's here about my heart : but it is no matter" (*Hamlet*, V. ii. 220-21). Horatio tries to dissuade him, and requests him to postpone the duel, but Hamlet persists :

> "...We defy augury : there's a special providence in the fall of a sparrow. If it be now, 'tis not to come; if it be not to come, it will be now; if it be not now, yet it will come : the readiness is all: ...."
>
> (*Hamlet*, V. ii. 230-34)

Hamlet was, in fact, stating a truth the ancient civilizations of the world had long been aware of. Paul Brunton indicates that the West is just "beginning to understand how strange faculties whose existence has long been known to hoary Asia may operate in perfect obedience to scientific laws; how telepathy, apparitions, thought-reading and thought-transference, mesmeric feats and all the marvel magic and miracle of primitive and medieval religious, mystical and yogic history may be factually based; and how the little-understood energy of "Karma" may be as universally and ceaselessly present as the equally mysterious energy of electricity and be just as precise in its working and effects."[20]

Robert H. West has, in fact, rightly observed that "Premonitions, dreams, prayers, curses, portents, the stars and apparitions bear in Shakespeare the general cast of the supernatural and may be literal confirmations of some power or system beyond the play's world of sense...."[21] Some of the best scenes in Shakespeare, are, in fact, rare expressions of psychic phenomena, indicating such planes of perception with an unusual, sensitive force, affecting a profound, subtle influence, transcending the limitations of time and place. Cassandra's intense crescendo is a fine illustration of her prophetic vision which foresees as immediate, the events yet to take place on the battlefield. Her breathless terror and agony at what is mentally perceived breaks through the intensity of her ulterance :

> Look how thou diest. Look how thy eye turns pale.
> Look how thy wounds do bleed at many vents,
> Hark how Troy roars; how Hecuba cries out;
> How poor Andromache shrills her dolours forth;
> Behold distraction, frenzy and amazement
> Like witless antics, one another meet,
> And all cry, Hector ! Hector's dead! O Hector!
>
> (*Troilus and Cressida*, V. iii. 81-87)

Likewise, the Soothsayer's prophecy regarding the 'ides of March' echoes through *Julius Caesar*, a play in which strange omens abound and Calphurnia dreams of her husband's statue, which

> "...like a fountain with an hundred spouts
> Did run pure blood, and many lusty Romans
> Came smiling, and did bathe their hands in it."
>
> (*Julius Caesar*, II. ii. 77-79)

The prophecy, the omens and the dream indicating Caesar's future assassination are all fulfilled. The curses of many queens echo through the history plays with an intensity, and sometimes an irony, that re-creates England's past, vividly focussing the highlight on human interactions and passions. King Richard III, an unredeemed villain, dreams, before his death on the battlefield of the ghosts of all those he had "murder'd" (*King Richard III*, V. iii. 204). Clarence, one of his victims, dreams before being killed, of 'that sour ferryman which poets write of / unto the kingdom of perpetual night" (*King Richard III*, I. iv. 46-47), and Romeo's dream foreshadows his death besides his lady, Juliet, who is seen breathing life into him again by her kisses. Whereas Romeo's prophetic dream is romantically transformed, the grooms outside Duncan's room in *Macbeth* are disturbed in their dreams, as Macbeth recalls :

> "There's one did laugh in's sleep, and one cried 'Murder !'"
>
> (*Macbeth*, II. ii. 2)

However, Macbeth himself can "sleep no more", since "only the innocent sleep" and "Macbeth has "murder'd sleep" (*Macbeth,* II. ii. 41, 37-42). The 'voices' that Macbeth 'hears' have their origin in the depth of his own being, as does the 'dagger' that he sees pointing towards him. Banquo's ghost unnerves him as nothing else can, and Lady Macbeth's 'sleep-walking' is also a denial of the "Balm of hurt minds, great nature's second course / chief nourisher in life's feast" (*Macbeth,* II. ii. 38-39).

The Indian view considers sleep also to be one of the aspects of cosmic energy, the Mother Goddess, to whom salutations are offered :

> "Yā devi Sarvabhūteshu Nidrarupena samsthita,
> Namas tasyei, Namas tasyei, Namas tasyei, Namo Namah."[22]

['Salutations to the luminous (goddess) who dwells in all living beings as sleep' — author's rendering.]

Macbeth has violated a profound moral law, being fully aware of the crime that he was committing in murdering his sovereign, the Lord's anointed, his kinsman and guest, the aged Duncan. The witches have only acted as catalytic agents. The weird sisters, in fact, appear to have penetrated right through the 'Tanmatras' — "causal elements" — or "the root materials from which the subtle and gross sense organs, organs of actions and the elements all evolve, and the common factor which allows their inter-connection."[23] Those who "come to master the Tanmatras...learn all the secrets of nature,"[24] Frawley indicates, and the witches can "look into the seeds of time/ And say which grain will grow and which will not" (*Macbeth*, I. iii. 58-59). Their prophecies to Macbeth and Banquo upon the heath are, moreover, part of a predetermined sequence of events. Though witchcraft was widely practised during Shakespeare's Age, there undoubtedly is "a curious majesty and even sublimity about the wayward creatures who meet Macbeth and Banquo upon the heath, that is not at all characteristic of ordinary witches,"[25] since they possess "a certain dignity and mysterious quality which inspires awe in the beholder and compels contemplation."[26]

Moreover, Hecate, who as part of a hierarchy appears to command them, is "both destroyer and preserver" and as Alex Aronson indicates, related to "the Egyptian Isis, the Canaanite Anath and the Hindu Kāli...."[27]

Kāli, the female form of Kāla (Time), symbolises the Creative Energy (Creatrix) at the root of existence, and her devotees, mostly Tantrics, are well-known for their occult powers or Siddhis, as that of vanishing "Into the air.... As breath into the wind" (*Macbeth*, I. iii. 81-82). The Tantrics are also known to perform group rituals, the Chakra-puja or 'circle worship' in secrecy, usually at deserted places or cremation-grounds. Moreover, they also intentionally speak in cryptic terms, mostly offensive and repulsive to those outside their cult. Having merged their individualities, they may also act as 'mediums' aiming ultimately to perceive the absolute, an undifferentiated unity of the positive and negative forces, symbolised by male and female energies. The witches in *Macbeth* appear to indicate similar traits and may suggest the existence of identical cults in the Western world. Zolar has, it seems, rightly remarked :

> "All Western peoples have a double line of ancestors : their own forefathers and Eastern civilizations...only very few prophetic beliefs are original to any group of people, because most beliefs are mankind's common heritage."[28]

A "profound philosophical significance"[29] is reflected in the final Romances which present an almost "magical sense of interaction between man and nature."[30] There is also "a deeply religious atmosphere, productive of "theophanies" or new revelations of the divines"[31] arising probably, from the depth of the causal plane in Shakespeare. Moreover, "the theme of music, typifying restoration of harmony, comes through at points of high emotional significance."[32]

Had Shakespeare also realized what the mystic-poet, Rabidnranath Tagore, after prolonged suffering expressed : "Only in the deepest silence of night the stars smile and whisper among themselves — 'Vain is this seeking ! Unbroken perfection is over all.' "[33]

Would it be unlikely that as play after play, throbbing with innumerable, individualized vibrant characters, emerged from the depth of his creative genius, Shakespeare probably did become aware of "the state of mere potency...the first ideating movement, from which at length, when finally perfected, the whole universe is evolved?"[34] It would perhaps be natural for such an artist to arrive at a close communion with "the ideating cosmic consciousness" which "becomes as the Supreme Speech (Parāvāk), the genetrix of the subtle and gross Śabda" (word) since "it is without idea or language, but is represented as gradually assuming the state in which it utters both and projects from itself into the sensual world the objects (Artha) which they denote."[35]

The Tempest does, in fact, suggest that Shakespeare had penetrated into the mystery of 'name' and 'form.' As the enacted revels of the spirits summoned by Prospero to celebrate Miranda's betrothal to Ferdinand come to a close, the magus observes :

> "....like the baseless fabric of this vision
> The cloud-capp'd towers, the gorgeous palaces,
> The solemn temples, the great globe itself,
> Yea, all which it inherit, shall dissolve,
> And like this insubstantial pageant faded
> Leave not a rack behind. We are such stuff
> As dreams are made on...."
>
> (*The Tempest*, IV. i. 151-57)

The dreamer himself dreams or 'creates' the dream in which he participates, as he also, at the same time witnesses it! "The cloud-capp'd towers, the gorgeous palaces" with all their glittering embellishments are 'real' as long as the dream lasts, but the 'stuff' that creates them is only the 'insubstantial' mind! This was the 'initiation' imparted to king Janaka, the 'Videha' by Sage Ashtavakra, and constitutes the most subtle essence of Indian thought.

The Tripura Rahasya clearly indicates :

"Just as the dream creations are pictures moving on the mind-screens, so this world, including yourself is the obverse picture depicted by pure intelligence and it is nothing more than an image in a mirror."[36] Hence "The object is sunk in illumination like the image of a city in a mirror."[37]

In the Hymn to Dakṣiṇāmūrti Shankarācharya also reiterates the same image :

> विश्वं दर्पणदृश्यमान नगरी तुल्यं निजान्तर्गतं
> पश्यन्नात्मनि मायया भू बहिरिवोद्भूतं यथा निद्रया।
> यः साक्षात्कुरुते प्रबोधसमये स्वात्मानमेवाद्वयं
> तस्मै श्रीगुरुमूर्तये नम इदं श्री दक्षिणामूर्तये।।

"To Him who by Māyā as by dream, sees within Himself the universe which is inside him, like unto a city that is seen in a mirror, (but) which is manifested as without : to Him who apprehends, at the time of awakening, His own non-dual Self : to Him, of the form of the Preceptor, the blessed Dakṣiṇāmūrti may this obeisance be!"[38]

However, such insight can only emerge from the causal body. Frawley states :

> "The causal body has the causal universe open to it (the formless realm of Divine truth principles) and can experience all creation as the manifestations of its own meditations, including creating universes of its own."[39]

Moreover, it is the state "in which we partake of the Divine mind and all its creative and transformative powers,"[40] and this, in fact, is what Prosporo has achieved.

The latest advances in Physics have also revealed that the known is "no less mental than the knowing element itself,"[41] and thinkers have acknowledged that to the enquiring mind "there is no mystery of the physical world which does not point to a mystery beyond itself,"[42] each sensation being "a purely mental response into which a nerve stimulus has somehow translated itself."[43] Hence, "every sensation is a private and individual matter, because it is an activity originating in one's own self."[44] Since we see the world "only through the immovable spectacles of the sense reports which we receive concerning it"[45] we "never know the panoramic external world in itself."[46] "Everything from infinitesimal microbe to infinite space is first an object of thought, an image or an idea",[47] hence all "sense experience is impossible without the association of an equivalent act of thought."[48]

It is therefore, undeniably true that :

"The entire planet itself offers...a curious example of great masses of solid, liquid and gaseous substances which are not what they really seem. For, if scientific investigation has not deceived itself, they are whirling winds of electrical energy...."[49] with particles living for "less than a millionth of a second"[50], a 'particle second' itself being "10^{-23} seconds which is a short-hand notation for a decimal number with 23 zeroes in front of figure 1 (including the one in front of the decimal point)."[51]

To know such mysteries of existence not only through intellectual analysis, but through direct perception in a state of attention focussed within the consciousness is a process of "returning" to true nature "and claiming our inherent mastery of all time, space, matter and energy."[52]

The vibrant force that endows Shakespeare's plays springs, undoubtedly, from that total absorption where the maestro of thought and expression fathomed the deepest origins of speech where "The Lord manifests Himself through his Māyāic power first as Parā Vāni in the Muladhara Chakra at the navel, then as Madhyamā in the heart, and then eventually as Vaikhari in the throat and mouth."[53]

Shakespeare, thus, is perceived by the Indian mind as the true devotee of the 'sattvic' form of Cosmic Energy, the Vāgdevi, Saraswati, who Śamkara Bhagwatpada extolls in ecstatic terms :

शरज्ज्योत्स्ताशुभ्रां शशियुत जटा जूट मकुटां
वस्त्रसत्रण रूटिकघुटिका पुस्तककराम्।
सकृन्न त्वां नत्वा कथमिव सतां संनिदधाते
मधुक्षीरद्राक्षामधुरिम मधुरीणा भणितय:।।15।।

"How will words, which are of the sweetness of honey, milk and grape-juice, not be in the command of such as have bowed even once to Thee, who are bright as the autumnal moonbeams, who hast as Thy crown the coiled plaited-hair with the (crescent) Moon on, and who holdest in Thy hands the boon-bestowing (and) security-affording (postures), a rosary of crystal beads and a book?"[54]

To a sensitive mind, each play of Shakespeare presents

a treasure of endless, unparalleled aesthetic experience, and a close study of his complete works from the early Romances, the History and the Roman plays through the tragedies to the final Romances unfolds a process of rapid, almost unmatched psychic evolution. *The Tempest*, his last play has truly been acclaimed as "the cornerstone of the total edifice of the Last Plays...presenting a philosophy which connects with all their themes and reflects a movement or a phase, which can now be more or less identified among the currents of European intellectual and religious history,"[55] as it affords "a clearer understanding of where this towering figure of William Shakespeare stands in the history" of not only "European thought and religion,"[56] but as the pinnacle of universal intellectual and aesthetic achievement originating from the eternal springs of consciousness itself!

REFERENCES

1. Frances A. Yates, *Majesty and Magic in Shakespeare Last Plays* (Boulder : Shambhala, 1978), p. 3.
2. William Hazlitt, *Lectures on the English Poets and the English Comic Writers*, ed. William Carew Hazlitt (London : George Bell and Sons, 1894), pp. 62-66.
3. Tom F. Driver, *The Sense of History in Greek and Shakespearean Drama* (New York : Columbia University Press, 1960), p. 121.
4. Fredrick Turner, *Shakespeare and the Nature of Time* (London : Clarendon Press, 1971), p. 82.
5. Kenneth Muir, *Shakespeare's Sources*, Vol. I (London : Methuen and Co. Ltd., 1957), p. 119.
6. Robert H. West, *Shakespeare and the Outer Mystery* (Lexington : University of Kentucky Press, 1968), p. 46.
7. A.L. Rowse, *Shakespeare the Man* (London : Macmillan, 1973), pp. 210-11.
8. J.I.M. Stewart, "Character and Motive in Shakespeare" quoted in Rowse, *op. cit.*, p. 212.
9. Rowse, *op. cit.*, p. 211.
10. *Ibid.*, p. 212.
11. Thelma Moss, *The Probability of the Impossible* (London : Routledge and Kegan Paul, 1976), p. 17.

12. Quoted in Naomi A. Hintze and J.G. Pratt, *The Psychic Realm : What You Can Believe* (New York : Random House, 1975), p. 83.
13. David Frawley, *Tantric Yoga and the Wisdom Goddesses : Spiritual Secrets of Ayurveda* (1994 rpt.; Motilal Banarsidass Publishers, Pvt. Ltd., 1996), p. 159.
14. *Ibid.*, p. 159.
15. *Ibid.*, p. 159.
16. *Ibid.*, p. 159.
17. *Ibid.*, p. 161.
18. D.K.C. Todd, *I Am Not Prince Hamlet* (London : The University Press, 1974), p. 173.
19. Frawley, *op. cit.*, p. 162.
20. Paul Brunton, *The Hidden Teaching Beyond Yoga* (1991 rpt.; Delhi : B.I. Publications, 1976), p. 308.
21. Robert H. West, *op. cit.*, p. 33.
22. *Durgasaptashati* (Gorakhpur : Geeta Press).
23. Frawley, *op. cit.* p. 161.
24. *Ibid.*, p. 162.
25. Walter Cylde Curry, *Shakespeare's Philosophical Patterns* (1937 rpt.; Peter Smith : Louisania State Univ. Press, 1968), p. 54.
26. *Ibid.*, p. 55.
27. *Alex Aronson, Psyche and Symbol in Shakespeare* (London : Indiana Univ. Press, 1972), p. 229.
28. Zolar, *The History of Astrology* (London : W. Foulsham and Co. Ltd., 1972), pp. 146-47.
29. Yates, *op. cit.*, p. 12.
30. *Ibid.*, pp. 12-13
31. *Ibid.*, p. 13.
32. *Ibid.*, p. 13.
33. Rabindranath Tagore, *Gitanjali : Song Offerings* (1913 rpt.; Madras : Macmillan India, 1977), p. 54.
34. Sir John Woodroffe, *The Garland of Letters* (Madras : Ganesh and Company, 1994), p. 114.
35. *Ibid.*, p. 127.
36. *Tripura Rahasya : The Mystery Beyond the Trinity* tr. Sw. Sri Ramananda Saraswathi Tiruvannamalai : Sri Ramanasraman, 1971), p. 101.

37. *Ibid.*, p. 163.
38. T.M.P. Mahadevan, *The Hymns of Śaṅkara* (1980 rpt.; Motilal Banarsidass Publishers, Pvt. Ltd., 1997), p. 2.
39. Frawley, *op. cit.*, p. 162.
40. *Ibid.*, p. 162.
41. Brunton, *op. cit.*, p. 278.
42. Lincoln Barnett, *The Universe and Dr. Einstein* (London : Victor Gollanz, Ltd., 1949), p. 23.
43. Brunton, *op. cit.*, p. 218.
44. *Ibid.*, p. 219.
45. *Ibid.*, p. 220.
46. *Ibid.*, p. 220.
47. *Ibid.*, p. 222
48. *Ibid.*, p. 222.
49. *Ibid.*, p. 236.
50. Fritjof Capra, *The Tao of Physics* (1976 rpt.; New York : Bantam Books, 1977), p. 213.
51. *Ibid.*, p. 214.
52. Frawley, *op. cit.*, p. 198.
53. Swami Sivananda, *Kundalini Yoga* (Shivanandanagar; The Divine Life Society, 1994), pp. ix-x.
54. Śri Śamkara Bhagwatpada, *Saundarya Lahiri*; tr. Pt. Subramanya Sastri and T.R. Srinivasa Ayyanger (1937 rpt.; Adyar : The Theosophical Publishing House, 1997), p. 81.
55. Frances A. Yates, *Shakespeare's Last Plays : A New Approach* (London : Routledge and Kegan Paul, 1975), p. 97.
56. *Ibid.*, p. 105.

7

Shakespeare's Great Tragedies : A Hegelian Perspective

—*Basavaraj Naikar*

HEGEL IS one of the most influential German philosophers who have tried to relate his philosophy to major forms of literature in a very profound way. His views on tragedy therefore have earned him worldwide acclaim. A highly original philosopher, he has offered his views in his own distinctive language, which appears to be more abstract than that of Aristotle. Whereas Aristotle appears to be more literary in his views on tragedy. Hegel strikes us as more philosophical.

It is common knowledge that conflict is the heart of drama and so of tragedy. That tragedy is a story of unhappiness ending in death is also a widely accepted view. But for Hegel mere suffering is not tragic. For him the cause of suffering is more important than the suffering itself. A.C. Bradley comments on Hegelian views :

> That tragedy is a story of suffering is probably to many people the most obvious fact about it. Hegel says very little of this, partly perhaps, because it is obvious, but more because the essential point to him is not the suffering but its cause, namely, the action or conflict. Mere suffering, he would say, is not tragic, but only the suffering that comes of a special kind of action.[1]

Hegel, thus, shifts the stress from suffering to the cause of it. The cause of suffering is ascribable to 'the tragic flaw' according to Aristotle. But in Hegelian theory, it is attributable to 'a special kind of action' born out of the conflict of the spirit.[2] Hegel uses the word 'spirit' in the wider sense which includes the entirety of man. The suffering of a tragic hero is caused by the conflict of spirit.

> The reason why the tragic conflict thus appeals to the spirit is that it is itself a conflict of the spirit. It is a conflict, that is to say, between powers that rule the world of man's will and action — his 'ethical substance.'[3]

Hegel, thus, highlights the ethical or moral significance of the conflict involved in a tragic action. The conflict need not always be between Good and Evil, but it can as well be between Good and Good each trying to assert itself to the exclusion of the other. Hence the collision. "The essentially tragic fact is the self-division and intestinal warfare of the ethical substance, not so much the war of good with evil as the war of good with good."[4] The incompatibility between the two forces produces the tragic conflict. There may thus be a conflict between personal love and honour or some social good or religion or science or national ideal. The collision happens because of the absolute demand of each force at the cost or negligence of the other. There is neither harmony nor cooperation or hierarchical obedience by the lower to the higher force. In a way conflict may be said to be the product of democratization or equalization of forces or beings. In other words, tragic conflict is caused by distention or magnification of one idea or value out of its natural proportion.

> It is the nature of the tragic hero, at once his greatness and his doom, that he knows no shrinking or half-heartedness, but identifies himself wholly with the power that moves him and will admit the justification of no other power.[5]

Hegel's perceptiveness and subtle philosophical observation may be seen in his recognition of the operation of eternal justice at the end of tragedy. At the final stage of the struggle or conflict, the absoluteness of the combatant forces is nullified by the ethical or cosmic justice, which shows the relativity of the combatant forces and demonstrates the final triumph of good over evil or of greater good over lesser good. Eternal justice because of its *raison d'etre* crushes or punishes the evil or the lesser good. Tragedy, thus, shows the story of the assertion or operation of external justice thereby teaching a moral lesson that those who violate Law are crushed by it. Tragedy, therefore, is not merely a story of suffering, but that of the inexorability of Law, or Fate or Necessity. What Hegel describes, as 'external justice' is parallel to Aristotle's concept of *hubris.* The solution shown by the resolution of conflict in tragedy is a negative one.

The same thing may be described in another fashion. The tragic hero is not only able to discriminate between good and evil or greater good and lesser good, but he indulges in action without any check or control. Thus his wrong thinking is followed by wrong action. Unable or unwilling to sacrifice the lower self to the higher self, he is doomed to sacrifice his entire life. The punishment, obviously, proves to be graver than he deserves.

The idea of 'reconciliation'[6] suggested by Hegel is a very important one. As the tragic conflict continues, the tragic hero begins to realize his folly or mistake stage by stage. He realizes not only his sin or crime but also the irrevocability of his action. He feels as if he is caught in the whirlpool, which proves stronger than his own poor self. This reconciliation mentally prepares him to accept his defeat or destruction. He has his self-realization and his conscience is awakened. But it is too late for them to save him.

Hegel makes a subtle distinction between ancient tragedy and modern. Whereas in ancient tragedy the pursuits are objective or substantial, in modern tragedy they are personal or subjective. Hegel offers *Orestes* as an example of ancient tragedy and *Romeo and Juliet* and *Hamlet* as examples of modern tragedy.

Another important observation of Hegel is that whereas the characters in ancient tragedy are relatively simple and more or less typical, those in modern tragedy are more complex, subtle and human with all their contradictions. Hence characterization assumes a greater significance in modern tragedies. *Macbeth, Othello, Richard* are offered as examples of this.

The endurance of physical pain is the most important aspect of a tragic hero. The grandeur of a tragic hero lies in his inability to endure the great pain (physical or mental or emotional) caused by his own weakness.

Bradley accuses Hegel of neglecting the element of exultation in tragedy. Even after realizing his folly, the tragic hero rises to the occasion and accepts his defeat or destruction heroically. It is this heroism that borders on the sublime and enlists our admiration for him.

Hegel's negligence of evil is specially noticed by Bradley who says that evil may not be in the character's mind, but it may inhere in a situation. Bradley wants Hegel to use the literary terminology of 'good' and 'evil' rather than two goods being at loggerheads with each other.

Bradley further complains that Hegel has neglected the idea of self-division or self-waste in the tragic character. Hegel's reference to the idea of conflict may be extended to the individual character also. Bradley is right when he says that the tragic hero enlists our sympathy because of his spiritual quality. Hegel has, of course, not worked it out elaborately, as he seems to have taken it for granted.

Bradley also points out correctly that the tragic hero is in the grip of evil even after realizing his folly. That is the reason why he does not repent about his wrong action in the midway. I personally feel that there is no concordance between his right knowledge and wrong action. It only means that he is half-wise and unable to translate his knowledge into action.

Hegel's emphasis on the affirmative function of eternal justice[7] which negates the tragic hero is a very significant contribution to criticism. We not only feel pity, fear and admiration, but also a security about the cosmic order. Otherwise we are simply depressed and horrified. Tragedy awakens in us a belief in the operation of superpower or justice or Fate or Necessity sitting in judgement upon human actions.

Othello[8] may be interpreted according to Hegelian concept of tragedy. In it we find an inevitable conflict between the protagonist and Cassio caused by Iago who is disappointed by the promotion of Cassio over against himself. Iago's professional jealousy and vengeance against both Othello and Cassio involves the innocent Desdemona in the evil game. The interracial marriage between Othello the Black Moor and the fair Christian Desdemona has already upset the people, especially the father of the girl, Brabantio. Iago wants to make the best use of this general disapproval of the marriage. Iago has another deep-seated suspicion that his own wife Emilia has been robbed of her chastity by both Othello and Cassio. It is thus the combination of professional jealousy and sexual jealousy that propels Iago to ruin the life of Othello and of Cassio.

Othello, who has married Desdemona much against the wish of her father, has complete faith in her integrity, especially in her sexual purity. But his belief in her chastity is shaken slowly and stage by stage by Iago. It is, obviously, the discordance between his willingness to believe in the ideal womanhood and the evidence to the contrary that upsets Othello thereby making him unhappy. The play satisfies the Hegelian expectation of tragedy by showing not only the suffering of Othello but also the cause of it all. The ideal of chastity suggests the other Elizabethan vice of cuckoldry. It was a matter of great shame and insult for an Elizabethan to be cuckolded by somebody. Othello is no exception to this phenomenon.

The real flaw of Othello consists not so much in his being cuckolded as in his gullibility. His belief in Iago's honesty and interpretation of Desdemona and Cassio is so firm that he does not endeavour at all to verify it properly. In Hegelian terms there is a conflict between Good and Evil in the play in which Othello the protagonist identifies himself with Evil *i.e.* Iago whole-heartedly by ignoring Good as expressed in the innocent purity of Desdemona and Cassio. He comes under the complete sway of Iago who goes on poisoning his mind about Desdemona's so-called adulterous relationship with Cassio. Iago who believes in the 'Divinity of hell' tries to arouse Othello's suspicion by making him see Desdemona and Cassio in privacy. Cassio leaves Desdemona, as he cannot face Othello on account of possible embarrassment. After slowly arousing Othello's suspicion, Iago alerts him in a generalized way. He awakens Othello to the idea of cuckoldry and precautions him. Othello is so much influenced by Iago's hypocritical tutoring that he does not want to verify the validity or otherwise of Iago's incrimination of Desdemona. Othello is shocked to know the so-called violation of woman's chastity. When he insists upon having some proof about the sin, Iago is clever enough to produce evidence like the handkerchief and Cassio's so-called confession about his affair with Desdemona. Besides, Desdemona's repeated requests to Othello about Cassio's reinstatement strengthen his suspicion. Gradually he loses the balance of his mind and consequently becomes more and more vindictive towards Desdemona. He identifies himself with the evil power of Iago so totally that he is not able or willing to recognize the point of view of the opposite party *i.e.* Desdemona. Even when Desdemona denies the charge levelled against her, Othello is not willing to accept or verify it and kills his dear and innocent wife high-handedly.

As Othello has violated the ethical or moral law of life by completely identifying himself with the evil force thereby neglecting the good force as incarnated in Desdemona, he has to pay the necessary price for the crime or sin. In Hegelian terms 'eternal justice' comes into operation by negating the protagonist who has tried to violate it. Though Othello, of course, realizes his folly, it is rather too late for him to do so. In the self-destruction of Othello can be seen the inexorability of Law or eternal justice. It affirms the cosmic order of life by denying the absoluteness of the combatant forces and establishing the balance between the two.

Though Hegel has not highlighted the grandeur of the tragic hero, we should not fail to grasp it. After having the right knowledge of the truth of Desdemona's purity, Othello grows very conscientious and repents his grave folly. But it is too late to be useful to him. He, therefore, stabs himself to death. Thus the awakening of his conscience results in self-destruction. As per the Hegelian canon, Othello's death shows the inexorability of Law. When Othello's identification with his instinct became absolute, the schism between it and the powers of Reason went on widening thereby resulting into a great conflict which was finally resolved by the Law negating Othello who tried to negate it. The resolution of the tragic conflict in *Othello* is followed by the negation of the protagonist and affirmation of the moral order in the universe.

Macbeth may be interpreted according to Hegelian theory of tragedy. Macbeth has to undergo a great ideal of tragic suffering which is caused by his own tragic folly *i.e.* overambition. The play fulfils the Hegelian expectation according to which Macbeth's suffering in itself is not tragic, but it is the subjective cause of suffering *i.e.* overambition which is the result of imbalance and split between his instinct and Reason. The schism between these two faculties starts widening in him the moment he meets the three witches who awaken in him the latent ambition of becoming the King of Scotland by illegal and foul means. The witches may, of course, be said to be dramatic externalization of Macbeth's dormant passion required for theatrical presentation. With the awakening of ambition in him, triggered off by the witches, Macbeth goes on losing his rationality and identifies himself with the evil *i.e.* ambition more and more closely. It is this lack of balance between his lower self and higher self that goads him to pursue the monstrous path of inviting the King, Duncan and murdering him in cold blood, of course, abetted by his own overambitious wife. Once he is on the track of evil, there is no controlling or checking him in the midway. His violation of the natural law of hospitality, of course, begins to rebound upon him in a very ruthless manner. When evil is invoked by his overambition, Good is also automatically awakened. When he murders Macbeth in his castle, he is disconcerted to know that King Duncan's son has escaped from there. Banquo and Macduff also have grown alert and try to thwart Macbeth's evil plans. Thus when Evil is ascendant, Good seems to be helpless and bidding its time. The conflict between Good and Evil has started in the play and fulfils the idea of Hegelian concept of tragedy. When Macbeth murders King Duncan, he cannot rest in peace, as his inner conscience has been awakened. He feels a sense of deeply disturbing insecurity because of the dire consequences awaiting him. He remembers the prophecy of the witches that Banquo will beget sons who would be the rulers of Scotland. He also fears the threat from Macduff. Suffering from a deep sense of guilt, he wants to blame the murder of Duncan on to his guards. When Macduff comes to know of Duncan's murder, Macbeth murders the guards for the 'supposed murder' of their own king. Thus he goes on committing a fresh murder in order cover up the old ones. One of the most important paradoxes of his life is that he has murdered his own sleep and therefore 'Macbeth shall sleep no more.' He is haunted by guilt and pursued by his own awakened conscience. He therefore feels that not all the perfumes of Arabia would wash the blood off his hands. In order to get rid of Banquo he has him murdered. But again as luck would have it, Banquo's son has escaped from there. Further, he has Lady Macduff and her son murdered at their own residence. The conflict between Good and Evil continues until Good begins to ascend in its power, when the young prince, son of the late King Duncan, gathers an army, with the help of Macduff and attacks Macbeth. Finally Macbeth is killed in the battle. Now the conflict is resolved finally by the triumph of Good over Evil. Macbeth who tried to negate the moral order or Law of Life is himself negated by it. The play, thus, shows the ruthlessness and inexorability of the Law. The affirmation of the Moral Order is shown through the concurrent negation of the protagonist, Macbeth who tried to negate it.

The root cause of Hamlet's tragic suffering, according to Hegelian concept of tragedy, is his over thinking. There is an imbalance between his intellect and emotion and between his head and heart. When goaded by the ghost of his father to take revenge against his uncle for robbing the former of his power of kingship and wife, Hamlet falls into deep thinking. The ghost of his father has revealed to him how his uncle has usurped his kingdom and wife by poisoning him. Now that the mystery is clear to Hamlet, he should have taken some action to avenge his father's death by trying to kill his uncle. But he does not do it because of his dilly-dallying. Perhaps one of the reasons for this protraction is his love for Ophelia, which is unfortunately unrequited. That is the reason why he curses her to 'Go to the nunnery.' On the one hand, he is upset about the sensuousness of his mother who has hurriedly married his uncle immediately after his father's death. On the other hand, he is frustrated in his love for Ophelia who has been warned by her father Polonius to keep away from him. He is frustrated in two ways in that his mother did not live up to his expectation as mother, and his beloved did not live up to his expectation as a beloved. Being a man of philosophical temperament, he goes on brooding about the ephemerality and mystery of life. It is the melancholic nature that prevents him from indulging in action. He pretends to be mad. Perhaps he feels lonely, insecure and helpless. He, thus, identifies himself more and more with intellectual faculty to the exclusion of the principle of action.

When Hamlet arranges for a dramatic performance by the touring actors, he wants to see the reaction of his uncle who witnesses the performance. The King who feels very guilty after seeing the play thinks that Hamlet's being alive would be a great threat to his own life and crown and therefore plots on his life. He asks Rosencrantz and Guildenstern to destroy Hamlet. It is Hamlet's obsession with his mother's sin that makes him go to her in a fit of frenzy and ask her to confess her sin. But he kills Polonius inadvertently. The murder of Polonius, of course, further aggravates the hostility of Ophelia and Laertes. The King's desire to get him murdered grows stronger and stronger. But when Hamlet, after his return from England, accepts the challenge and fights with Laertes, he is wounded by the poisoned sword. His mother has died by drinking the poisoned wine. Hamlet, after knowing the King's treachery, forces the poisoned wine down his gullet. He has, of course, fulfilled his father's desire by taking revenge upon his uncle, but at what cost? It may be said that he angers his uncle by awakening his guilt and vindictiveness and by killing Polonius in an inadvertent manner. It is the murder of Polonius, which drives Ophelia to suicide, and Laertes to wound Hamlet mortally. Though Hamlet achieves his goal, he gets negated by the Law of life. He is punished for his melancholic brooding and delayed but irrational action. The tragedy, thus, shows the negation of the protagonist and the concurrent affirmation of the moral order of the universe.

According to Hegelian idea of tragedy, *King Lear's* suffering is in itself not tragic, but the cause of his suffering. When, for example, King Lear wants to distribute his kingdom according to the proportion of love that each one of his three daughters bears towards him, he has in Hegelian terms, committed the tragic mistake. His gullibility may be said to be an additional folly. In his decision to distribute the property among his three daughters according to their love shows his lack of practical wisdom, which is so necessary for him on such an occasion. When he is ready to believe the painted words of his 'pelican daughters' like Goneril and Regan, he is not willing to believe the frank words of his youngest daughter Cordelia, one can easily see how his concealed egoism is fed by the elder daughters and pricked by the youngest one. It is this egoism which overpowers his reason. He is unable to maintain a balance between his instinct (*i.e.* egotism) and Reason and allows the former to override the latter. In Hegelian terms, there is thus a division in King Lear's 'ethical substance.' Further he makes the mistake of whole-heartedly identifying himself with the instinctual, egoistic power that moves him thereby suppressing or ignoring the other, rational faculty in him. When angered by Cordelia's frank realistic words, he decides to distribute his entire property between the two elder daughters only thereby making Cordelia lose even her legitimate share of property. It is the irrational identification with his instinct that happens to be the root cause of his tragic suffering later. Once he has violated both legal and moral law, he has to be subjected to the inexorable law in a very merciless fashion. As soon as the elder daughters take charge of their property, Lear not only ceases to be a king for them but even becomes a burden to them. His senility, of course, adds to his unwantedness. That is the reason why his eldest daughter Goneril does not tolerate the din and noise of his hundred servants and his own all too liberal behaviour. She wants to cut down the number of his servants from hundred to fifty. Shocked by the filial ingratitude, Lear goes to Regan's palace where he is treated in the worse manner and where Regan wants to cut down the number of his servants from fifty to only five. It is only now that he realizes the gravity of his folly. Deeply insulted by the callous treatment by his daughters, he rushes out in the dark and stormy night. Thus Lear has to undergo all this suffering because it is all rooted in his own personal folly. He refuses to return to his elder daughters though advised by Kent to do so. Whereas Lear continues to suffer on account of his total identification with instinctive (egoistic) force, the evil on the other hand asserts itself more and more vehemently. Goneril and Regan try not only to defeat the French army, but even to have Lear killed. Thus the conflict between good and evil becomes very tense. It is because of the conflict that tragedy; in this case, *King Lear* attains the artistic height, according to Hegel. In the conflict evil goes on growing more and more powerful. In the war that ensues between Britain and France, the French army is defeated by the British army. Consequently Lear and Cordelia are taken prisoners. Lear has, of course, gone mad because of his folly and helplessness. He is heart broken to see that his beloved daughter Cordelia is hanged by Edgar's captain. The end of King Lear is complete now. He loses not only his daughter but his own power, property and precious life. Thus King Lear is ultimately negated by the Law as a punishment for his negating it. After committing the grave folly of neglecting Cordelia and parting with his property to his pelican daughters, King Lear seems to have been reconciled to his lot, as per Hegelian observation. His reconciliation with his present condition is also suggestive of the awakening of wisdom in him, though in a belated manner. What endears Lear to us is his heroic or noble endurance of his suffering. The tragedy strengthens our faith in the moral order by showing the affirmation of Law through the concurrent negation of the protagonist who had tried to defy it.

REFERENCES

1. A.C. Bradley, *The Shakespearean Tragedy* (London : Oxford University Press, 1904), p. 68.
2. G.W.F. Hegel, *Aesthetics* : *Lectures on Fine Arts,* trans. T.M. Knox (Oxford : Oxford University Press, 1985), p. 351.
3. A.C. Bradley, *op. cit.,* p. 71.
4. G.W.F. Hegel, *op. cit.,* p. 344.
5. *Ibid.*, p. 355.
6. *Ibid.*, p. 358.
7. *Ibid.*, p. 360.
8. Shakespeare, *Complete Works,* ed., Peter Alexander (London : The English Language Book Society and Collins, 1964). All the subsequent references to great tragedies are to this edition only.

8

Predeterminism and Free will in Shakespeare's Tragedies

—Sudhir Dixit

'EDMUND'S MISTAKE is this.... He recognizes no fate, but only free will'[1] argues G. Wilson Knight in 'The Lear Universe.' That is also Bradley's mistake when he analyses the Shakespearean universe, 'The dictum that, with Shakespeare, "Character is destiny" is no doubt an exaggeration...but it is the exaggeration of a vital truth.'[2] The Bradley bias is based on the 'free' actions of the protagonists, 'We find practically no trace of fatalism.... Nothing, again makes us think of the actions and sufferings of the persons as somehow arbitrarily fixed beforehand.'[3]

However, in Shakespearean tragedies protagonists do not bring upon themselves their doom; their actions are not always of free choice; they are often beguiled by the subtle workings of fate; their intentions are always good and yet the end-result is always catastrophic. In most of his tragedies, there's a divinity that shapes their ends, rough-hew them how they will. Shakespearean tragedy bears the hallmark of a palpable fatalistic design, an eerie impression that sufferings are 'somehow arbitrarily fixed beforehand.'

Fate is largely responsible for the tragedy in the Shakespearean universe, as it used to be in the Greek tragedy. In *Oedipus Tyrranus*, the most famous Greek tragedy, we find that Oedipus is not really responsible for his deeds. The patricide and incest were not the deeds of his choice, these were rather thrust upon him. The last play of Sophocles, *Oedipus at Colonus*, highlights this helplessness of mortals.

> "Come, tell me this : if to my father God's oracles were bringing a message to say that he should die by his child's hands, how couldst thou fairly reproach me therewith, who was not yet begotten or conceived, but was then unborn."[4]

Even Aristotle's *hamartia* was an outcome of the Greek concept of *hubris*, as evidenced in *Ajax*. If tragedy issues from tragic flaw, then men ought to be free to choose either the good way or the bad way, and that is exactly what is denied to Shakespearean heroes or Sophoclean heroes. The destiny in Shakespeare is mostly 'predetermined' and Shakespeare's technique of plot-construction makes this point very clear in the beginning itself. Macbeth, Julius Caesar, and Romeo get the warnings of fate in the very first act; Gloucester's speech on eclipses in Act I sets the very pattern of the tragedy of *King Lear*. Antony and Richard III are also forewarned in the course of the play.

In spite of the *prima facie* causal connection, deep down the hero's doom is already sealed, even before he acts or makes any choice at all. If Macbeth's fate was not predetermined how could the witches foresee that he 'shall be king hereafter' or that 'none of woman born shall harm Macbeth.' Had everything depended on human action, the future could not have been foretold and it would have been impossible for the witches to show '*eight kings in a line*' who would come to rule England in future. If astrology is true, then the theory of free will has to be fallacious. If the planets govern human thoughts, decisions and actions, then men are simply puppets in the hands of Destiny. Elizabethans believed in astrology and all major playwrights including Marlowe, Lily and Webster used astrological jargon in their plays.

In Shakespeare's England people believed in God and as we have forsaken our faith in God, we find it difficult to believe in the theory of predeterminism. Being atheistic, the modern age believes in the concept of free will and interprets Shakespeare's heroes guided by the modern concept, and not by the Shakespearean concept. In Elizabethan times people believed that man's actions and thoughts are not determined by his free will, but by his destiny. Spinoza's words succinctly sum up this metaphysical standpoint, 'There is no such thing as free will, everything in nature is determined.... Man thinks he is free because he is ignorant of the causes of his decision. Thus the falling stone, if it became conscious would regard itself as free.'[5]

St. Augustine thought that God 'has settled from all eternity what is going to happen to every individual.'[6] Even the stoics believed that 'Everything is absolutely determined, even the human will.'[7] The Renaissance was an extension of this medieval belief in predeterminism. The majority of the people believed that destiny determined human situation externally as well as internally. The external workings of destiny were through chance or accident, the internal workings of destiny were by influencing decision-making faculty and compelling man to choose the destined path. Shakespeare must have believed in the prevalent religious faith in predeterminism or, even if he did not believe it personally, being a dramatist catering to popular public taste, he must have respected it.

In most of his tragedies, the hero's fate has been foretold by means of prophecies. The oracles of Delphi and prophecies of Teiresias and Cassandra played a crucial role in Greek drama. Shakespeare, like Greek dramaturgists, used several foretelling-devices in his plays like auguries, prophecies, curses, omens and dreams and also innovates on his Greek predecessors by including palmistry and astrology in his stock.

The role of chance or accident is too significant to be summarily dismissed. Romeo never got the Friar's message, the Friar arrived a little too late to prevent Romeo's suicide, Juliet did not awake from her sleep a minute sooner : such are the accidents or rather, the series of accidents in *Romeo and Juliet*. In *King Lear*, Edmund's confession comes a little too late to save Cordelia. In *Hamlet*, the stabbing of Polonius, the letter-replacement, the attack of pirate-ship, Ophelia's death, Gertrude's death are all accidental. In *Othello*, Desdemona's fatal loss of her handkerchief and Bianca's timely arrival to meet Cassio are chance events of crucial importance. In *King Richard II*, the Welsh army deserts the king at the most crucial moment of his life and this chance event causes his downfall. In *Julius Caesar*, Artemidorus' warning letter is not perused by Caesar in spite of persistent persuasion and the speech of Artemidorus, prior to his pleading, is significant enough to be quoted :

> 'If thou read this, O Caesar? thou may'st live :
> If not, the Fates with traitors do contrive'
>
> (II, III, 15-16).

In most of his plays, destiny shapes Shakespeare's plots or to be precise, Shakespeare shapes plots to show the dominance of destiny over human free will. The foretellings of the witches in *Macbeth* are already discussed. In *Julius Caesar*, a soothsayer warns Caesar *'Beware the ides of March'* (I, ii, 17). To highlight the supremacy of destiny, Shakespeare makes him reappear to repeat his warning on the very day of his public murder. Caesar jeers at the soothsayer, 'The ides of March are come,' and the soothsayer aptly replies, 'Ay, Caesar, but not gone' (III, i, 1-2). On the fatal morning Caesar discusses his wife's nightmare in which she has seen Caesar's statue bleeding. Even the augurers forbid Caesar 'to stir forth today' as they could not find a heart within the beast. In *Antony and Cleopatra*, the soothsayer predicts Antony's downfall at the hands of Caesar, 'O Antony! stay not by his side.' Other omens include the departure of Hercules on the eve of the battle and the nests of swallows built in the ships. In *King Richard II*, there are many prophecies, curses and ghosts; and all of them predict correctly. Romeo anticipates his disaster even before he meets Juliet, rather too early and too clearly in the very first Act. In Shakespeare *Destiny is*

Character and Shakespeare has taken pains to make it quite clear.

In *Hamlet, King Lear* and *Othello*, there are no prophecies, but there are many chance events and accidents. In all these plays chance plays a great role as discussed already. In addition to this, in these plays we find a plethora of metaphysical questions, discussions and arguments about predeterminism and free will. In *Othello*, Iago discusses and advocates free will. In *King Lear*, the continual references to stars, gods and fate are too many to be bypassed.

'It is the stars,
The stars above us, govern our conditions'
(Kent, IV, iii, 33-34)

'As flies to wanton boys are we to the gods;
They kill us for their sport,' (Glo. IV, i, 35-36)

'These late eclipses in the sun and moon
Portend no good to us' (Glo, I, ii, 105-6)

'Men must endure
Their going hence, even as their coming hither. Ripeness is all. (*Edgar, V, ii,* 7-9)

In *Hamlet*, the protagonist, after the four Acts of metaphysical questioning, comes to accept the doctrine of fate in the fifth Act.

'There's a divinity that shapes our ends
Rough-hew them how we will.' (V, ii, 10-11)

'There's special providence in the fall of a sparrow.' (V, ii, 227-28)

'Readiness is all.' (V, ii, 230)

Free will in Shakespeare is always associated with the villains. Iago advocates the doctrine of free will,

''t is in ourselves that we are thus and thus.'
(I, iii, 320-21)

Cassius in *Julius Caesar* does so, while inciting Brutus to rebellion,

'Men at some time are masters of their fates :
The fault, dear Brutus, is not in our stars,
But in ourselves, that we are underlings.'

(I, ii, 138-40)

In *King Lear*, Edmund rejects the existence of Fate by placing too much confidence in himself,

'When we are sick in fortune (often the surfeit of our own behaviour), we make guilty of our disasters the sun, the moon, and the stars.' (I, ii, 120-23)

The taint to free will has come from the Original Sin. God gave Adam and Eve the freedom to choose between good and evil but they, disobeying God, chose evil. This concept of the Original Sin makes the idea of free will dangerous.

Shakespeare has made his villains the mouthpieces of the philosophy of free will and it is significant that no Shakespearean protagonist is endowed with it. 'Who can control his fate?' Othello asks (V, ii, 270), and the obvious and only answer in the Shakespearean universe is *'none.'*

REFERENCES

1. Knight, G. Wilson, *The Wheel of Fire,* Methuen Paperbacks, London, 1964, p. 186
2. Bradley, A.C., *The Shakespearean Tragedy,* Surjeet Paperbacks, New Delhi, 1995, pp. 7-8.
3. *Ibid.*, p. 21.
4. Sophocles, *Oedipus at Colonus,* II. 970-8.
5. Thilly, Frank, *A History of Philosophy,* Henry Holt & Co., New York, 1955, pp. 328-29.
6. *Ibid.,* p. 187.
7. *Ibid.*, p. 135.

9

Offstage Action in the Plays of Shakespeare

—*B.G. Tandon*

IN CONSTRUCTING the plot of his drama a dramatist is confronted with two vital problems : what parts of the play are to be transacted on the stage and what parts are to be relegated to offstage presentation? If the dramatic plot involves falling in love, conspiring, eating, joking, fighting, dying, travelling, hanging, sermonising, and marrying, the problem is : which of these are to be onstaged and which are to be offstaged?

The Western theorists since Plato came out with their own individual answers. Plato accepted tales in praise of gods and heroes for onstage presentation and banned those that were irreligious, immoral and irrational. Aristotle permitted emotion on the stage but, like Plato, he too prohibited the irrational from onstage enactment. Horace added that the events that are horrible should also be offstaged. During the Renaissance, the Italian critic Lodovico Castelvetro brought in an independent concern with the problem of stagecraft, stating that what was not actable credibly must be kept out of the stage. Sir Philip Sidney added to this list of the non-presentables two more actions, those happening in disparate times and in disparate places : that is, actions happening a few days ago or a few miles away must not be performed on the stage. Ben Jonson raised the problem of stage limitation : that which could not be performed on the stage realistically must be offstaged. Such was the answer of the theorists when Shakespeare came upon the dramatic scene.

Shakespeare was fully aware of the problem of offstage action in drama. He knew it well that there were certain actions that could not be adequately represented on the stage, that they could be pieced together only by the imagination of the audience. An attempt at realistic presentation would be ridiculous, the best was to stimulate creative imagination of the audience. To one Shakespeare thus there would be a thousand dumb Shakespeares. In the various choruses of *Henry V* he admits the deficiency of the stage in presenting mighty themes and he appeals to the imagination of the audience to make good this deficiency :

Can this cockpit hold
The vasty fields of France? Or may we cram
Within this wooden O the very casques
That did affright the air at Agincourt?
O, pardon! since a crooked figure may
Attest in little place a million;
And let us, ciphers to this great accompt,
On your imaginary forces work.

(*Henry V*, Chorus to Act I, 11-18)

There is a similar appeal to the imagination of the audience in *A Midsummer Night's Dream* where Hippolyta and Theseus converse about the interlude of the Clowns :

Hip. This is the silliest stuff that e'er I heard.
The. The best in this kind are shadows; and the worst are no worse, if imagination amend them.

(V, i, 208-10)

In *Pericles* Gower as Chorus appeals to the imagination of the audience to bridge the long gap of time.

But Shakespeare sorted out the problem in his own unique way without respecting the principles laid down by the theorists. Thus, the theorists demanded that death scenes must be offstaged because they are horrible. In Shakespeare there are numerous death scenes that are enacted, and there are quite a few that are narrated, that of Banquo is enacted; Desdemona dies on the stage; Ophelia dies off the stage; Romeo and Juliet die in full view of the audience; Henry IV and Falstaff die behind the curtain; King Lear dies onstage, his Fool offstage.

Similarly, many other ghastly and repugnant scenes are shown before us, and many are relegated behind the scenes. The stabbing of Caesar, the blinding of Gloucester, murder of Macduff's son, are all enacted, while the mutilation of Lavinia, the torture of Aaron, the murder of two Princes in *Richard III*, are all narrated.

In respect of the irrational also, of which one variety is the supernatural, Shakespeare disregards Aristotle's advice of keeping it offstage. There are onstage appearances of the Ghost in *Hamlet*, witches in *Macbeth,* fairies in *A Midsummer Night's Dream*, and of spirits in *The Tempest*, and they meddle in the affairs of man. The ghost also appears in *Julius Caesar* and in *Macbeth* : Brutus encounters the ghost of Caesar, and Macbeth that of Banquo. But the ghosts also make offstage appearance in dreams, to Richard and Richmonds in *Richard III*, to Posthumus in *Cymbeline*, to Katharine in *Henry VIII*, and more.

It would appear that dreams have to be offstaged, and there are many examples of offstage dreams in Shakespeare — Joan la Pucelles' dream of Virgin Mary in *1 Henry VI*, Gloucester's dream of death in *2 Henry VI*, Calpurnia's strange dream in *Julius Caesar,* Clarence's dream of death in *Richard III*, the dream of Antigonus in *The Winter's Tale,* Cleopatra's dream of Antony in *Antony and Cleopatra,* and Caliban's poetic dream in *The Tempest*. But so bold and daring was Shakespeare's imagination that he put even dreams on the stage, some fine examples being the dream of ghosts in *Richard III,* sleep walking scene in *Macbeth*, the vision of Diana in *Pericles*, and the dream of angels in *Henry VIII.*

Shakespeare is not restrained even by stage or acting or audience limitation, though he was fully conscious of their inhibiting power. He puts many unstageable scenes on the stage, the finest being the shipwreck in *The Tempest.* He does defy their curbing power, but, as in other matters, so here, he submits to it also and offstages the unstageable, the examples are the sea fight between Antony and Caesar in *Antony and Cleopatra,* Turkish expedition against Cyprus in *Othello,* Hamlet's escape from the pirates, the burning of Saint Joan in *1 Henry VI*, the drowning of Ophelia, and the like.

Likewise, some battles are acted and some narrated. The battle between Macbeth and Malcolm, the War of Roses, parts of the battle of Agincourt, are onstaged, while the French invasion in *King Lear*, Irish Rebellion in *Richard II,* the Roman invasion in *Cymbeline*, are offstaged. Shakespeare realised the crudity of war on the stage, yet showed many of them, depending, as said earlier, upon the imagination of the audience.

The same is true of the mass scenes. Many mob scenes in *Coriolanus* and *Julius Caesar* are shown before us, but the mob scene in the *Merchant of Venice* in which the street boys chase the distraught Shylock, the crowd gathering around Bolingbroke in *Richard II*, the first procession in *Julius Caesar,* are negotiated behind the curtain.

Further, the funeral procession of Ophelia in *Hamlet* and that of Henry VI in *Richard III* are shown on the stage, but the funeral procession of Caesar, of Juliet to the family vault, of Polonius and of Hamlet are narrated.

From the above discussion it may appear that Shakespeare's management of offstage action in drama was erratic and irregular, and that he had no logic behind it, that he onstaged and offstaged the same action indiscriminately. The fact is that there is an exquisite workmanship in his manipulation of such action and that it is the business of criticism to discover it.

The first thing to remember in this matter is that Shakespeare had his own list of non-presentables. While there are numerous marriages in his plays, not one marriage ceremony is shown on the stage : the possible reason could be that such ceremonies tire the audience. Likewise, there are no onstage bed-scenes in the whole of Shakespeare. Romeo is seen climbing up and climbing down the wall of Juliet's bed-chamber, but the intervening bed-scene is kept out of sight. Similarly, Lavinia in *Titus Andronicus* is raped by Demetrius and Chiron, the sons of Tamora, but the scene is described and not displayed. Another typical non-presentable is the coronation scene, for example, the coronations of Macbeth, Claudius, Bolingbroke, Richard, and of Henry V. But here there is one exception : the coronation of Queen Anne in *Henry VIII* is presented on the stage. The reason for keeping them offstage could be the limitation imposed by the huge expenses involved in enacting such scenes. Similarly, hangings and executions are always offstaged in Shakespeare, and this is surprising in the face of the fact that the Elizabethan audience enjoyed watching the hangings in real life. It is my conjecture that Shakespeare offstaged the hangings because he was opposed to Capital punishment. Another typical offstage action in Shakespeare is a mother crooning over a babe in arm : the reason could be the embarrassment such a scene could cause to the boy actors. The list of these non-presentables is really not very long. Mostly Shakespeare did not formulate regular categories.

The important fact is that Shakespeare judged each action by its individual merit. He had an uncanny eye on he theatrical. His magnificent dramatic insight could instantly enable him to see the theatrical potential of an action. If he felt that it would be effective on the stage he onstaged it, and, on the other hand, if his dramatic perception made him believe that it would be more effective in narration, he offstaged it. I may illustrate my point by a few examples.

My first example is from *Henry V* : it concerns the death of Falstaff. Falstaff figures in four plays of Shakespeare — *I Henry IV*, *2 Henry IV*, *Henry V*, and *The Merry Wives of*

Windsor — and yet his death is described and not displayed : the Hostess graphically narrates it in *Henry V*, II, iii. Why does Shakespeare do that? Has he wasted a potentially theatrical situation? My speculation is that the onstage presentation would have been interlarded with two undramatic possibilities : first, it would have interfered with the Shakespearean design of showing Henry V as larger than Falstaff, Falstaff might have then run away with the drama, the drama would have then belonged to him and not to Henry V. Shakespeare had to minimise his role. Second, the enactment would have brought out the pathos but not the humour that characterized Falstaff. By committing such comic errors as using the words 'Arthur's bosom' for 'Abraham's bosom' or 'rheumatic' for 'lunatic' the Hostess blends poignant pathos with sympathetic humour, and without this the reminiscence of the merry knight would have been incomplete. So here the offstage presentment proves better than onstage enactment.

My second example is from *Hamlet,* it concerns the death of Ophelia which is narrated by Gertrude. Why does Shakespeare not show it on the stage? The fact is that Ophelia's death offstage shows Shakespeare's innate good taste even in a tragedy of blood. He cannot see Ophelia, an embodiment of innocence and loveliness in this revenge drama, to be involved in the ghastliness of the last scene where the stage reeks with blood. The Queen's description of her death is such as sounds fully appropriate : it is the end of a person who was beautiful even in madness. She was flowery in life and dies a flowery death. There would have been no place for her in the bloody deaths of the tragic close. By offstaging her death Shakespeare has shown a superb dramatic sense.

My third example is from *Richard III* and concerns the offstage dream of Clarence. Why is it offstaged while in the same drama the dreams of Richard and Richmond on the eve of the battle of Bosworth are onstaged? Let me recall the scene at some length. Imprisoned in the Tower, Clarence narrates a ghastly dream to the lieutenant of the Tower, Robert

Brakenbury. He tells him that he dreamt that his brother Richard had pushed him into the sea. Harrowed with the pain of drowning, with dreadful noise of waters in his ears, he saw a thousand shipwrecked hulks, ten thousand men gnawed upon by fishes, heaps of gems scattered in the slimy bottom of sea, some lying in dead men's skulls, some settling in their empty socket. The envious flood smothered his soul and panting body, but the dream continued even after his death. His soul passed the melancholy flood and reached hell where he was confronted by his father-in-law Warwick who accused him of betraying him. Then came Prince Edward whom he and Richard had murdered, calling him false, fleeting, perjured Clarence, and asking the Furies to seize on him. With that, a legion of foul fiends surrounded him and howled in his ears such hideous cries, that with the very noise he trembling waked, and for a time could not believe that he was in hell. After narrating this dream, Clarence confesses to Brackenbury that he has done sinful things for Edward who is now treating him ungratefully. Such a dream, of course, could not be shown on the stage. But Shakespeare's real motive in offstaging it must have been to show what goes inside the mind of a man soaked in sin. The onstage presentation could not show what lay in the unconscious layers of Clarence's mind which the narration does through the symbols of the slimy bottom of the deep and through the furies charging him in the hell. Besides, the image of jewels hanging in the skulls and in the empty holes of the eyes symbolise the futility of the pursuit of power and riches by the wrangling lords, something which could be done more effectively by poetry.

The examples could be multiplied, but such as are given sufficiently clarify the remark that each action of a Shakespearean drama is selected for onstage or offstage presentation on its own individual strength and not on the basis of what was laid down by the theorists from Plato to Ben Jonson. The imagination of Shakespeare brooked no commandments : it was free and unfettered.

10

Is there a 'Mother' in this Text?*

—*Rama Kundu*

"I AM sick of hearing of the sublimity of Milton, the elegance and harmony of Pope, and the original, untaught genius of Shakespeare. These cursory remarks are made by some who know nothing of nature, and could not enter into the spirit of these authors, or understand them." — M. Wollstonecraft[1]

In a study of Shakespeare the question — (after Stanley Fish) 'Is there a mother in this text' is bound to rebound.

In spite of the wide range of female characters who are often remarkable in their own ways, the 'mother' remains more or less conspicuously absent from the plays of Shakespeare. This seems intriguing in view of the stronghold of the patriarchal ideology of motherhood in his contemporary England.

Motherhood as an experience, being essentially a woman's experience, had understandably remained an 'unwritten story' till the other day. It is the women writers who have self-consciously gone back to the work of reviving the mother, and it has emerged as a major theme only in the recent decades in contemporary women's literature. But motherhood as an institution has a long history. Over the ages the role of the mother has been universally imposed upon women as their sole identity, their proper identity, above all others.

---

* Presented in the World Shakespeare Conference, held by the Shakespeare Society of Eastern India, in Calcutta, from 3-6 December, 2000.

As Simone de Beauvoir suggested — and subsequent feminist critics took the cue from her — the ideology of motherhood was a construct of pre-Christian cultures across the globe which deified woman as Mother Deity, Mother Goddess, Earth Goddess, etc.; and the ideology got only more firmly entrenched during the Christian centuries. The icon of the virgin mother kneeling before her divine son epitomised the sanctification of the subjugated and enslaved woman. The Freudian school also admits that Christianity integrates a preconscious acknowledgement of the maternal feminine. Though marriage and subsequent motherhood, supposed to be significant events of the woman's life, were also presage to the denial and extinction of her self, still tradition extolled this very denial and extinction as passport to the category of the 'good' woman. Celebration of motherhood in this sense of an institution has been common in cultures across the globe. Today the 'unwritten story' of the 'mother' as a person is just beginning to be told as a result of women's struggles, — their 'search' of their 'mothers' gardens,[2] and their interrogation of the so-called 'joys of motherhood' which is even identified (to the horror of many) as 'a beautiful funeral.'[3] But in the sixteenth century England nobody would have imagined of speaking about motherhood in that fashion. Thanks to the pre-eminence of the virgin mother cult in England and Europe since the Middle Ages motherhood had already come to mean for Shakespeare's contemporaries the supreme identity for woman, whose sanctification was taken for granted, and its implications of subjugation and enslavement to physicality forgotten. The excerpt from Gervase Markham, *The English Hus-wife* (1615) in Dover Wilson's *Life in Shakespeare's England* allows us a glimpse of this aspect of Shakespeare's England.

> ...our English housewife, who is the mother and mistress of the family, and hath her most general employments within the house; wherefrom the general example of her virtues, and the most approved skill

> of her knowledges, those of her family may both learn to serve God, and sustain man in that godly and profitable sort which is required of every true Christian (273).[4]

Ruskin's lecture "Of Queens' Gardens" (1865) and Coventry Patmore's *The Angel in the House* (1854-56) which represent the dominant Victorian attitude toward 'the lovely angel' show the continuity of the same ideology through the centuries.

Also the experience of motherhood — a unique one to women — was interpreted for them through male authorities since ages, and the subject apparently had its fascination for the male author/artist, — especially as he envisaged the mother-son/mother-child relationship. Thus 'Madonna' has been central to European arts through the Middle Ages, as well as the Renaissance and afterwards. The Eurocentric culture in which Shakespeare's works are rooted, upholds the 'madonna' cult and ideology in its sculpture, painting and literature.

In view of the above it is surprising that Shakespeare, in spite of being so great a dramatist with so great psychological insight, was never apparently interested in the traditional role of mother in human relationship and human life. Shakespeare seems to have been not only indifferent to the potential of the subject. He also seems to evidence a degree of uneasiness regarding the 'madonna.'

Let's have a quick look at the plays, not in order to register details of their overt presentation of mother, but to note their covert non-representation of the 'mother.'

Some of the plays, admittedly, have their exclusive focus on erotic or romantic or martial situations where the 'mother' — at least traditionally seen — may not figure. But even when there is no such situational compulsion the 'mother' — either as role or as person — does not often get entry to the Shakespearean stage. A long list may be drawn up of children and youths, especially daughters, who lose their mother either at the moment of their birth or at an early age;[5] or otherwise they are separated from the mother in babyhood/childhood for a long period, — sufficiently long for them to grow up and get settled/unsettled in marriage. By the time they get reunited it is usually the last scene of the play; thus the audience gets no chance of viewing the evolvement of a relationship between the woman and her offspring. Again, more often than not, one has to infer from the situation that the children are motherless; even a specific reference to the event of a death or the cause of the absence of the mother is missing.

Thus Prospero, on his dangerous journey across the seas has to take the baby-girl along with him. She grows up under the care of her father without any experience or memory of motherly love. Both Miranda and the audience are only given this much assurance that she is surely Prospero's own daughter since

> "Thy mother was a piece of virtue, and
> She said thou wast my daughter" (I : 2).

The mothers often belong to the realm of "was", *i.e.* past; they are often banished from the present, relegated to the past and/or to some non-space outside the stage. Sometimes we do not even know whether they had ever existed at all but for the simple biological fact that the child required a womb to be born (or are they all potential Macbeth-killers — man [woman too] of no woman born!). Thereafter she becomes redundant and disposable; and finds no mention in the subsequent sequences, either as a living presence or a past memory in the life or consciousness of the child. For example, Silvia in *The Two Gentlemen of Verona* is introduced (in the list of 'Dramatis Personae') as "the Duke's daughter, beloved of Valentine." But who is her mother, and where is she? Julia, the other lady in the play, moves about with remarkable freedom, disguises herself as a page to be near her lover; but no parents are around to help or hinder her. In *Much Ado about Nothing* Hero and Beatrice are introduced as daughter and niece to Leonato respectively, but we get no glimpse of their mothers, dead or alive. Jessica (*The Merchant of Venice*) is presented as Shylock's daughter; Hermia (*A Midsummer Night's Dream*) is the daughter of Egeus. But where are their mothers?

Whereas even the ghosts in Shakespeare's plays reappear in human shapes and with audible voices, this voicelessness and invisibility of mothers is intriguing. We do not even always know whether they are dead or alive. They are simply absent, — not only physically but also from the consciousness of the children. Rosalind (in *As You Like It*) is "daughter to the banished Duke," and Celia the daughter of Frederick. Neither do the mothers of the girls figure in the list of 'Dramatis Personae,' nor do the daughters remember them; they could have been non-existent as well. Rosalind is sad because she fails "to forget a banished father" (1 : 2). But she has forgotten a mother 'banished' from the scenario, from her memory, from her consciousness. Similarly Celia says : "You know my father hath no child but I, nor none is like to have" (1 : 2); but she does not explain why. We are not even told that their mothers have died. They are simply forgotten and thus reduced to the status of non-existence. Even a dead person can be very much present depending on the way people remember her. In *Twelfth Night* Viola and Sebastian, the young twins, have no parents, neither does Olivia have any, though she has an uncle. Viola mentions 'father' once : "I have heard my father mention him (Orsino) (1 : 3). About Olivia we learn that she is the daughter of a count who has died, and that she had a brother who has also died. Sebastian introduces himself : "...my father was that Sebastian of Messaline.... He left behind him myself and a sister, both born in an hour..." (2 : 1). Neither of the twins does mention their mother. Who she is/was? Where is/was she? Did she die of child-birth, or afterwards? We are not told. When the estranged twins are reunited at the end (5 : 1) they recall the mole on their father's brow, the day he died, but nothing about their mother. It seems she has been completely erased from their memory as well.

In *All's Well* the countess introduces Helena as the "gentlewoman (who) had a father," but is silent about the other parent (1 : 1). The list of such unidentified, unlocated, absented mothers is long indeed, including the mothers of Lavinia (*Titus Andronicus*), Ophelia, Laertes (*Hamlet*), Goneril-Regan-Cordelia (*King Lear*), Imogen (*Cymbeline*), among others.

We also do not hear of the mother of Claudio and Isabella. Isabella mentions her once, but she does so not as a personal memory but as a shockingly contemptuous comment. In order to show her indignation at Claudio's desperate suggestion Isabella says something which denigrates her mother :

"Heaven shield my mother play'd my father fair!
For such a warped slip of wilderness
Ne'er issu'd from his blood" (3 : 1).

Bertram's (*All's Well*) disrespectful allusion to Diana's mother —

"And now you should be as your mother was
When your sweet self was got" (4 : 1)" —

may be read as an oblique way of dethroning the mother and reducing her to a sex symbol. Diana's protest that she was honest, duteous at the moment of the sex act does not help to shift the focus.

Among the few mothers who remain alive some are separated from their children through the best part of the play; *The Comedy of Errors, The Winter's Tale, Pericles* may be cited for example. There are another few who remain alive and are allowed onstage appearance. But barring exceptional cases they do not appear to play a supportive role or show any great motherly emotion. Mistress Page (*Merry Wives*), busy with her 'sport' (5 : 5) and mirth, is indifferent to Anne's feelings or problems. In *King John* the two mothers, Queen Elinor and Constance vie with each other in promoting their own ambitions through their sons. When the son would have been contented the mother goads him on (3 : 1). Both John and Arthur meet unnatural death. The way King John receives the news of his mother's death may be noted; he does not feel it as a personal loss but rather as a practical political inconvenience (4 : 2). Volumnia also plays a similar destructive role in her son's life (*Coriolanus*). Her ambition moulds her son's life and nature and finally she persuades him to take a course which destroys him. Coriolanus knows this even before he sets out to meet his death. One may recall his moving speech :

> "O mother, mother!
> What have you done? Behold...
> The gods look down, and this unnatural scene
> They laugh at. O my mother, mother! O!
> You have won a happy victory to Rome;
> But for your son — believe it, O, believe it! —
> Most dangerously you have with him prevailed,
> If not most mortal to him." (5 : 4)

This, studied alongside Volumnia's accusation and claim, offers an interesting case of mother-son relationship :

> "Thou hast never in thy life
> Show'd thy dear mother any courtesy,
> When she, poor hen, fond of no second brood,
> Has cluck'd thee to the wars, and safely home
> Loaden with honour." (5 : 4)

Hamlet's mother is instrumental behind her son's tragedy. Cymbeline's second wife is the appropriate mother of her bad son with whom she is in league as schemers.* The Duchess of York (*Richard III*) dissociates herself from her murderous son in a most unequivocal manner. She takes the side of the right and does not hesitate to denounce her villainous son :

> "Take with thee my most grievous curse,
> Which in the day of battle tire thee more...

---

* Tamora (*Titus Andronicus*) offers a grotesque and horrible example of a vengeful mother who encourages her sons to rape an innocent girl and herself seeks out carnal pleasure of adultery at the same time.

Bloody thou art; bloody will be thy end.
Shame serves thy life and doth thy death
attend" (4 : 4)

Here she appears to be less a mother than a queen; the strong condemnation indicates a degree of objectivity which is remarkable.

If we stopped here we could come to some clear, simplistic conclusions about Shakespeare's mysogynic treatment of the mother. But Shakespeare, being what he is, does not allow us that pleasure. What seems intriguing is that Shakespeare was also perfectly aware of the mother's pains, anguishes, joys *via-à-vis* her child. Duchess of York herself represents this other face of the mother, the bereaved woman mourning over the death of her child, a common paradigm[6] which Shakespeare has used on certain occasions with remarkable success.

The daughter of Clarence asks her grandmother, the old Duchess of York :

"Why do you weep so oft, and beat your breast,
And cry 'O Clarence, my unhappy son!'" (2 : 2)

The old lady expresses in her dignified way the grief of a bereaved mother, which is enhanced by shame in the surviving son (2 : 2; 11, 49-54). As mother her sorrow surpasses all :

"Alas, I am the mother of these griefs!
Their (the widows' and orphans') woes are parcell'd,
mine is general" (2 : 2)

At the same time it is tormenting for her that her own son is the cause of this woe :

"O my accursed womb, the bed of death!
A cockatrice hast thou hatch'd to the world,
Whose unavoided eye is murderous" (4 : 1).

As Arthur (*King John*) is captured and sent to England to be put to death his mother Constance goes mad with grief and dies. In *Henry VI, Pt. I* (3 : 3) Pucelle or Joan uses a touching analogy of a mother's agony as she watches her dying child, in order to move her countrymen :

"Look on thy country...
As looks the mother on her lowly babe
When death doth close his tender dying eyes...."

In *Henry VI, Pt. 3* we watch the unbearable sorrow of a mother mourning over her murdered child. As the prince is killed Queen Margaret implores "O, kill me too!" The intense pathos of her speech is unmistakable :

"O Ned, sweet Ned, speak to thy mother, boy!
Canst thou not speak?...
No, no, my heart will burst, and if I speak —
And I will speak, that so my heart may burst...
Butchers and villains! bloody cannibals!
How sweet a plant have you untimely cropp'd!
You have no children, butchers; if you had,
The thought of them would have stirr'd up
remorse." (5 : 6)

That Shakespeare knew of the tenderness, the anguish, the suffering and the sentience of a mother is evident from the above. He could, when he would, capture the poignant pain as also the majestic grandeur of motherly suffering.

Shakespeare shows a similar sensitivity towards the feelings of a mother who is forcibly or accidentally separated from her child. One may recall Aemilia's disclosure at the end of *The Comedy of Errors* :

"Thirty-three years have I but gone in travail
Of you, my sons; and till this present hour
My heavy burden ne'er delivered." (5 : 1)

Or to cite Hermione's spirited speech when her children are snatched from her and she is threatened with death :

"Sir, spare your threats.
The bug which you would fright me with I seek...
(because) my second joy

And first fruits of my body, from his presence
I am barr'd, like one infectious; my third comfort,
Starr'd most unluckily, is from my breast —
The innocent milk in it most innocent mouth —
Hal'd out to murder...." (3 : 2)

Again, an instance of a most adequate response of the child to its mother may be noted at the end of *Pericles* when Marina finds her long-lost mother :

"My heart
Leaps to be gone into my mother's bosom." (5 : 3)

Sebastian too (*Twelfth Night*) once mentions 'mother' to Antonio :

"...my bosom is full of kindness, and I am yet so near the manners of my mother that, upon the least occasion more, mine eyes will tell tales of me" (2 : 1).

However, it is not clear whether the reference is to a personal memory or to a general notion that gentleness and emotionality were but feminine traits, unbefitting a male.

The most lovable mother-figure in the Shakespearean gallery is perhaps the Countess in *All's Well* who, in her tender loving way, not only presents a satisfying mother-son relationship, but also becomes a second mother to Helena. No wonder, Shaw (even Shaw) admires her as "the most beautiful old woman's part ever written" (Halliday 29).

At the same time it remains an enigma that the same author could evoke the grotesquely paradoxical image of a monstrous mother through Lady Macbeth's famous analogy for frustrated ambition :

"...I have given suck, and know
How tender 'tis to love the babe that milks me —
I would, while it was smiling in my face,
Have pluck'd my nipple from this boneless gums,
And dash'd the brains out...." (1 : 7)

To conclude, Shakespeare remains an enigma when we consider his treatment of 'mother.' Though he has largely exiled mothers offstage, and on the few occasions of their appearance onstage he has not unfrequently highlighted departures from the 'ideal' rather than the standardized norm, still it cannot be said by any means that Shakespeare was insensitive to or impercipient of motherly feelings or sentiments. On occasions (rare though) he even seems to betray a degree of fascination for the pervasive image of motherhood. Then how to explain his relative avoidance of the subject? Does this indicate his refusal to subscribe to any stereotype, moulded by any fixed ideology, when the 'piece of work' in question was a human! And thus does this refusal show indifference to or insight into the 'piece of work?' Or could there be other explanations, say stage compulsions or biographical factors, for example?

The great masterpieces, as has been claimed by Marcel Proust, exist for many years before they come properly to be understood. Harry Lavin in his summing up of "Critical approaches to Shakespeare from 1660 to 1904" explains this : "It is mainly because they must emerge through zones of preconception unfavourable to their very originality. Therefore, in a sense, they must prepare their own way; gradually the artist must communicate not only his novel perceptions but, to some extent, his unique mode of perceiving them." So, though Dover Wilson claims in the preface to his book on life in Shakespeare's England : "It will be frequently observed how closely Shakespeare's thoughts and phrase resemble those of his contemporaries" (13), Shakespeare was likely to have transcended contemporancity in his thought and perceptions; and thus the very absence of the paradigmatic mother only emphasises the presence of the 'absent' mother in the auditor's perception.

Finally, a text preexists 'a reading' (of the same) and no text has a single, essential, untransformable meaning to which, when all criticism is said and done, we can finally return.

"We make texts mean", as Terence Hawkes says in the conclusion of his essay on Shakespeare, "and the positions from which we do so constitute a major aspect of the meanings we produce."

NOTES

1. *Thoughts on the Education of Daughters : With Reflections on Female Conduct in the Important Duties of Life* (1787). Clifton, N.J. : Augustus Kelley, 1972, pp. 52-53.
2. Reference is made to the title of Alice Walker's well-known work — "In Search of Our Mothers' Gardens" in her 1983 collection of nonfiction writings with the same title.
3. Reference is made to Buchi Emecheta's *The Joys of Motherhood* (New York : George Brazillier, 1979).
4. Markham's elaborations prescribe servile piety for the "good woman" who is viewed as but a loyal and dependable servant to the house of her husband (274-75).
5. Elaine Showalter in her review of E. Bronfen's book *Over Her Dead Body* (1992) underscores the male artist's unease with the woman as the living 'Other', which according to her, explains the preponderance of dead women in the arts through the ages.
6. The mourning mother has been a very popular paradigm across time and space, from the Greek myth of Persephone to the Noh plays of Japan, the poems of Thomas Hardy to the writings of Tagore.

WORKS CITED

Beauvoir, Simone De, *The Second Sex* (1949); (Eng. trans. 1953); Penguin Modern Classics, 1983.

Halliday, F.E., *A Shakespeare Companion,* Penguin Books, 1954.

Hawkes, Terrence, "Shakespeare and New Critical Approaches", *The Cambridge Companion to Shakespeare Studies* (Ed. Stanley Wells), Cambridge : CUP, 1986, pp. 287-302.

Levin, Harry, "Critical Approaches to Shakespeare from 1660 to 1904". *Ibidem*, pp. 213-29.

Shakespeare, W., *Complete works.* London : The English Language Book Society, 1964 (Quatercentenary Edition).

Wilson, Dover, *Life in Shakespeare's England* (1911), London : Pelican Books, 1944.

11

The 'Two Othellos' : A Folkloric Perspective

—Rama Kundu

THE CONTROVERSY over the swift transformation of Othello from the heroic lover and caring husband to a furious wife-baiter and a debased murderer, — a transformation that has continued to baffle readers, audiences, and critics, — provides a sort of index to the changing and conflicting priorities in Shakespeare criticism through time. Othello, who begins as a glamorous hero and soon, in a changed scenario, discloses himself as a brute and criminal has elicited varied critical responses including uneasy justification as well as shocked condemnation. If Laurence Lerner's thesis of the "two Othellos"[1] represents one extreme condemnatory stance regarding the case, Helen Gardnar's vision of 'the' "Noble Moor"[2] would uphold the opposite view.

While neo-classical critics sought to identify certain moral premises in Shakespeare, the Romantics praised him for his amorality, his extension of sympathies even to the sinner, for the 'negative capability' which could find equal delight 'in conceiving an Iago as an Imogen.' Twentieth century showed its departure from the Romantic tradition by beginning to view Shakespeare with detachment and even satire. Eliot's well-known jibes (that Hamlet had died rather 'too pleased with himself' and Othello died 'cheering himself up') provided the cue to be taken up by F.R. Leavis and his followers who had mercilessly criticised Shakespeare protagonists. This trend of underscoring a single and judgmental point of view continued till the sixties when literary criticism took yet another turn and began to acknowledge the multiplicity of responses, even if conflicting, that could be elicited by a single text. Alistair Cooke represents this new trend when he describes Shakespeare as the 'king of the foxes' (based on Archilocus's distinction between the fox and the hedgehog — the fox "knows many things" and the hedgehog "knows one big thing").[3]

However, it is interesting to note how some recent critics, ever as they introduce quite interesting perspectives, or cast illuminating sidelights, would be underscoring the same old issue of choice and responsibility while writing on Othello's transformation. These critiques offer to construct a new meaning by adopting a kind of midway between the two older premises, *i.e.* the Romantic critics' attempt to rationalize 'the evil in them'[4] (Shakespeare's heroes) and the mid-twentieth century critics' conviction that those characters were to be morally castigated for their error or folly. Ebun Clark's folkoric interpretation[5] is a case in point; he tries neither to justify nor to reprove the hero directly. Mr. Clark, originally from the University of Lagos, Nigeria, uses the Nigerian folkore of the 'Complete Gentleman' to explain the tragedy as a focus "on the gap between appearance and reality." The basic outline of the African story, which is found in a number of slightly varying versions in different regions of the continent, is as follows : Beauty wilfully chooses a handsome outsider and thus flouts her society by asserting individual decision in regard to marital choice. Despite warnings and forbidding she follows the stranger to a wilderness where he begins to return his borrowed limbs one by one to their original owners until only the skull remains. Beauty is now taken by force to the house of 'Skulls' to undergo terrible humiliation and torture. According to some versions of the tale Beauty is killed here, while in some others, as in the Nigerian, she is rescued, thoroughly chastened in the meantime and made dumb by the trauma, and given away by her father in marriage to the man of his choice who happens to be the rescuer. There are, indeed, certain striking points of resemblance between this tale and Shakespeare's play, as Mr. Clark so carefully analyses : the hero and the heroine in both; the sequence of events; the tragedy that inheres in the shocked perception of a sudden change in the loved one. But what finally emerges from the comparison is an unequivocal message based on a patriarchal value-system. Clark also candidly confesses that in his society a girl's independent choice of spouse is still frowned upon. The lesson that has been thrust home here is unambiguous : if the woman is wilful, disobedient, choosy, adventurous, or non-conformist in any way, she must suffer. This is also apparently in tune with those mid-twentieth century American essays "on the indiscretions of Desdemona and the misdemeanours of Juliet," both of whom, it was argued, "got just what was coming to them for disobeying their fathers."[6] That is putting the blame squarely on the disobedient daughter and thereby upholding the assumption of parental authority. Indeed, the notion of the father's uncontested authority over the daughter till she is married off and thus handed over to another authority is a generally accepted patriarchal norm over the world. The Church ritual of 'giving the bride away' and the Hindu ritual of *Kanya-sampradan*, still very much in vogue, are but indications of the same assumption. Don Lewis cites a number of curious English customs in his industriously compiled book *Curious and Humorous Customs*. Among "some of the customs familiar to our forefathers which have remained to this day"[7] "an old custom was for the bride's father to give the groom one of his daughter's shoes on the wedding day, showing that he was giving him authority over his daughter. The groom tapped his bride on the head with it to exercise his authority as soon as possible."[8] Of course, it is to be noted in this context that whereas in Cinthio's story, which is supposed to be the source of *Othello*, Desdemona repents her firm disobedience[9], Shakespeare does not make her do so.

However, apart from stressing a common patriarchal motif in this marital tragedy, Mr. Clark also suggests the possibility of treating the text from another significant perspective. After reading Clark's unique 'Nigerian' interpretation of *Othello* the reader is struck afresh with a renewed awareness that Shakespeare's continued relevance across time, space and cultural frontiers has been possible due to, among other reasons, his ability to touch and stir some memories implanted deep within the 'collective unconscious', memories which get manifested in certain archetypes, myths, lores — registering some common anxieties and fears, dreams and hopes of the race itself.

Indeed, the story Clark finds so relevant in analysing Desdemona's plight represents a typical motif to be found in the folklores of various places including India and Japan. The crucial place of marriage in Indian folklore may be recalled in this context :

"Marriage, indeed, marks the beginning of all crises in the life of the girl. It is as if both dreams and nightmares have come alive. At the height of vulnerability and sensitivity, this is the time women remember most throughout their lives, spinning stories around it to immortalise it."[10]

* * *

The observation, though meant specifically to explain the situation *vis-à-vis* Indian context, may also apply to a broader arena. A common predicament of the bride — her lonely, terrified disillusionment after she leaves her own people behind and comes to a strange house (as is obligatory under patriarchal system) has stirred popular imagination so deeply and sometimes so painfully that the anguish has found expression in macabre folk-tales of transformation found in various parts of the globe; these tales directly relate the bride's disillusionment to the discovery of a beast in the spouse. At the centre of a number of these tales there is the newly-wed bride, or the would-be wife, waking up to a shocked perception of the hidden bestiality in the male partner. Among the tribal Folk-tales of Assam there is to be found the story of 'Chiasung and Manghan.'[11] Chiasung, a girl falls in love with Manghan, a boy from a distant village. After a brief period of courtship the lovers get married. It is only after coming to her husband's house that the wife discovers to her terror that they are a family of tigers, with their own tiger-rituals and tiger-diet including human blood. After some time she manages to run away by stealth and is received back in her parental family. The husband arrives again, in his human shape, to renew his wooing. One night, however, a huge tiger is found sleeping in the garden and is killed by the girl's father. 'The story of the Tiger-Man and His Beloved'[12] also gives the tale of a stranger proposing marriage to a beautiful girl. As the girl's parents accept him celebrations take place, but the bridegroom and his friends do not take any food. At night they are discovered by the maid of the house as eating raw meat. This act evidently proves their identity as 'tiger-men' and the girl's parents naturally refuse to give their daughter away in this marriage. But the villagers are afraid lest their cattle are eaten up by the angry tiger-man, and so force the girl to marry him. This shows the plight of the girl who is sacrificed to a mismatch and consequent torture for the sake of the community. However, a tail-piece is added, possibly in the way of wish-fulfilment, about the girl's ultimate escape from the tiger's clutch by killing him.

'Pushpamala', a widely known folk-tale of Bengal, collected and presented in printed form by Dakshinaranjan Mitra Majumdar[13], is the story of a princess, who, in order to honour her parental vow, marries low; the couple flee the country to evade the king's wrath. The princess helps her husband through a number of ordeals including a deadly encounter with dacoits. But Chandan, the husband, turns into a big goat under the magic spell of the envious wife of a gardener, and follows this woman, leaving his sleeping wife alone to fend for herself in a strange land amidst strange people.

Thus we have different versions of the same story of transformation, underscoring either a violent treatment or a collous one being meted out to the bride; these tales are marked by an unmistakable note of sadness and/or horror. Different versions of the story of a transformed bridegroom are also found in Japan. "The Serpent Suitor" is recounted by Richard M. Dorson as "one of the most popular of all Japanese tales, occurring both as fiction and as legend."[14] Hiroko Ikeda reports ninety-seven versions of the same tale collected from all over Japan besides other instances of the "Snake husband" or "The Girl as the Bear's Wife" tales from Korea, China, Formosa.[15] Also the four forms of snake-bridegroom tales classified in the *Minzokugaku Jiten* (Japanese Folklore Dictionary compiled by the Folklore Institute of Japan, Tokyo, 1951)[16] form part of the same group. "The Serpent Suitor" story (as cited by Dorson) is as follows :

"Once there lived a village headman named Shiohara in aikawamura, One-gun. He had a lovely daughter. Every night a nobleman visited the daughter, but she knew neither his name nor whence he came. She asked him his name, but he never told her about himself. At length the girl asked her nurse what to do. The nurse said : 'When he comes next time, prick a needle with a thread through his skirt, and follow him as the thread will lead you….'

The next day the girl puts a needle in the suitor's skirt. When he departed, the girl and the nurse followed him as the thread led them. They passed through steep hills and valleys and came to the foot of Mt. Uba, where there was a big rock cave. As the thread led inside, the girl timidly entered the cave. She heard a groaning voice from the interior. The nurse lighted a torch and went into the cave. She peered within and saw a great serpent, bigger than one could possibly imagine. It was groaning and writhing in agony (as)…the needle…was thrust into the serpent's throat.

The girl was frightened and ran out of the cave, while

the nurse fainted and died on the spot. The serpent also died soon."[17]

It is interesting to note how the same motif operates, though in a more complex and less explicit way, in some South Indian legends. In Kerala, for example, there is a legend about 'Mannarassala', a Nambootri family, which is supposed to have control over the serpent population. Whereas priesthood is the male's prerogative far and wide, here it is the chief woman of the family who is the priestess of the serpent gods. "Legend has it that the first priestess in the family herself gave birth to a five-headed serpent which disappeared into the interior chamber of the family house."[18] In interior villages of Kerala *tottam* song, *i.e.* spontaneous community songs freely recreating epic themes, are still sung by rustic singers. "One such interesting *tottam*," as well-known Malayali playwright, K.N. Panikkar informs us, "deals with story of a girl giving birth to an elephant ."[19] Do these anecdotes hint at the idea of some mismatch, painful union taking place between beast and human spouses, the obvious prelude to and explanation of the story of such strange birth? Again, the tradition of *Vilppattu*, *i.e.*, oral songs sung to the accompaniment of bow and pot is still in vogue in parts of South Kerala. 'Panchavan Kattu Nili', a widely known *Vilppattu*, gives the story of a priest falling in love with a *Devadasi*. The girl's mother, on finding the youth penniless, turns him out. The girl leaves home in search of her beloved husband, meets him on the way. But Nambi kills his wife while asleep, and leaves the place appropriating all her ornaments, though to die soon by snake-bite. Here also the same transformation theme is underscored; only this-time it is presented in a more realistic projection *i.e.* the wooer turned killer, the loving humane appearance giving way to the different reality, — an abysmal brutality.

It may be worthwhile to recall in this context the several bestial images in *Othello*. It is Iago alone who knows the depth of degradation to which *Othello* could be made to sink, and Iago refers to him as "ram", "horse", "devil." Othello's transformation, considered from the perspective of the pervasive myth of the 'beast-husband' above-mentioned, may lend insight into a typical post-marital phenomenon by which the latent brutality of the possessive owner could surface to cause misery to the newly-wed bride who is now forced to realise the gap between appearance and reality, between the premarriage tender wooer, and the post-marriage insensitive husband exercising his prerogative of wife-beating and wife-baiting. (Incidentally, wife-beating is an ageless practice still very much in vogue even in so-called progressive countries including China and Japan. How many wives are still killed every year in India by their husbands and in-laws? Any daily newspaper would substantiate the contention.)

In exploring the source of Keralite folk-tales, Mr. Panikkar analyses the process by which "a very private event in the life of a person can sometimes transcend its limit and create social repercussions and when it gets transferred into collective memory it assumes mythical dimensions."[20] Thus, the stories mentioned above could have their initial source in some real event of a private tragedy, resembling, say, that of Shakespeare's play. And as Panikkar shows further, "a real event loses its rationale which it has in its origin and gets generalised, taking into its fold a totally different rationale which attributes to it the colour and dimension of a myth."[21]

II

Another strain of ancient memory may not be altogether ruled out as an operative influence behind the lore of the transformed stranger — an attractive stranger turning out to be a beast or demon in the long run. Frazer, in his characteristic meticulous manner, describes the mistrust and fear with which the stranger was held by the ancient tribes when men believed in witchcraft and magic, and feared a stranger as being capable of anything. A stranger was necessarily a suspect, male or female. One never knew what a stranger had up his sleeve. Othello is introduced as "an extravagant and wheeling stranger" (I, i), just the type to be mistrusted, precisely because of his attractive exoticism. As Frazer writes :

> "...of all sources of danger none are more dreaded by the savage than magic and witchcraft, and he suspects all strangers of practising these black arts. To guard against the baneful influence exerted voluntarily or involuntarily by strangers is therefore an elementary dictate of savage prudence."[22] (194)

Travellers from a distance are potentially more dangerous than outsiders from a comparatively nearer place.

> "More dreaded...than the evil spirits of the neighbourhood are the evil spirits from a distance which accompany travellers."[23]

This original mistrust of the stranger also finds expression in two typical forms of folklore : the stranger turned husband is found out to be a beast/serpent/demon; the stranger turned wife is found out to be a witch/beast/demon. (One familiar theme in the folk-tales of Bengal is the prince's encounter with an exotic, charming woman, usually in a dense forest, who after coming to the palace as queen, proves herself a demon.)

It is also possible to consider these tales as projecting a kind of psychological insight, though in a quite nascent and crude form. It is not improbable that in those twilight days of civilization the undefined and only dimly perceived areas of consciousness could not be scientifically analysed; nevertheless, when these submerged areas of the mind surfaced on occasions, they surely sent tremors of shock and terror around. It also appears significant that some of these tales showing the suffering and death of the subhuman partner are indeed pathetic. In a large number of these tales one notes a particular sympathy on the narrator's part for the beastly partner who, after being unable to conceal his/her bestiality, yet retaining some fine humane qualities, suffer a lot and often die a sad death. The tribal folk tales of Assam and legends of Japan abound in such anecdotes.[24] To claim *Othello* as a tragedy falling in the line of these tales of transformation may seem rather far-fetched, but nevertheless this helps us to consider the play and particularly the issue of 'two Othellos' in a new light, especially in view of Jung's analysis of the "collective unconscious." Jung defines the contents of the "collective unconscious" as "the inherited brain-structure. These are the mythological association — those motives and images which can spring anew in every age and clime, without historical tradition or migration."[25] Jung's term for mythological associations is "archetypes of the collective unconscious" or universal patterns of behaviour expressed in mythical forms : "a universal homogeneous substratum whose homogeneity extends into a worldwide identity or similarity of myths and fairy tales; so that a negro of Southern States of America dreams in the motives of Grecian mythology, and a Swiss grocer's apprentice repeats in this psychosis, the vision of an Egyptian Gnostic."[26]

III

One of the typical explanations of Othello's transformation is his jealousy. It is also generally agreed but for a few abnormally determined critics that this jealousy is unfounded. The question then naturally arises : why is Othello so ready, almost eager to suspect and mistrust Desdemona? Iago gleefully serves as the instrument of severance between wife and husband, like the typical Elizabethan villain who gloats over his skill in separating lovers, brothers, friends. But why does he attain such easy success in carrying out his aim of destroying this marriage? Ebun Clark justifies the change as "a tragedy of cultural conflict and cultural isolation." It is true that the couple's mutual ignorance of their respective cultural demands, along with their complete isolation from the respective families may have served as the base of the tragic plot. At the same time, however it is also to be admitted that isolation but helps to bring out into the open what has been lying dormant there all the time. Here again it is possible to relate the case to the "collective unconscious" in which mistrust of women is only too deeply embedded. In the myths and legends of the West handed down through generations the accepted twin images of women have been those of beauty manifest and evil incarnate.

In *The Iliad*, the West's epic of growth — which, unlike an epic of art, is supposed to draw largely on the folk-tradition — Helen emerges as an epitome of this combined image of beauty and evil, an image simultaneously fascinating and repulsive to the possessive male ego. Helen means temptation, sex-allurement; she attracts because she is evil. Reactions to Helen — of her husband, of Paris, of Greece, of Troy, show the inherent ambiguity of the male approach. The beautiful woman infatuates, and because she infatuates she is suspected to be a potential betrayer, who should be loathed accordingly. Hilda Dolittle in her verse-narration *Helen in Egypt*[27] challenges the traditional image of Helen, as she has been made out in the margin of men's texts, by creating her afresh. But even Hilda's Helen, who is the replica of the twentieth century self-conscious woman, has to struggle through the accumulated misconception and slander of centuries in order to find her true identity, and there are moments when she almost totters under the burden of this old image. Thus as Hilda's Helen wonders alone in Egypt she is overwhelmed by the hatred heaved on her head — "Helen hated of all Greece", and she is filled with guilt :

> "How could I hide my eyes!
> How could I veil my face!" (16)

This is the patriarchal mythology about woman's despicable nature; the central image of woman here is that of the representative of the flesh who tempts man to evil and wrongdoing through her sexuality. The same myth thus operates at the heart of both pagan and Christian 'wisdom.' Adam an otherwise obedient boy of God, is only allured by the temptress Eve, to perform the act of 'man's first disobedience' and consequently cause all the suffering of mankind. The Hindu ethos is also obsessed by a similar idea, which brands the woman as the 'doorway to Hell'; the same suspicion of beautiful woman forms the basis of the 'Arabian Nights' series. In view of this age-old belief in the possible notoriety of a beautiful woman it appears only natural for the 'lusty Moor' and the base Iago to level charges of sexual betrayal against their wives, and so unquestioningly take the women's treachery for granted.

Adultery, suspected or real, is a common theme in Elizabethan and Jacobean drama. The treatment of the theme usually underscores the male partner's (and also often the writer's) ready belief in the female's vulnerability. It is an accepted notion that Othello's tragic folly is his jealousy. But jealousy is rooted in possessiveness which finds expression in one's mistrust of one's partner. That's why Othello's jealousy is so quickly roused by Iago. The possessive husband had all along been lurking behind the caring lover. Iago only causes it to take frontstage.

Spivack voices a common notion whens he contends that Iago is the residue of the Vice, evil incarnate, who appeared in the Morality plays.[28] But is it not a way of externalizing the evil that but lives within one? And isn't it equally true that Iago is also a projection of something within Othello, something firmly rooted within his psyche — the savagely possessive male ego, whose basis is mistrust of and contempt for 'the other', the woman! (in a way, *The Iliad* and *The Ramayana* are but slightly varied presentations of the same story of male possessiveness, and of injured male ego engaged in frenzied operation!)

The patriarchal society has its set norms regarding the woman. Thus Desdemona who is praised as "maiden never bold/Of spirit so still and quiet that her Motion/Blushed at herself" is perceived overnight as a treacherous creature, once she defies authority. Hence the father's warning to the husband — the other contender for authority over the girl :

"Look to her, Moor, have a quick eye to see,
She has deceived her father and may thee",

Iago later takes up the same cue :

"She did deceive her father, marrying you;
And when seemed to shake and fear your looks
She loved them most."

And when the woman is equated with deceit the idea seems to sell easily to the male ego. After the couple's reunion in Cyprus, Othello, in his extreme happiness, says :

"My soul hath her content so absolute,
That not another comfort like to this succeeds...."

Ironically the same man attributes to his wife before long "a will most rank", and degenerates to the level of imploring Iago;

"Set on thy wife to observe."

Readily he jumps to the conclusion about "her stolen hours of lust" and to the vulgar denouncement :

"I had been happy, if the general camp Pioneers and all, had tasted her sweet body, ...etc." This reminds the Indian reader of a sequence in *The Ramayana* where Rama, after defeating Ravana, denounces Sita in a most vulgar language in the presence of "the general camp", asking her to choose any of his monkey soldiers as mate. This is the voice of jealousy stirred by an injured ego and finding an ugly expression in foul words, Othello too insults and degrades Desdemona, for no fault of her own, in presence of Lodovico, and as she silently weeps he jeers : "Each drop she falls would prove a crocodile...." It is significant that Othello is open to Iago's insinuations but not to Emilia's insistent assertion that Desdemona is innocent. His only reaction is — "this is a subtle whore." When finally Iago suggests strangulation instead of poisoning Othello agrees because,

"The justice of it pleases."

Even after killing her, when others grieve, Othello

insists : "O, she was foul!" It takes another death, the death of Emilia, another wronged woman, killed by her husband, to convince him of the value of his "pearl." Thus when Emilia says to the dazed, grief-stricken Desdemona, "I would you had never seen him", and exclaims "these men, these men!" she is but voicing a poignant cry of agony and disappointment which has remained central to "Her Story." Without much ado Othello replaces one image of Desdemona by the other, the loved idol smoothly making way for the despicable "whore", and simultaneously he himself slips from the status of the valiant fighter to that of a debased murderer. The cause of this smooth transition appears to have been entrenched in the male psyche itself since the seeds of the mistrust have been there within him all the time, nourished by religious myths and secular lores alike.

Othello may thus be seen as the legendary bridegroom with his mad possessiveness which so quickly fans murderous jealousy, and Desdemona, the legendary bride, the maltreated, misunderstood, long-suffering wife. Iago and Emilia, in this sense, may serve as but cruder parallels to the glamorous couple, — Iago paralleling the suspicious, jealous husband, Emilia the wronged, murdered wife.

It is only after the two women are killed that Othello slowly comes back to his sense, and then, only then, he realises the value of the 'pearl' he has thrown away. It is only in death that his male consciousness can come to terms with Desdemona's uniqueness. And even before she dies, one has the apprehension that Othello can be at peace only when she is dead, and not so long as she is alive :

"Be thus when thou art dead, and
I will kill thee
And love thee after."

Janet Wolft, in an interesting review-article 'Death and the Maiden : Does Semiotics Justify Murder?' raises the issue of death-obsession and particularly the preoccupation with dead women that has been so common in narrative.[29] Elizabeth Bronfen in *Over Her Dead Body : Death, Femininity and the Aesthetic* analyses the way death and femininity have been made to intersect in various literary texts and contends that a certain necessary connection prevails between Woman and Death, both in representation and in 'psychic economy.' She examines certain typical textual themes and tropes — dead brides, hysterical women, speaking corpses, the dead beloved as muse. Through this examination she demonstrates the psychic mechanisms by which a patriarchal culture defines alterity and sustains the illusion of identity. Even without totally accepting Bronfen's claim it may be acknowledged that, seen in this light, Othello's murderous frenzy acquires a further significance. Like "Porphyria's Lover" he may also be seen as representing the male psychic obsession with femininity as a possible threat to stability whose "eradication produces a recuperation of order, a return to stability."[30] Even our great Rama in *The Ramayana* is more at ease with the golden statue of Sita by his throne, than the real living Sita accusing him face to face. A major bulk of Rajasthani and Punjabi folk-tales[31] end with the scene of funeral pyre and double corpses.

V

Lawrence Danson in his essay 'Twentieth-Century Shakespeare Criticism; the Comedies' underscores the importance of "anthropology, which invests myth and folk-tale with significance (and) has been a great stimulus to interest in comedy."[32] Also C.L. Barbar, among Shakespeare scholars, is known to have exercised remarkable anthropological insights in *Shakespeare's Festive Comedy* (1957). Although Barbar's focus is on Shakespeare's comedies, what he suggests, applies to the tragedies as well, that anthropological as well as historical and psychoanalytic insights can help to exfoliate the intricate inter-dependencies of literature and society."[33]

Again, in his essay on the Roman plays of Shakespeare G.K. Hunter observes : "It is a notable mark of Shakespeare's ability to turn round and around the value systems he works with."[34] Roman integrity, the central claim to virtue in both Brutus and Titus, is shown as "much less a virtue than a limitation." Similarly in *Othello* Shakespeare seems to subject to scrutiny some of the common complacent assumptions of a patriarchal culture and its value system which could cause disaster in human relationship. Although there are critics who claim to have found affirmation in *Othello* of age-old assumptions regarding the woman's role, the tragedy of Othello in its ultimate effect, appears rather to challenge than to reinforce the male or phallocentric *status quo*. Shakespeare used the original 'brutal' story of Cinthio with very little change in *Othello*; it is a sordid story dealing with the degradation of love between man and woman, "a subject on which", according to Granville-Barker "about this time he was finding varied material, both for tragedy and for such so-called comedies as *Troilus and Cressida* and *Measure for Measure*."[35] Shakespeare gives us a world which is basically one of man-woman interdependence.[36] Shakespeare finds the interdependence essential yet fraught with tragic potentials. In *Othello* he seems to be probing into the cause; why and how does the mutual expectation and trust, the very basis of conjugal relationship, get shattered and on what rocks? Is it due to the 'evil' within one or is it due to the 'evil' ideas — taboos, inhibition, obsessions imbibed by and retained within the collective memory? At least *Othello* invites us to look within ourselves, to examine our own bias and ego in relation to the collective memory, and thus attain a better self-knowledge leading to more sympathy and understanding for the 'other.'

A Shakespeare reader, on the brink of the twenty-first century, will surely, bring his/her own preoccupation to the sixteenth-century writer, and test his relevance by that standard. Amazingly, or perhaps not amazingly at all, the old man still does not fail the test.

REFERENCES

1. Laurence Lerner, "The Machiavel and the Moor", *Essays in Criticism*, IX, 4, Oct. 1959. (The change, Lerner argues, "can never be blamed on another, human or diabolic, without abandoning all belief that people are responsible for their actions"; and Othello changed because he was basically "a Negro, a barbarian, and a Pagan.") The notion of 'two Othellos' — the savage and the civilized, may also be traced back to August Wilhelm Schlegel's *Lectures on Dramatic Art and Literature* (trans., John Black, London, 1815) where Schlegel remarks :

   We recognize in Othello the wild nature of that glowing zone which generates the most raging beasts of prey and the most deadly poisons, tamed only in appearance by the desire of fame, by foreign laws of honor, and by noble and milder manners. His jealousy is not the jealousy of the heart, which is incompatible with the tenderest feeling and adoration of the beloved object; it is of the sensual kind from which, in burning climes, has sprung the disgraceful ill-treatment of women and many other unnatural usages. A drop of this poison flows in his veins, and sets his whole blood in the most disorderly fermentation : The Moor seems noble, frank, confiding, grateful for the love shown him; and he is...a hero...a worthy leader...; but the mere physical force of passion puts to flight in one moment all his acquired and accustomed virtues, and gives the upper hand to the savage in him over the moral man....

2. Helen Gardner, "The Nobel Moor", *Proceedings of the British 1955*, pp. 189-205.

3. Alistair Cooke, "Shakespeare in America" in *Shakespeare : Pattern of Excelling Nature*, ed. David Bevington and J.L. Halio (London, 1978), pp. 17-28.

4. Helen Gardner, "Milton's 'Satan' and Theme of Damnation in Elizabethan Tragedy", *Essays and Studies*, 1, 1948, pp. 46-66.

5. Ebun Clark, "Othello the Complete Gentleman! An African Folkloric Interpretation", *Journal of Commonwealth Literature*, XXV, 1, 1990.

6. Harriett Hawkins, *The Devil's Party : Critical Counter-interpretations of Shakespearian Drama* (London . Oxford Univ. Press, 1985), p. 3.

7. Don Lewis, *Curious and Humorous Customs* (London : Mowbroys, 1972), p. 11.

8. *Ibid.*, p. 43. Also Achebe's *Things fall Apart* bears evidence to the African marriage-custom, including bride-price and the husband's authority over the wife.

9. "I begin to fear that my example will teach young women never to marry against their parent's consent"..., Cinthio's *Hecatommithi* (1565), Translated by W. Parr in *Shakespeare's Library*, ed. W.C. Hazlitt, (London : 1875), quoted by B. Spivack (N.Y. Columbia Univ. Press, 1958), p. 240. The "fear", of course, may also be interpreted as apprehension rather than repentance.
10. Swati Bhattacharjee, "Folk-tales : A Distorted Prism", *The Telegraph*, Calcutta, 17 March, 1994.

    Also the short chapter "The Sex War" in Rosalind Miles's *Female Form Women Writers and the Conquest of the Novel* (1987) gives an excellent treatment of this; she refers to a shocking description of a prenuptial ritual in Ahdaf Soueif's *Aisha* (1983) which shows the kind of torture and humiliation that a 15-year old bride Zeina has to undergo as part of the marriage custom.
11. S.N. Barkataki, *Tribal Folk-tales of Assam* (Gauhati : Publication Board, Assam, 1970), story no. 53.
12. *Ibid.*, story no. 59.
13. Dakshina Ranjan Mitra Majumdar, *Thakurdada's Jhuli* (Grandpa's Bag) (Calcutta : 1907; reprinted Calcutta : Mitra & Ghosh, 1997), pp. 105-50.
14. Richard M. Dorson, *Folk Legends of Japan* (Tokyo : Charies E. Tuttle Company, 1962), p. 117.
15. Miroko Ikeda, *A Type and Motif Index of Japanese Folk-literature,* Doctoral Dissertation, Indian University, 1955, pp. 25-26.
16. Quoted by R.M. Dorson, *op. cit.*, p. 117.
17. *Ibid.*, pp. 117-18.
18. K.N. Panikkar, *Folklore of Kerala* (New Delhi : National Book Trust, 1991), p. 54.
19. *Ibid.*, p. 105.
20. *Ibid.*, pp. 24-25.
21. *Ibid.*, p. 25.
22. James Frazer, *The Golden Bough* (Hertfordshire : Wordsworth Editions Ltd., 1993), p. 194.
23. *Ibid*, p. 195.
24. The tales of 'The Story of Nara' (No. 45), 'The Girl who Turned into a Tiger' (No. 52) 'The Story of a Man called Vaingam — (No. 65) S.N. Barkataki, *op. cit.*, tales of 'The Blind Serpent-Wife', Two daughters who became Serpents' 'Hachiro's Transformation' cited by R.M. Dorson, *op. cit.*

25. C.G. Jung, *Psychological Types* (trans. from the German by H. Gordwon Baynes (London : 1946), p. 616.

26. *Ibid.*, p. 624.

27. Hilda Dolittle, *Helen in Egypt* (N.Y. : Grove Press, 1961).

28. *Op. cit.*, p. 194.

29. *Critical Quarterly*. V. 35, No. 2, Summer 1993.

30. E. Bronfen, *Over Her Dead Body* (Manchester : Manchester Univ. Press, 1992), p. xii.

31. The Punjabi folk-tales of "Hir Ranjha", "Sassi Punnu", 'Purna Bhagat', H.V. Singh, *Punjaber Upakatha*. New Delhi : N.B.T., 1990. The tales of 'Seni-Vijanasid,' 'Naghi-Nagwanti', Binjha-Sorath', H. Maheswari, *Rajasthani Literature*. New Delhi : Sahitya Akademi, 1985.

32. In *The Cambridge Companion to Shakespeare Studies*, ed. Stanley Wells (N.Y. : Cambridge Univ. Press, 1986), p. 234.

33. *Ibid.*

34. 'Shakespeare and the Traditions of Tragedy', *Ibid.*, p. 135.

35. H. Granville-Barker, *Prefaces to Shakespeare* (London : B.T. Batsford Ltd., 1963, ed.), p. 135.

36. "If...Shakespeare offers us no model of a heroine who is a complete success in coping with the world independently of man, it is difficult to think of a Shakespearean hero who is known to be a complete success in coping with the world independently of women...." H. Hawkins, *op. cit.*, p. 147.

12

Hamlet : The Only Son and the Lonely Prince

—Sahadeo A. Chougule

"Read on this book, That show of such on exercise may colour your loneliness."

(Polonius to Ophelia III, i)

IN THE medieval times the institution of family dominated man's social behaviour. The members of a family were bound to one another by several ties of social customs and economic systems. Economic co-operation between members of the same family was a matter of security, with each one bringing the share of income to run the family. Husband and wife collaborated with each other and the women generally depended upon the men. But this situation underwent a conspicuous change with the advent of the philosophy of individualism in the Renaissance. The spread and growth of the intellectual atmosphere in this period, in addition, taught and trained people to obey their individual voices. This new climate was greatly responsible for the beginning of disruption of family harmony and by and by it caused among its members a growing sense of being estranged from it. The shift of attitude from the divine to the secular also ushered in a great change in man's mode of sensing and perceiving the world of his habitation. His mind was filled with doubt, for the old he could not completely give up and the new he could not live up to. Against the background of the vast world discovered and yet discoverable the individual man of the time began to feel neglected and belittled. The gulf between man and man increased and eventually resulted in his alienated condition. In their "Introduction" to *Man Alone* Eric and Mary Josephson have the following to say about man's alienation in the Age of Renaissance :

> It is historical emergence of the individual as we know of him, of man alone, that makes alienation so crucially a modern problem. In the past, ...men felt anxiety or despair particularly when they lost the status that identified them and offered them some security. But when the medieval system collapsed, the likelihood of alienation increased appreciably. Indeed; only with the release of the individual from medieval bonds could alienation become a widespread social problem. In his *Literature and the Image of Man*, Leo Lowenthal has summed up this historical process : 'The breakdown of the feudal order forced man to fall back upon himself; he had to learn how to cope with countless problems and decisions that were once taken care of by worldly and spiritual hierarchies. But together with the anxieties generated by this new autonomy he sensed a great promise, for in the period of formation of the national state and the development of a mercantile economy his own future seemed to have infinite possibilities. At the end of the curve, in our century, he begins to feel threatened by the encroachment of powerful social forces emanating not only from his own corner of the earth but from every part of a contracting world.'[1]

Hamlet (1600-1601) was written on the threshold of the seventeenth century which opened new facades to the world. In this play Shakespeare has done his best by presenting the hero who represents some of the traits of his time and yet transcends them. Hamlet makes us aware of several things that we have failed to realize. He has thus become the yardstick by which various generations have measured themselves out and attempted to grasp the unfathomable and the mysterious in life. Hence our interest in this scholar, courtier and soldier has always been on the crescendo. *Hamlet* the play and its hero have always been looked upon from different stand-points, which, in turn, have resulted in the enrichment and growth of his personality. We have a variety of critical opinions : logical and theological, analytic and psychoanalytic interpretations of the play are in abundance. Critics and scholars have been alert and adept in explicating Hamlet's delay and dilemma, his failure about his poetic imagination which is inventive to an unusual degree, about his madness, real or feigned or both, and so on. Even the characters in the play have proved good critics on Hamlet : Polonius, Claudius and Gertrude have propounded forth their own theories about his puzzled and puzzling behaviour. The more we know about him the more we know that the less we know. The inadequacy of our knowledge of him instigates us to investigate him thoroughly. But he seems to abide by Polonius' moto : "Take each man's censure and reserve thy judgement" (I, iii, 69).[2]

This paper, in its moderate aim, essays to discuss Hamlet as the only son and the lonely prince simply because it is the son and the prince that have posed before him certain personal and political problems and imposed on him certain obligations which he wants to discharge. There are, among others, two immediate and urgent problems before him : the filial, the revenge for the assassination of his father; the political, the usurpation of the throne by Claudius and his consequent deprivation from it. He struggles, all by himself, to find proper solution to them. His is a single man's battle against the evil forces of which Claudius is the author and representative. He attempts with all his might to get at the roots of reality, both emotionally and intellectually. Consequently he becomes a split personality whose mind is torn and tortured, and consciousness divided. He becomes aware of large vacuum in his life which not only leaves him lonely to count himself as the "king of infinite space" (II, i, 248) but also devours and destroys him altogether. He feels an acute sense of being alienated from Society, Family and his own Self and thus becomes a prototype of the lonely modern man. As the domestic and dynastic facts that have taken place in the Castle at Elsinore are greatly responsible for his loneliness, we will discuss first his loneliness caused by his alienation from his family.

I

Paternal as well as maternal relationship is central to *Hamlet*. Its hero Hamlet is the only son of the late king Hamlet and Gertrude, loved by both. The fact that he has no brother or sister is of paramount significance in this tragedy where the Ghost of his father will perforce speak to him alone to reveal the secret Claudius has hitherto kept hidden from the public eye or ear : "This spirit, dumb to us, will speak to him" (I, i, 71). His father's Ghost is Hamlet's sole support and source of initial information by means of which he is going to take steps to restore justice and to set things right in the rotten state of Denmark. At the opening of the play the Hamlet family is already disintegrated in that Hamlet's father has been assassinated by Claudius and that his mother has remarried within the prohibited degrees of kinship. One of the parents already dead and the other being no more the member of his family, Hamlet comes to look upon himself as a lonely creature in a world where lust of flesh and power, pretence and preferment are rampant, where means and not ends, policy and not philosophy counts. In this world "man" to him is nothing but "a strange piece of work", separate, lifeless, movable and even disposable when unwanted.

Hamlet had been "at school in Wittenberg", had already suffered the pangs of loneliness caused by his severance from his family at Elsinore in Denmark. Now his feeling of loneliness is aggravated by the fact of his father's death, the feeling which is embodied in his sad and desperate utterance:

"That I the son of a dear father murdered" (II, i, 546). The Ghost reveals to him the pre-play acts and tacts — murder and adultery — and imposes on him a heavy task of revenge from which Hamlet would rather shirk initially. Now to believe or not to believe in the Ghost is the question : he thinks, he wavers and the Ghost comes again to whet his "almost blunted purpose" (III, iv, 110). Hamlet here is confronted with a predicament similar to that of Macbeth on seeing and hearing the witches' prophecy : "This supernatural soliciting / Cannot be ill; cannot be good"[3] (I, ii, 130-131). The Ghost's revelation upsets Hamlet's mental make-up and consequently he comes to feel that all the filial bonds are turned topsy-turvy, the conjugal relations broken up and renewed in an uncanny manner and that love and its roots are smothered and strangled. The murder of his father by Claudius (whose name echoes 'claw' and 'odious') not only shocks him but also leaves him soul-shaken and conscience-stricken. He learns from the Ghost of his mother's adultery, comes to distrust womankind : "Frailty thy name is woman" (I, ii, 146). He blames his own flesh and blood, which, he feels, is stained. Hamlet has now to live in a world which is "mad in pursuit and in possession so," and where "The expenses of spirit in a waste of shame / Is lust in action."[4] His first soliloquy of "sullied flesh" has for its main theme the incest of his mother whom he curses, condemns and calls several bad names. He wishes that his "sullied flesh" should "thaw and resolve itself into a dew", ponders on suicide and thinks that God should not have "fixed / His canon against self-slaughter." His mother's "over-hasty marriage", her disloyalty to her late husband and her choice of Claudius as her husband create in him a sense of estrangement from his family. The following lines record his utmost boredom, desperation, weariness and loneliness :

> "How weary, stale, flat and unprofitable
> Seem to me all the uses of this world!
> Fie on't! ah fie! 't is an unweeded garden
> That grows to seed — things rank and gross in nature

Possess it merely...
...why, she would hang on him
As if increase of appetite had grown
By what it fed on. And yet within a month...
Let me not think on't...
Frailty, thy name is woman
A little month or ere those shoes were old
With which she followed my poor father's body,
Like Niobe, all tears, why she even she
(O God! A beast that wants discourse of reason
Would have mourned longer) married with my uncle,
My father's brother, but no more like my father
Than I to Hercules — within a month,
Ere yet the salt of most unrighteous tears
Had left the flushing in her galled eyes,
She married. O most wicked speed, to post
With such dexterity to incestuous sheets!
It is not nor it cannot come to good...
But break my heart, for I must hold my tongue" (I, ii, 129-159).

His mother's second marriage with Claudius sets Hamlet in a perplexed mood as it has posed before him the problem of relationship itself. Now his uncle has become his 'uncle-father' and his mother the 'aunt-mother.' Here the family relationship itself is out of joint. He becomes ill at ease at the Castle as he feels that the pull between the individual as a constituent of family and 'home' is lost; consequently the sense of human responsibility for others is found nowhere, the high ethical code is observed by none. It is our feeling of being drawn to the home that makes us restful there; Hamlet, instead, feels withdrawn from it as it is reduced to a prison-ward in Denmark as prison. Even Claudius' speeches throw light on Hamlet's alienation from his family. He addresses Hamlet as "my cousin Hamlet and my son" (I, ii, 64) and Hamlet's typical response follows thus : "a little more than kin and less than kind." After assuming the reins of the state, Claudius behaves like a shrewd politician and a wary ruler and makes the following speech which points out the broken familial bonds :

> Therefore our sometime sister, now our queen,
> Th' imperial jointress to this war like state,
> Have we, as it were with a defeated joy,
> With mirth in funeral, and with dirge in marriage,
> In equal scale weighing delight and dale,
> Taken to wife....

The very syntax of this jerky sentence indicates that even Claudius was not much happy when he took Gertrude to his wife. The separation of 'we' in this quotation from its predicate 'taken to wife' is a grammatical parallel of the prospective separation between Claudius and Gertrude.

Hamlet's alienation from his family can also be discussed against the background of Polonius' 'losing' his daughter to him and of using her beauty as a bait to trap him. Hamlet's love for her, so far, has been honest and sincere, but now he is disillusioned about her as well, as she turns out to be another instance of woman's frailty. He speaks very cynically to Polonius : "Conception is a blessing, but / Not as your daughter may conceive" (II, ii, 184-185). The Nunnery speech is a remarkable example of Hamlet's estrangement from his prospective family life. He rails against Ophelia thus :

> "It thou dost marry, I'll give thee this plague for thy dowry. Be thou as chaste as ice, as pure as snow, thou shall not escape calumny. Get thee to a nunnery, go! Farewell! Or if thou will needs marry, marry a fool; for wise men know well enough what monsters you make of them. To a nunnery go, and quickly too! Farewell" (III, i, 132-137).

The love between them has failed to grow into a conjugal relationship of which both may have dreamt. Ophelia's natural reaction to Hamlet's reproaches against her is that the heavenly powers should restore him, restore the noble mind thus overthrown. Then Hamlet comments very bitterly and cynically on the institution of marriage itself and reflects his disinterest about it in the following speech :

> "I have heard of your paintings too, well enough.... You jig, you amble, and you lisp, and nickname God's creatures, and make your wantonncss your ignorance.... I say we will have no marriages. Those that are married already, all but one, shall live, the rest shall keep as they are. To a nunnery go" (III, i, 139-145).

Hamlet's off-stage cry "Mother, mother, mother" (III, iv, 6) is a cry of a lonely son deprived of his parents : "How stand I then, / That have a father killed, a mother stained" (IV, v, 56-57). The broken family ties are given an apt expression in the following dialogue where Hamlet and his mother pull in different directions, accuse each other and reflect how they have lost the common ground for communication between them. What comes out of these accusations in but nothing :

> "Hamlet : Now mother, what's the matter?
> Queen : Hamlet, thou hast thy father much offended.
> Hamlet : Mother, you have my father much offended.
> Queen : Come, come, you answer with an idle tongue.
> Hamlet : Go, go, you question with a wicked tongue.
> Queen : Why, how, now Hamlet!
> Hamlet : What is the matter now?
> Queen : Have you forgot me?
> Hamlet : No by the rood, not so.
> You are the Queen, your husband's brother's wife.
> And would it were not so! You are my mother"
> (III, iv, 8-16)

After Ophelia's death by drowning, Hamlet's mother also voices his alienation from his prospective bride in these lines : "I hop'd thou shouldst have been my Hamlet's wife. / I thought thy bride-bed to have decked, sweet maid / And not have strewed thy grave" (V, i, 219-221).

II

Hamlet's alienation from his family is a prelude to his self-alienation. His father's murder and his mother's mortal sin leave his personality shaken to its roots. His discovery and knowledge of the horrible secrets in the Castle harasses and embarrasses him, consequently he is unable to grasp the events and happenings there : "there is something in this more than natural, if philosophy could find it out" (II, ii, 342-343). His philosophical and intellectual stand and his emotional involvement in the affairs at the Castle have made him a remarkable combination of an unusual degree of sensitivity, intellect and intuition. A young man of reflective bent of mind, he looks within to look without. He is an alienated character whose centre of feeling and thinking is unable to hold all the stuff that he is made of. He fails to communicate his thoughts and feelings plainly and properly as a result of which he becomes a sphinx, a person with a divided self.

We notice in Hamlet a sharp conflict between impulse and intellect, between flesh and spirit. The impulse that becomes a young man like him hastens him to take revenge for the murder of his father; at the same time as an intellectual doubter he announces : "I'll have grounds / more relative than this" (II, ii, 566-569). Being an idealist-intellectual, his way of feeling and thinking clashes with that of the world. He stumbles in the world which has given itself to material and practical pursuits, and yet he prefers to go his way alone.

Hamlet does not experience himself as the centre of his own world. He feels cut off from the basic facts of his existence, the facts that he struggles throughout to know. His self-alienation is enhanced by his typical temperament of breaking through the routine of sleeping, eating, drinking and dreaming in order to get to the fundamental realities of existence. The characters in the play express their reactions to Hamlet's behaviour in various ways. Claudius, Hamlet's antagonist, for instance, cannot even dream of the fact that has kept Hamlet "so much from the understanding of himself"

(II, ii, 9) and speaks of "Hamlet's transformation" "Since nor the exterior nor the inward man / Resembles that it was" (II, ii, 6-7). Claudius wants Rosencrantz and Guildenstern to know why Hamlet has put on "this confusion / Granting so harshly all his days of quiet / With turbulent and dangerous lunacy" (III, i, 3-4). Gertrude also speaks of her "too much changed son" (II, ii, 36). Polonius asserts that "though this be madness, yet there is method in it" (II, ii, 202). Guildenstern tells Claudius and Gertrude of Hamlet's destraction and "crafty madness" (III, i, 8). As Opehlia informs her father, Hamlet "raised a sigh so piteous and profound / As it did seem to shatter all his bulk / And end his being" (II, i, 94-96). These foregoing remarks by various characters amply point out that Hamlet is alienated from himself. His own utterances, too, throw a flood of light on his self-alienation. He feels that his father's Ghost has visited him "making nights hideous, and we fools of nature / So horridly to shake our disposition / With thoughts beyond the reaches of our souls" (I, iv, 54-56). After learning from the Ghost that Claudius is the murderer of King Hamlet, he decides to "put an antic disposition on" (I, v, 72), *i.e.*, to assume a clownish pose, indeed a device to "find direction out" by "indirections." He ejaculates that "Denmark is a prison" (II, ii, 238) where his "wit's diseased" (III, ii, 294). He tells Horatio that in his heart "there was a kind of fighting, / That would not let me sleep" (V, ii, 4-5). He desires that Horatio should try to know how he is punished with "sore distraction" (V, ii, 205).

Hamlet does not experience himself as the centre of his own world, as the creator of his own acts. His reactions to Polonius' death illustrate this point well. He says :

> "I do repent, but heaven hath pleased it so,
> To punish me with this and this with me,
> That I must be their scourge and minister
> I must be cruel only to be kind" (III, iv, 172-177).

He wants us to know that the murder of Polonius by him was a pre-ordained act : "There is a divinity that shapes our ends" (V, ii, 10), hence he is partially responsible for it. Later on, he comes to rely on and resigns to God in this calm assertion of trust in Him :

"Not a whit, we defy augury. There's a special providence in the fall of a sparrow. If it be now, 't's not to come. If it be not to come, it will come now. If it be not now, yet it will come. The readiness is all" (V, ii, 195-199). Hamlet, a neurotic and neurasthenic character, reflects the traits of self-anesthesia, self-elimination and self-idealization. The world, to him, is an unweeded garden and yet he prefers to stay in it. He looks upon Denmark as a prison and yet lives there. He puts on 'an antic disposition' to avoid the consciousness of his own self. The loss of his previous self is expressed in Ophelia's observation and account of him in the following lines :

> "O what a noble mind is here o'erthrown!
> The courtier's, soldier's, scholar's, eye, tongue, sword,
> The glass of fashion and the mould of form.
> The observed of all observers, quite, quite down!
> Now see that noble and most sovereign reason
> Like sweet bells jangled, out of tune and harsh."
>
> (III, I, 146-154)

His self-elimination expressed in his self-reproaches and self-abnegation in the following ironical lines of his soliloquy are indicative of his self-alienation :

> "Now I am alone.
> O what a rogue and peasant slave am I!
> ... ...
> Yet I,
> A dull and muddy-mettl'd rascal, peak
> Like John-a-dreams, unpregnant of my cause,
> And can say nothing, no, no for a king
> Upon whose property and most dear life
> A damn'd defeat was made. Am I a coward"
>
> (II, ii, 509-565)

In the same tone and tempo he chides Ophelia and even himself thus :

> "Get thee to a munnery. Why wouldst thou be a breeder of sinners? I am myself indifferent honest, but yet I could accuse me of such things that it were better my mother had not born me.... What should such fellows as I do crawling between heaven and earth? We are arrant knaves all, believe none of us..." (III, i, 121-129).

Hamlet's self-alienation also results in his indulgence in the ideal self. At the close of Act I we notice his idealization of his own self in this assertion : "The time is out of joint. O cursed spite / That ever I was born to set it right" (I, v, 189-190). 'After killing Polonius, he comes to look upon himself as God's scourge and minister.' At one time in the play he tells Claudius, "I see a cherub that sees them" (IV, iv, 46). At the end of the play he asks Horatio to narrate the story of his life and work properly "to the unsatisfied" (V, ii, 316), and leaves the last stamp of his noble and ideal characer in this declaration : "I do prophesy the election lights on Fortinbrass. He has my dying voice" (V, ii, 331-332).

III

Hamlet's alienation from his Family and Self results in his social isolation. He has lost his faith in his kith and kin, his beloved and his school fellows. Nobody or nothing delights him. He comes to feel that both life and death are meaningless, and hence "to be or no to be" is the question before him. He feels helpless and powerless in a world of corruption, dishonesty and deception as he cannot exercise any control over it, let alone alter it. He regards himself as a wanderer with no place of rest or resort and consequently feels an acute sense of lack or loss of companionship : he is utterly lonely. As far as the grouping of the characters in the play is concerned, he forms a very negligible minority with Horatio, his only confidant and declares to Laertes that he is of the "faction that is wronged" (V, ii, 213). He feels that he is spied on almost by everybody and everywhere : "I am most dreadfully attended" (II, ii, 259). He finds it difficult to have contact and communication with the people whose conduct and conversations pull in different directions, are in contrast to each other. It is his experience that man's facial expression and the response of his heart go contrary to each other : "One may smile and smile and be a villain" (I, v, 108). He knows that "to be honest as this world goes is to be one man / Picked out of ten thousand" (II, ii, 178-179). Here in the world of Denmark people are not what they seem and seem what they are not. Consequently, he does not feel at home in this strange world and "as a stranger give(s) it a welcome" (I, i, 165).

Hamlet, who has written letters to Horatio and Claudius from his voyage to England, is a man completely estranged from the society of Denmark. Having known the evil intentions of Claudius, he changes the contents of the letter by Claudius and brings about the deaths of Rosencrantz and Guildenstern, and himself returns to Denmark. His letter to Claudius with the word 'alone' in the postscript throws ample light on his social isolation.

Hamlet is the heir apparent to the throne of Denmark but he is kept away from it. He says, "I lack advancement" (III, ii, 311). He wanted to be the king of Denmark but Claudius had "popped in between the election and my hopes" (V, ii, 65). Obviously, he feels politically alienated. Murray Levin's concept of political alienation in the following pithy passage helps us a lot to understand Hamlet's political alienation :

> "Political alienation is the feeling of an individual that he is not a part of the political process. The politically alienated believe that their vote makes no difference. This belief arises from the feeling that political decisions are made by a group of political insiders who are not responsive to the average

> citizens — the political outsiders. Political alienation may be expressed in feelings of political powerlessness, meaninglessness, estrangement from political activity, and normlessness."[5]

Though Hamlet is rightfully one of the 'political insiders' he is actually one of the 'political outsiders.' He has no voice, no influence in determining the political events in Denmark; eventually his political alienation enhances his social isolation. He lives, throughout the play, as the only son and the lonely prince. His total alienation — from the social and the cosmic pattern — can be seen as fully expressed in the following speech by him :

> "I have of late, but wherefore I know not, lost all my mirth, foregone all custom of exercises, and indeed it goes so heavily with my disposition that this goodly frame the earth seems to me a sterile promontory, this most excellent canopy the air, look you, this brave o'erhanging firmament, this majestical roof fretted with golden fire,-why, it appears no other thing to me than a foul and pestilent congregation of vapours.... Man delights not me...no, nor woman neither" (II, ii, 284-296).

The modern problem of loneliness caused by man's alienation from God, Nature, Society, Family and Self is a steady growth from the beginning of the Renaissance to our own times. Hamlet in this respect is our prototype. Harry Levin has aptly pointed out that "it is this isolation from all others, this alienation from his environment, that has made Hamlet the spiritual patron of many a disinherited modern hero.... Furthermore, their decoy, Ophelia, is on stage, reading a book of devotion to 'colour' her 'loneliness' — to serve as a pretext for apparently being unaccompanied.... His loneliness needs no colouring. The convention of the soliloquy, treating his speech as if it were unheard by the other actors, isolates him further from them and brings him closer to us."[6]

REFERENCES

1. Eric and Mary Josephson, "Introduction", *Man Alone*, ed. Eric and Mary Josephson (New York : Dell Publishing, 1962), pp. 19-20. Hereafter cited as *Man Alone*.
2. William Shakespeare, *Hamlet : Prince of Denmark*, ed. Kenneth Grose (London and Glasgow : Blackie and Sons Ltd., 1969), p. 17.

   All references, unless otherwise mentioned, are to *Hamlet : Prince of Denmark*.
3. William Shakespeare, *Macbeth, Complete Works*, ed. Peter Alexander (London and Glasgow : The English Language Book Society, 1964), p. 1002.
4. William Shakespeare, "Sonnet 29", *Complete Works*, p. 1330.
5. Murray Levin, "Political Alienation", *Man Alone*, p. 230.
6. Harry Levin, *The Question of Hamlet* (New York : Oxford University Press, 1959), pp. 52-53, 68.

13

Raktaksi : An Example of a Cultural Adaptation of *Hamlet**

—*Basavaraj Naikar*

SHAKESPEARE WAS such a great genius that his plays have not lost their appeal and relevance even today. His vision of life is so universal that it can easily transcend the barriers of time, place and even culture. An illustration of such a phenomenon may be seen in the cultural adaptation of *Hamlet* by the great Kannada poet, critic, dramatist and novelist Kuvempu (or Dr. K.V. Puttappa, the Jnanapitha Award Winner for his epic *Sri Ramayana Darsanam*) who has tried to respond to Shakespeare in his own creative manner.

It is a matter of common knowledge that translation is an adventurous task of transforming one linguistic code into another, which obviously requires a bilingual competence and creativity. But this process of translation becomes all the more difficult when the translator has to translate not only the linguistic code, but also the cultural code. In fact, the cultural transplantation of the theme happens to be more difficult and challenging than the normal linguistic translation especially when the source culture and target culture happen to be radically different from each other, like, for example, the western and the eastern; or the British and the Indian; or the

* Paper presented at an International Seminar, "Shakespeare and India," conducted jointly by the English Department of the University of Delhi. The Shakespeare Society of India, and La Trobe University, Australia, in February 1998.

Christian and the Hindu. Thus cultural dissimilarity poses a great challenge to the translator who, when he cannot find exact equivalents in the target cultural codes, has to make minor changes in the plot or structure, characters and texture to convey the essential vision of the source cultural codes in a manner acceptable to the readers and spectators of the target culture. Such an adaptation (or *rupantar*) may involve the process of altering the scenic sequence, the number of characters, the units of action and the chronotope etc., to suit the expectations of the audience for whom the work is primarily meant. Nothing that jars on the sensibility of the spectators of the target culture has to be retained in the text by the cultural translator. Such circumstances demand a creative but marginal change in the structure as well as the texture of a work of art, especially a play that achieves its completion in the presence of a live audience. Such a problem was faced by myself when I tried to Indianize J.M. Synge's *The Playboy of the Western World* and Bertolt Brecht's *The Caucasian Chalk-Circle* and *The Good Woman of Setzuan* in my cultural translation into Kannada.

Kuvempu faced the same difficulty in his cultural translation of *Hamlet* into *Raktaksi*. We all know that *Hamlet* is one of the great tragedies of Shakespeare giving expression to his tragic vision against the background of British, Elizabethan and Christian culture, in the linguistic code of the sixteenth century of England. Kuvempu who is separated from Shakespeare in time by four hundred years and in space by about three thousand miles and in culture to a great extent has not only accepted the challenge but also happily succeeded in it to a large extent.

The first thing that strikes our attention is the conspicuous change that Kuvempu has brought in the title of the play. Instead of retaining the proper name of Hamlet for the play, he has named it as *Raktaksi* which means "The bloody eyed girl," which suggests the preponderance of bloodshed that is typical of a tragedy. In Kuvempu's play, it is Ophelia who is named as Rudrambe who becomes a 'bloody eyed girl.' Thus the play being named after a lady instead of being named after a man holds a mirror to Kuvempu's creative shift of emphasis from the inactive male to the active female which is in tune with the Hindu philosophical belief that woman is a manifestation of *Sakti* or cosmic energy as well as with the modern feminist philosophy which considers woman not only as equal but even superior to man. Kuvempu has given a very appropriate name to the heroine Ophelia by calling her 'Rudrambe' which comes from the Vedic god Rudra and which connotes the terrific or the ferocious element and sentiment.

Kuvempu has exercised his creative imagination in the very selection of the historical story of a Virasaiva royal family of Karnataka, which can be the nearest equivalent to that of Hamlet and which can, therefore, be amply adequate to express the tragic vision of Shakespeare without upsetting the cultural norms of Indians, especially Hindus. His selection of a story of a Virasaiva royal family of Keladi Kingdom in the seventeenth century Karnataka helps him to appropriate it for the expression of Hamletian predicament. The relationship between the members of the royal family and between the Kingdom of Keladi and that of Hyderali of Mysore and the usual political intrigues obtaining between them have been intelligently employed by Kuvempu by being invested with the tragic spirit of Shakespeare's play. Once the story of a royal family and its relationship with a neighbouring kingdom is selected, the translator has to adhere to the cultural codes also presupposed by these kingdoms. Any value that is not acceptable to the story structure of the target culture has to be eliminated inevitably. Thus Kuvempu being himself a poetic dramatist in Kannada, has exercised his creative discrimination in eliminating certain scenes and characters of Shakespeare's *Hamlet* in line with the cultural requirements of the story as well as the technical and contingent requirements of the Kannada stage. Thus in the process of trans-cultural transplantation what is lost in one respect is gained in another qualitatively if not quantitatively.

The chief cause of action of *Hamlet* happens to be the unjust murder of the King of Denmark by his queen Gertrude and his younger brother Claudius and the usurpation of his throne by the present king, Claudius. The central action of *Hamlet* thus happens to be double dimensional *i.e.* sexual and political. This core theme of *Hamlet* has been properly captured by Kuvempu, but he has made some minor changes in the positions, if not in the relationship between the characters. Basavappanayaka happens to be the king who has been unjustly murdered by Captain Nimbayya (equivalent to King Claudius) and Rani Cheluvambe (equivalent to Queen Gertrude). But an important difference between Claudius and Nimbayya is that Claudius has occupied the position of a King and that of a husband of Gertrude. Thus both his kingship and husbandhood have been legitimized although not wholly approved by Hamlet. But in *Raktaksi*, Nimbayya remains only a Captain of the army and not the legitimate King. Similarly he remains a clandestine lover of Rani Cheluvambe and never married to her publicly. Thus his political and sexual power remain illegitimate and clandestine and therefore, acceptable to the Indian, especially Hindu culture which is a hiding culture as against the exhibitive culture of the West. Had Kavempu made Nimbayya the King of Keladi and married him to Rani Cheluvambe, the plot would have suffered from the violation of the law of probability in the Hindu context and therefore, unacceptable to the Hindu spectators who are likely to view such action as shameless.

The murder of the King of Denmark has taken place before the beginning of the play, *Hamlet*. The similar situation is retained by Kuvempu in *Raktaksi* where King Basavappanayaka has already been murdered and appears in the form of a ghost initially seen by a sentinel called Kenchanna who is an equivalent of Bernardo. Kuvempu has retained one sentinel instead of two *i.e.* Bernardo and Francesco, in order to reduce the number of characters to the minimum possible ones for achieving the theatrical economy and cohesion of dramatic effect on the Kannada spectators nourished on concise plays of various kinds.

The supernatural appearance of the ghost of Basavappanayaka is noticed by the sentinel Kenchanna who goes on publicizing it among the members of the palace. He tells the news to Honnayya (which means the 'goldenman') who is an equivalent to Horatio. Honnayya is also surprised by the appearance of the ghost of Basavappanayaka. Both of them compare their experiences and confirm the veracity of the same.

The incest motif which is central to Shakespeare's tragedy has been slightly altered by Kuvempu in *Raktaksi*. Rani Cheluvambe's illegal and secret relationship with Captain Nimbayya is parallel to Gertrude's with King Claudius. Her name 'Cheluvambe' is significant in that it denotes the meaning 'a pretty lady' and seems to be deliberately chosen by Kuvempu. Her physical beauty has perhaps made her prone to the illegal sexual attraction for Captain Nimbayya who happens to be a cunning and clever person. Prince Hamlet's philosophical and melancholic nature making him oversensitive to his mother's incestuous indulgence has been qualitatively maintained by Kuvempu. Prince Basavayya broods philosophically about the complexity of life and wishes he were never born. Although Kuvempu has invested Prince Basavayya with a philosophical nature, he has been careful enough to give a Hindu, especially Vedantic flavor to his philosophization. For example, Prince Basavayya never wishes to be born again because of his awareness that every birth is followed by the balance of *Karma* like a shadow. At times, Kuvempu has retained the secular, universal and essential element that is ingrained in Hamlet's philosophical speech. Prince Basavayya curses his stepmother as a Sani (*i.e.* planet Saturn) who has started an illegal relationship with Captain Nimbayya before the grass has grown on his father's grave and before the tears of the mourners are dry. He exclaims rhetorically, "O frailty, is not your name woman?" He invokes the thunder to clap on his mother and her paramour.

On the whole, Hamlet's melancholy, philosophical brooding

and poetic waxing is brought out well and beautifully by Kuvempu, although the context is generally Hindu, especially Vedantic. Prince Basavayya suspects that there is some fraud in the death of his father Basavappanayaka. But Somayya, son of Captain Nimbayya (equivalent to Laertes, son of Polonius in Shakespeare's play) tries to console him by reminding him of the Vedantic lesson taught by his guru that birth and death are but part of *maya* and that man should not worry about them. But Prince Basavayya finds it difficult to accept sorrow as part of *maya*. He soliloquizes about the fraud — whether it is in others or in him. He expresses his sorrow homologically by comparing the world to a colourful dome, which hides the truth that is white. In his opinion, a fool likes a fool and a wise man appears like a fool in a majority of fools.

In Shakespeare's *Hamlet*, King Claudius revels at midnight. But this scene is eliminated by Kuvempu in *Raktaksi* perhaps because of his own puritanical nature or because of his desire to make the play concise. When Hamlet worries about the death of his father, his suspicion is removed and his vindictive motivation is intensified by the ghost of his father. Kuvempu has wisely retained this central scene in *Raktaksi*. Prince Basavayya dreams a dream in which he sees his father shedding tears and later he meets the ghost of Basavappanayaka at midnight (not in the palace but outside the city of Bidanur in a nearby forest). The encounter with the ghost is not presented directly but is reported by Prince Basavayya. He tells Minister Linganna that he has seen his father's ghost who appeared to him in the moonlight in a dignified manner; that it, while shedding tears, narrated the event and divulged the secret. He has learnt from the ghost that it was Rani Cheluvambe and Captain Nimbayya who got King Basavappanayaka killed by mixing poison with medicine and cleverly getting it administered to the ailing King; that Rani Cheluvambe has been dallying with her lover Captain Nimbayya thereby neglecting the family honour; that the ghost ordered for the burning of the two culprits so that it could have a sense of satisfaction; that Basavayya should save his own life and protect the Kingdom both of which are likely to be snatched away by Captain Nimbayya. Thus Prince Basavayya's subjective fear is corroborated by the objective event of encounter with the ghost. The event shown in direct action on the stage in Shakespeare's play is presented through indirect action in Kuvempu's play.

Hamlet suffering from the emotion of love is common to Shakespeare's play as well as Kuvempu's. In *Raktaksi*, Rudrambe (equivalent to Ophelia) is a sixteen-year young lady who is as delicate as strong and terrible. Kuvempu appropriately describes her as pretty as a far-off lightning. Unlike in Shakespeare's play where Ophelia is precautioned to be careful with Hamlet and to cold-shoulder him, Rudrambe in Kuvempu's play is asked by her father, Minister Linganna to entertain Prince Basavayya and ease the burden of his soul. Rudrambe appears to be slightly more mature than Ophelia, as she wants to share her lover's happiness as well as sorrow. She requests him to tell her the cause of his suffering. Although initially he hesitates to reveal the real reason for his suffering, finally he expresses it frankly. But Rudrambe finds it difficult to believe in the evil intention of Rani Cheluvambe. On the whole, the relationship between Prince Basavayya and Rudrambe is characterized by a lyrical beauty and sweetness and mutual trust. Kuvempu's depiction of the Prince and Rudrambe appears to be more affirmative than Shakespeare's depiction of that of Hamlet and Ophelia. In Shakespeare's play, Hamlet's love for Ophelia is tinged with melancholy and Ophelia's response to Hamlet is one of suspicion, distrust and caution. Ophelia does not reciprocate his love properly. Hamlet, therefore, curses her to go to the nunnery. She never understands the intensity of Hamlet's love, which is not equalled by the love of even forty thousand brothers. But Kuvempu's picture is slightly different from Shakespeare's in that Rudrambe is never cold and rigid like Ophelia in her relationship with her lover. Rudrambe shows a sense of trust in the value of love. Likewise, Prince Basavayya loves her sincerely but never to the extent of going mad or losing the balance of his mind. Kuvempu has given a clarity of motivation to Prince Basavayya and Rudrambe, whereas Shakespeare has brought in an element of ambiguity and abnormality in his characterization of Hamlet. Kuvempu has eliminated the character of Laertes *i.e.*, brother of Ophelia totally from his play. Instead, he has created a rival for the Prince in Sivayya (Somayya's friend) for the love of Rudrambe. Such an emotional rivalry is not to be found in Shakespeare's play.

Once Hamlet learns from his father's ghost the crime of Claudius and Gertrude, he decides to take revenge upon his uncle in power. But before that, he accidentally gets a chance of arranging a stage-play entitled *The Mousetrap* with the help of Rosencrantz and Guildenstern and to catch the conscience of the King. The meta-dramatic device used by Shakespeare happens to be one of the most interesting scenes in *Hamlet*, which enables the over smart protagonist to watch the awakening of the conscience of King Claudius and Gertrude. The scene has a psychological as well as moral dimension about it. Hamlet becomes a drama-director in order to expose the drama of his uncle and mother. The whole situation with many of its details is conspicuous by its absence in Kuvempu's *Raktaksi*. Kuvempu's elimination of the whole situation has undoubtedly impoverished the play by avoiding the psycho-moral dimension of the play within the play. The reason for Kuvempu's removal of this situation cannot be accounted for in clear-cut terms, though one can, of course, attribute it partially at least to his taste and temperament if not to the theatrical requirements of the Kannada stage. The liberty that he has taken with Shakespeare's play happens to be too blatant to be excused, especially when we know that he had the creative capacity to retain it and make the best out of it.

In *Hamlet*, King Claudius and Gertrude's conscience is pricked by the spectacle of the play arranged by the Prince. But in *Raktaksi*. Captain Nimbayya and Rani Cheluvambe are alerted by the public opinion, which makes them feel guilty as well as apprehensive about the imminent coronation of

Prince Basavayya. They feel that the event of coronation will defeat the very purpose of their illegal sexual relation and grabbing of political power. They, therefore, think of getting Prince Basavayya and Minister Linganna initially imprisoned and subsequently murdered. A good deal of political intrigue is brought in by Kuvempu to develop the theme to its logical end. Captain Nimbayya tries to brainwash Rani Cheluvambe and make her agree to the fact that the Kingdom of Keladi should go to his own son Somayya after the murder of the Prince. Rani Cheluvambe who is deeply under the sexual influence of Captain Nimbayya seems to agree to his suggestion. But the Kingdom belongs to the subjects as well. The public opinion, thus, begins to be mobilized by the well-wishers of the Kingdom like Minister Linganna and others. People are eager to coronet Prince Basavayya as the King of Keladi. Thus the two antagonistic groups begin to work against each other through espionage and counter-espionage, intrigue and conspiracy so common in the political life of any kingdom. Kuvempu shifts the emphasis from the private conscience of the Prince to the public conscience of the Minister, courtiers and other administrators who try to restore the political and moral order in the Kingdom.

Timmajetti, for example, who had poisoned King Basavappanayaka, has been now appointed to murder Prince Basavayya also. But even such a hired murderer feels the pricks of conscience and hesitates to carry out the order. He feels totally helpless as he can neither obey nor dare disobey the secret orders of Captain Nimbayya. Since Kuvempu has eliminated the character of Laertes from *Raktaksi*, he has made a few suitable changes in the plot according to his own creative imagination. He has also avoided the scene where Polonius eavesdrops Hamlet's conversation with his mother and where he accidentally kills Polonius hiding behind the arras. Kuvempu suddenly jumps to the situation where Prince Basavayya and Minister Linganna are led to the prison. The imprisonment of such two noble personalities upsets the moral conscience of other courtiers and people who are about to rebel against it, but Captain Nimbayya has worked out a systematic conspiratorial plan of getting the persons out of the prison and have them murdered conveniently in the nearby woods. But the operation of moral order is shown through the external political force of Hyderali of Mysore and his army. Counter-spying overtakes spying. Ramaraya, a spy of Hyderali, who has assumed the guise of a sanyasi learns the secret of murder-order from Timmajetti, tries to avoid it systematically. He gives sleep-inducing medicine to Sanganna, the guard of the prison and helps Sivayya and Honnayya to take out Prince Basavayya and Minister Linganna from the prison. While the two persons *i.e.* Sivayya and Honnayya are taking out the two prisoners separately, the sanyasi gives a letter to Prince Basavayya and asks him to hand it over secretly to Hyderali of Mysore camping at Sivamogge.

One of the innovations brought into the plot by Kuvempu is that he creates in Sivayya, a rival for Prince Basavayya for the love of Rudrambe. Sivayya knows that he cannot have the love of Rudrambe as long as Prince Basavayya stays alive. He, therefore, tries to cheat the Prince on the way to Sivamogge. He tries to prejudice him against Rudrambe though the Prince is not easily convinced by him. Finally he deceives the Prince by drawing his attention to the beauty of Nature around him. When the Prince is looking down the valley, Sivayya pushes him down and is happy to imagine that the Prince is dead. Prince Basavayya screams and moans piteously and curses the treachery of Sivayya who rides away hurriedly from there.

A little later, when Honnayya brings Minister Linganna to the same spot, they hear the moaning of the Prince in the valley and learn from him the treachery of Sivayya. Before dying, Prince Basavayya hands over the letter to Minister Linganna and asks him to reach it to Hyderali camping at Sivamogge and to avenge the death of King Basavappanayaka.

Sivayya has already met Hyderali at Sivamogge and gives him a false impression that he is Prince Basavayya himself. But Minister Linganna comes there at the right time and exposes the double-dealing and pretension of Sivayya. Hyderali, convinced by the honesty of Minister Linganna and exasperated by the hypocrisy of Sivayya, understands the chaos that is prevalent at the Kingdom of Keladi. He orders Sivayya to be arrested and promises to help Minsiter Linganna defeat Captain Nimbayya and his paramour Rani Cheluvambe. This part of the play is strikingly different from that of *Hamlet* and holds a mirror to Kuvempu's creativity. The agent of moral order or justice comes from outside the Kingdom of Keladi. While Kuvempu has retained the law of vengeance which is a kind of wild justice and the chief motif in *Hamlet*, but has adapted it to suit the cultural context of Karnataka. He has creatively shifted the operation of the law of justice from the palace to the outside force represented by Hyderali of Mysore. This alteration in the plot contributes a great deal to the capturing of the attention of the Kannada audience who know the political relationship between the Kingdom of Keladi and that of Hyderali, father of Tippu Sultan of Mysore.

Captain Nimbayya and Rani Cheluvambe are afraid that the situation has gone out of their control. When they learn that Minister Linganna has escaped from the Kingdom of Keladi and sought the help of Hyderali and that there is a rebellion of the native citizens also, they grow desperate and wish to win the war through foul means *i.e.* by squandering money on soldiers. The lover and the beloved grow more and more dependent upon each other and decide to live or die together.

The whole situation connected with the young lady Rudrambe is a new one created by Kuvempu and not to be found in Shakespeare's *Hamlet*. Kuvempu, for example, has avoided the situation of the duel between Hamlet and Laertes and the Queen drinking the poison accidentally and Hamlet and Laertes dying by mutual wounding. In Kuvempu's play,

Prince Basavayya has already died, but the law of vindictive justice has come into operation.

In *Raktaksi*, Kuvempu has brought in his own changes. In order to please Captain Nimbayya, Honnayya has taken upon himself the crime of murdering the Prince although the latter is actually murdered by Sivayya. Honnayya is a well-wisher of the Prince secretly. He, therefore, arranges a decent burial for the dead Prince.

But Honnayya's fake confession of being the murderer of the Prince has exasperated Rudrambe, beloved of the Prince. The course of action takes an unexpected direction. It is here that Kuvempu's creative innovation and cultural adaptation can be felt very strikingly. He has made Rudrambe not a very innocent girl like Ophelia, but a figure bubbling with the elemental vitality. When Rudrambe learns the false news that Honnayya has killed her lover-prince, she grows ferocious and wants to kill Honnayya. In the outer lane of Bidanur, she comes clad in old rags and in a fierce mood of anger and despair and behaves in a mad fashion in the moonlight. She addresses the stars as merciless and the shine of the moon as sepulchral and wants to kill the moon. She feels a blankness in her and requests the mountains and forests; the sky and the ocean; the sun and the moon and the stars, the cosmos, time and space to fill in her blankness. She is eager to kill Honnayya, the murderer of her lover. She claims to be a "bloody-eyed girl" *i.e.*, Raktaksi. Just a little while after Honnayya has rendered a decent burial to Prince Basavayya, the rag-covered Rudrambe rushes to the spot where she stabs Honnayya indiscriminately. Honnayya feels sorry that he could not reveal the truth to Rudrambe earlier. He cannot identify Rudrambe but after knowing her identity, he tells her that it was Sivayya who murdered the Prince but that he took the blame on himself just to give the dead Prince a decent burial. Now that Rudrambe realizes the truth, she falls on Honnayya and repents of her indiscriminate and incorrigible action. Before dying, Honnayya reminds her to wreak vengeance upon Sivayya according to the last wish of Prince Basavayya. Honnayya dies happily as he now has the satisfaction of revealing the truth of events to Rudrambe. True to her name, Rudrambe assumes a terrific mood and invokes the spirit of Lord Siva and invites Him to suck her poisonous milk; she requests the three-eyed Lord (Siva) to burn her as He burnt Kama; she invokes Lord Bhairava to inspire her and to spark off an untimely thunder and to enable her to fulfil her lover's wish. She also prays to the Lord not to shake her faith in Him. After crying like this, Rudrambe remembers something and begins to dig up the mud of the grave with a spade lying about there. Kuvempu has thus invested the character of Rudrambe with a greater liveliness and energy than Shakespeare's Ophelia who appears to be relatively cold, passive and weak with a suicidal tendency. Rudrambe becomes a striking medium of the operation of the law of justice or vengeance initially broached by the ghost of King Basavappanayaka.

Whereas Rudrambe is the internal agent of vengeance, Hyderali of Mysore with his large army happens to be the external agent of vengeance. The two agencies combine to punish the culprits and restore the law and order in the Kingdom. For example, Captain Nimbayya and Rani Cheluvambe are unhappy to know that their messengers are captured by Hyderali of Mysore. Captain Nimbayya orders Rudrayya to keep the army ready and burn the palace as soon as the enemies attack it. He wants to take his paramour Cheluvambe away from the city through a secret passage. But all their expectations are nullified. The messengers come and report that the army of Hyderali has attacked the city of Bidanur. Rani Cheluvambe is deeply worried. Captain Nimbayya tries to enhearten her by promising to take her to a safe place and return to the battlefield. Both of them change their dress and try to escape in disguise, but to their surprise, they discover that the door has been locked from outside. The external agency and the internal agency of vengeance are combined at this juncture. They see Rudrambe through the peephole. They order and even request her to open the door, but she refuses to do so and accuses them of having had Prince Basavayya murdered. The two lovers remain totally helpless. Rani Cheluvambe repents of her sin and crime and invokes the spirit of her late son Basavayya and sags to the floor. But Captain Nimbayya hardens himself to die along with his beloved in the overwhelming flames. In Hyderali's camp at Sivamogge, Hyderali thanks Ramaraya who was in the guise of a sanyasi. Hyderali is happy to have punished the evil but unhappy not to have protected the good people. He is unhappy about the death of Prince Basavayya. Minister Linganna is worried about the whereabouts of his daughter Rudrambe. Muhammadali, Captain of Hyderali's army wants to send his soldiers to search for her. Hyderali suggests that Minister Linganna should punish the culprits, but the latter refuses to punish them in spite of his despair. He wants everybody to be happy. His only wish is to see his daughter once. He wants to bless everyone and never tries to curse anyone. This line of action is, obviously, in line with the Hindu philosophy of life, which is highlighted by Kuvempu. By that time a soldier comes and reports that a mad girl rushed into the prison and murdered Sivayya and stabbed herself. Minister Linganna is heart-broken to learn this tragic news. The dead body of Sivayya is lying in a pool of blood. Rudrambe is dying slowly. Minister Linganna comes there and falls on his dying daughter in a very sorrowful manner. Hyderali and Muhammadali also come there and witness the tragic scene helplessly. Thus the play *Raktaksi* ends with a lot of bloodshed and death thereby suggesting a sense of tragic waste and affirming the moral order of the universe.

Raktaksi, thus holds a mirror to Kuvempu's creative ability to transplant Shakespeare's tragic vision from the British and Christian cultural setting to the Indian and Hindu cultural setting. Although he has taken liberty with the original play *Hamlet* by eliminating certain characters and situations, he has retained the basic motifs like the illegal sexual relation, the supernatural element (of the ghost of King Basavappanayaka and its instruction to the Prince), the revenge motif, the court intrigue, the reflective tone about death and ephemerality of life and the sense of tragic waste by adapting them to the Kannada cultural pattern thereby making it acceptable to the Kannada spectators. One of the striking changes that Kuvempu has made in the characterization of Hamlet is that he has made Prince Basavayya relatively more firm and clear in his attitude to life than Hamlet. Hamlet's interminable oscillation or dilemma has been minimized by Kuvempu in the creation of Prince Basavayya's character. Consequently we see in the character of Prince Basavayya less psychologization and morbidity and relatively more action than in Hamlet. But the reduction of Hamletian dilemma and psychologization and enlargement of action cannot be quantified exactly though it can be felt by any sensitive reader of *Raktaksi*.

A comparative overview of Shakespeare's imagery in *Hamlet* and Kuvempu's in *Raktaksi* shows a world of difference between the two. Kuvempu's translation of the British and Christian cultural codes into Indian and Hindu cultural codes may be seen in the texture expressed in the native imagery employed by the various characters in the play. Whereas the images of disease and corruption are predominant in *Hamlet* and contribute to the morbid atmosphere of the play, *Raktaksi* is studded with a variety of typically Hindu images drawn from Hindu religion, myths, superstition, philosophy, yoga and Nature. Although the images of disease and corruption are not very dominant in *Raktaksi*, there are many Hindu images, which qualitatively reveal the idea of corruption. The images of snake, snake-hole, kiss of a snake, the *Kalakuta* poison of Lord Siva, the graveyard of sky, funeral pyre, dark night, *Sunya* (Void), hell, planet Sani's (Saturn's) adverse effect, *Karma* and Yama's servants create an atmosphere of corruption, disorder, unhappiness, tragic death and futility. The universal images like labyrinth, net, prison, scissors are also used by Kuvempu at appropriate places but these images are combined with those drawn from Nature and cosmos also. Kuvempu who happens to be an excellent lyrical poet in Kannada and who is deeply steeped in Kannada classical poetry, has tried to bring in the images of Nature and cosmos at all the opportunities in *Raktaksi*. The images of the sun, the moon, the moonlight, thunder, lightening, rainbow, pole star, spring, autumn, garden, river, crocodile, tree, lotus etc., are employed by many characters in *Raktaksi*, especially by Prince Basavayya. These images provide a qualitative balance to the ones connoting death and to tone down the melancholic atmosphere of the play.

Linguistically, Kuvempu provides a parallel to *Hamlet* by mixing prose and verse in *Raktaksi*. Being a lyric poet as well as an epic poet, Kuvempu is known for his poetic prose. In *Raktaksi*, he has employed prose for the depiction of normal situations, but poetry for the expression of intense moments of experience. For example, Prince Basavayya's philosophical reflection about death and ephemerality of life, the frailty of woman; his poetic description of Nature; Honnayya's philosophization about the illusionary nature of *maya* etc., and even Captain Nimbayya's amorous dialogues with Rani Cheluvambe are fine examples of poetic passages known for their beautiful metaphors and mellifluity.

Raktaksi is, thus, an example of how Shakespeare can be presented to the twentieth century Kannada readers and spectators and how the barriers of time, place and culture can be overcome by the creative genius of writers like Kuvempu. The extraordinary popularity of *Raktaksi* in Karnataka is proved beyond doubt by the very fact that it has run into ten reprints by now, although it was originally published in 1932. It is a fine example of how one great poet of one country receives the vision of life of another great poet of another country and transforms it in the alchemy of his imagination.

WORKS CITED

Shakespeare, *Hamlet*, ed. Edward Hubler, Twelfth Reprint, (New York : Signet Classics, 1963).

Kuvempu, *Raktaksi*, Tenth Reprint, (Mysore : Udayaravi Prakasana, 1993).

14

Nirvana as the Leitmotif : A Study of *King Lear*

—O.P. Budholia

WILLIAM SHAKESPEARE, a born genius, myriad-minded, a skilled artist and a mystery man, has revealed a world of multifarious aspects of human life in his tragedies. In his four major tragedies, — *Hamlet, Othello, King Lear* and *Macbeth*, Shakespeare displays four-fold aspects of human life : social, ethical, political, and spiritual. In *King Lear*, the dramatist unfolds a complicated world of human relations, human nature, varying mental states, filial ingratitude, demented human emotions and above all hero's long journey from passions to self-realizations. This paper is restricted to exploring the gradual progression of Lear from passions to his final regeneration.

Like *Hamlet, King Lear* has also a parallel running of two plots, and each stamps the validity of *nirvana* in it. The sub-plot of this play consists of three main characters : Gloucester, Edmund and Edgar. The main plot of the story rotates around the old King and his three daughters, Regan, Goneril and Cordelia. The two plots are thus patterned for symbolic revelation of the varied group of human relations. The main plot analyses the psychic aberrations of Lear through two streams as the projections of his mind : the Goneril-Regan nexus and the Cordelia-consciousness. The Gloucester part of the story also symbolizes the degeneration of human and moral values and finally its merger in Act III for the wider vision of life.

As an old man, Lear wishes to be "unburthen'd" by the authority of his kingdom. He thus intends to divide his kingdom into three parts. Being a man of self-love and with egoistic reflections he longs to have the emotions of self-love satisfied by his daughters. He puts a question before them : "Which of you shall we say doth love us most."[1] The reply of Goneril brings a soothing-effect to his passion-ridden psyche :

> Goneril : Sir, I love you more
> Than words can wield the matter
> Dearer than eyesight, space and liberty.
>
> * * *
>
> As much as child e'er loved, or father found;
> A love that makes breath poor, and speech unable.
> Beyond all manner of so much I love you (I, i, 45-52)

Regan also agrees with Goneril and confesses "that self-metal" of which Goneril is made of Lear thus makes sure of them for their share in the kingdom. His third and the youngest daughter, Cordelia, does not satisfy the sudden stimulated passions of his mind. Her reply becomes an example of the unsheathed truth :

> Good, my lord,
> You have begot me, bred me, loved me : I
> Return those duties back...
> Why have my sisters husbands, if they say
> They love you all? haply, when I shall wed,
> That lord whose hand must taken my plight shall carry
> Half my love with him, half my care and duty;
> Sure, I shall never marry like my sister,
> To love my father all (I, i, 87-95)

Cordelia with her naked truth shakes the unconscious passions that lie slumbering in Lear's mind. The phrase "dragon and his wrath" (I, i, 14) symbolizes the psychic level of Lear's mind. The noun "dragon" is followed by another noun "wrath" with a possessive "his" in the context of the Cordelia-consciousness, symbolizing the demented human emotions. Lear in a fit of his passions, is at his wits' end for distinguishing between good and evil. He thus deliberately confines himself to the inexorable laws of karma. Over-laden with passion and the violent anger, Lear commits distressingly two mistakes : Kent's exile from his kingdom and depriving Cordelia of her share in the estate. Before Burgundy, Lear acknowledges that "her price is fallen" (I, i, 189). As Cordelia symbolizes the truth of life, she does not please Lear with "glib and oily art" (I, i, 116). Once again, the often repeated word "wrath" comes to the mouth of Lear and he curses Cordelia : "Better thou / Hadst not been born than not have pleased me better" (I, i, 127). King of France, Burgundy surprises at Lear for demeaning of human emotions. The reply of Cordelia so influences Burgundy as he observes many apparent contradictions of human qualities in her :

> Fairest Cordelia, thou art most rich, being poor;
> Most choice, forsaken; and most loved, despised
> Thee and they virtues here I seize upon.
> ...queen of us, of ours and of our France....
> Bid them farewell, Cordelia, though unkind :
> Thou losest here, a better where to find (I, i, 345-46)

Out of Lear's violent anger, there crops up an aversion in him not only towards Cordelia, but also towards the Cordelia-principles of life. Bound with the 'wheel of fire" or by the non-convergence values of life, Lear makes his ingrained passions the sole formula for his future actions. He even forgets the courtesy which begins at home for his blood relations. He bids Cordelia farewell without his "grace", "love" and "benison" Cordelia, the most-loved daughter, knows her father well. She beholds the impetuous passions of lower instincts in him. She also suspects the villainy of human nature in her sisters :

> I know what you are
> And like a sister, am most loath to call
> Your faults as they are named (I, i, 261-63)

The sub-plot of the play consists of three main characters — Gloucester, Edgar and Edmund. This part of the play deals with the moral dilemma of father and his two sons, Edgar and Edmund. Gloucester's past full of lascivious passions creates rashness in his mind. His bastard son, Edmund becomes the sole cause of his violent anger and temperamental aberrations. Edmund misguides Gloucester against Edgar by presenting a forged letter. Gloucester like Lear in a fit of wrath (*krodha*) casts out Edgar. In the main plot, Cordelia as "a spirit", "a soul in bliss", and "a fair daylight" lays down apparent contradictions with the dark world of Lear's passions. Edgar as the higher self of Gloucester teases him for his past in Edmund. Edgar thus stirs him momentarily with a negative rush of human emotions. The entire human relations in this play become symbolic and emblematic. The predominance of human nature (manav prakriti) becomes associative and reconcilable to higher prakriti for outlining the cosmic vision of Shakespeare.

According to Indian *dharma*, the human nature assimilates the three gunas of the higher prakriti — *sattva, rajas* and *tamas*. As a tragedy of human nature, *King Lear* fits in to the analysis of the three gunas of human nature. Thus, the leitmotif of this tragedy lies in the incessant persuasiveness of the hero for the release of a Karmic life. An Indian critic of Shakespeare, Syed Mehdi Imam has beautifully explored the influences of gunas in Shakespearean tragedy, more especially in *King Lear* :

> From the perusal of Shakespeare's tragedies, three general principles of tragic drama emerge — the principle of play (Lila), of Disillusionment (Maya) and Release (Mukti)...in *Lear* is the play of the dualities of gratitude and ingratitude, a disillusionment (Maya) and release (Mukti).[2]

Thus, on the basis of this analysis of the text, there emerges the formation of the triangular which shows the complicated world of human relations on the attributes of gunas :

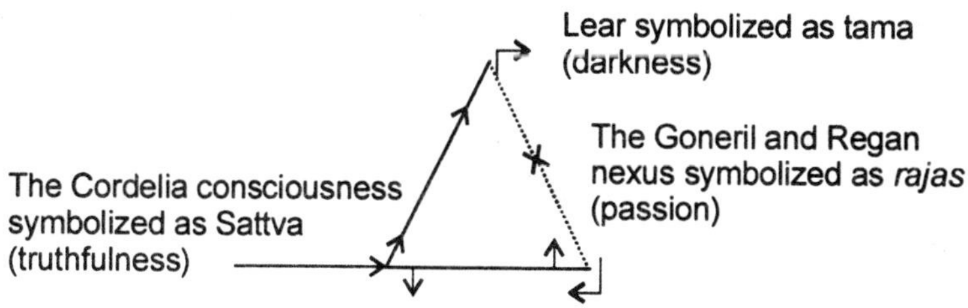

The deeper reality of human mind lies behind the surfacial values of human sentiments and emotions. Therefore, it seems appropriate to weigh scientifically and psychologicallly the role of the symbolic expression in human life. Gerald S. Blum, a noted psychologist, brings in to being the relations of the symbolic expressions with the deeper reality of human mind :

> The symbol is an indirect representation which stands for something else, thereby contributing to the disguise of unacceptable impulses. The process is facilitated by the fact that thoughts are typically translated into pictorial images in dreams. Various principle of association — such as physical resemblance, similar function, part whole relationship, contrast, and occurrence together in time — lend themselves to the substitutive disguise.[3]

In this way, triangular sketched above symbolizes Lear as tama and his three daughters become symbolic of *rajas* and *sattva*. The Goneril-Regan nexus represents *rajas* while the Cordelia consciousness stands for *sattva*. The individual attributes of each guna can be analysed according to Indian way of life thus : the *sattva guna* produces a deeper sense for goodness, beauty, virtue, observance of duty and freedom from desire and; *rajas* (passion) produces desire and action;

tamas produces ignorance, darkness, indifference and dullness. The modern psychologists regard unconscious as the store of all ideas. Man's each idea is governed either through *ego* or *super-ego. Id* being a sensual desire enhances a concrete shape to them by its associative role. The association of *Id* with *ego* creates *rajas* and *tamas* and the dissociation of the two leaves *Id* to be reconciliatory with *super-ego* or guilt consciousness or super-consciousness creating the eternal values of *sattva guna*.

Modern critics of Shakespeare have explored the problem of psycho-analysis in *King Lear*. In fact, the problem of father-fixation cannot be denied fully in this play, but to deal with it in detail means to deviate from the core of our discussion. To be with the concept of *nirvana* in *King Lear*, a few slokas of *Srimad Bhagavadgita* deserve to be quoted in context to Lear's journey towards super-consciousness or *nirvana* :

> With the preponderance of *rajas*, Arjuna, greed, inactivity, undertaking of actions with an interested motive, restlessness and thirst for enjoyment make their appearance.

Again,

> With the growth of *tamas*, Arjuna, obtuseness of the mind and senses, disinclination to perform one's obligatory duties, frivolity and stupor — all these appear.[4]

Lear's association with the Goneril and Regan nexus results in arousing *tamas* in his mind. His dissociation with the Cordelia-element means his deviation from the universal validity of moral values. He even observes "the sacred radiance of the sun (I, i, 100) in Cordelia, yet the preponderance of passion (*rajas*) makes him to compel her to mend the truth :

> Mend your speech a little
> Lest it may mar your fortune (I, i, 85-86)

Almost in all Shakespearean tragedies, a man in action

limits his predicament. Shakespeare lets Lear free to choose his action from either ways of life. And he chooses the wrong one due to the thrust of human nature or the attributes of gunas :

> The emblematic...situation erupts the mysterious thrust of psychic energy that we call a choice, an act; and the waiting coil of consequences leaps in to threatening life, bringing with it, as every act considered absolutely must, the inscrutable where we had supposed all was clear, the unexpected though we thought we had envisaged all contingencies and could never be surprised.[5]

Oedipus Rex is not an example for Shakespeare for deciding the karma of the hero only on the basis of destiny. In the world of Lear, there are two extremes : the extreme good and the extreme evil. And Lear chooses in the beginning of the story the extreme evil. Man in Shakespearean tragedies is patterned neither by the Gloucester-formula ("As flies to the wanton boys / Are we to the gods; they kill us for their sport" IV, i, 36-37) nor through the Edgar-formula ("The gods are just and of our pleasant vices make an instrument to plague us" V, iii, 171-72); but Shakespeare considers the Edmund-formula seriously and reconciles with it for the theory of karma ("The wheel is come full circle; I am here" V, iii, 75-76).

Lear is the most passive character among all his tragic heroes. Each action of Lear begins and ends in the psychic depth of his mind. The total sum of Lear's actions reveals the psychic reaction. The attraction and repulsion of desires make this tragedy *sui generis* for its tragic elan.

As Cordelia is the truth personified in human being, it arouses in Lear the momentary emotional stimulus response, causing a rush of uncontrollable passions. Thus, his judgement towards the truth of Cordelia is based on "primary process mode of thinking and the operation of the pleasure principle."[6] The association of *tamas* and *rajas* creates the momentary excitement in Lear. One discerns a purblind impetuous embrace of the diabolic intellect of Goneril and the unbridled malice of Regan. The spell of Lear from passions is bound to break. Breaking, it brings a moral awakening in his slumbering conscience. This sudden awakening makes him yield to the Cordelia-element of life or *sattva* which may be renamed as the true self of Lear. Thus, Lear overcomes his lower impulses by the gradual process of jnana (knowledge).

As an archetypal hero in Act I, Lear suffers not from the inexorable laws of destiny, but from his own flaws from the demented human emotions. Both Goneril and Regan observe a change in him. The phrases apply to the alchemy of his mind — "poor judgement", "the unruly waywardness", "choleric year" exhibit the declining vales of reasoning of his mind. Here is Goneril's opinion about his reasoning power :

> Gon : come, sir,
> I would you would make use of that good wisdom,
> where of I Know you are fraught, and put away these
> dispositions that of late transform you from what you
> rightly are. (I, iv, 4-8)

What kind of transformation is it? Certainly it is of "dispositions" and of human nature. In fact, it is his movement from *sattva* to *rajas* that Goneril observes in him. When Goneril reminds him his true human nature, he undergoes the metamorphosis in to a moral being that now begins to realize the Cordelia-element of life :

> Darkness and devils !
> Saddle my horses; call my train together
> Degenerate bastard; I'll not trouble thee
> Yet have I left a daughter (I, iv, 38-41)

Too much attraction to any thing binds one in bonds of karma and "seething excitement." The unfulfilled passions of Lear fill him with the violent anger. As a man of negative thoughts, he becomes obsessive to the Cordelia-consciousness or tragic elan. This makes him kneel with reverence before

Cordelia and creates an abhorrence to the lower impulses of human nature. Like an Indian sage, he curses Goneril for her filial ingratitude :

> In to her womb convey sterility,
> Dry up in her the organs of increase;
> And from her derogate body never spring
> A babe to honour her!...
> Let it stamp wrinkles in her brow of youth
> With cadent tears fret channels in her cheeks;
> Turn all her mother's pains and benefits
> To laughter and contempt; that she may feel
> How sharper than a serpent tooth it is
> To have a thankless child! Away, Away
>
> (I, iv, 64-75)

The impact of Goneril and Regan is so piercing in his mind as he feels the shaking of his "manhood" : "I'll pluck ye out, and cast you, with waters that you loose to temper clay" (I, iv, 290). Thus, he overcomes the blood-smearing coil of the passions. The killing of passions, giving up selfish motives, attraction and repulsion, jealousy, malice, greed and other psychic aberrations make Lear again a man of total integrity. Sometimes, the suppression of lower desires does not suit our moral purpose, as they enter the subconscious regions of human psyche. They come in the form of mental disease while lying long inactive and in passive conditions. But all natural desires are not detrimental to human personality as few of them create the sense of guilt. The sense of guilt in psychology is linked with the super-consciousness. The guilt-ridden conscience in man makes him release a kind of liquid which relieves him from all passion and makes him calm and submissive. Prof. Blum analyses beautifully the inner traits of a guilt-ridden man thus :

> Guilt or super-ego anxiety has a host of reactions associated with it. Confession, the seeking of atonement, acts of reparation all stem from unconscious forces related to moral standard.

> Seemingly self-destructive behaviour can serve to gratify a need for punishment and expiation of one's sins. An individual may, without conscious awareness, place himself in a situation where an accident is likely to befall him.[7]

In absence of Cordelia, the companionship of Fool creates a moral height and a "trembling sensibility"[8] in Lear's mind. As a personification of the Cordelia-consciousness, Fool always follows him in his miseries. As Blum suggests of any accident to a guilt-ridden man, the Fool brings one to our notice when he reminds Lear the fruits of altruism :

> Let go thy hold when a great wheel runs down a hill, lest it break thy neck with following it; but the great one that goes up the hill, let him draw thee after. (II, iv, 66-69)

The sense of guilt acts thus as a purgatory process to the tension-tormented human psyche of Lear. He now follows the path of *nirvana*. Gautama Buddha teaches his disciples to give up, rather to burn entirely the dross and dirt accrued from the images of attraction and repulsion to a loved-one object of our lower sensual order for attaining the perfect peace of mind :

> Just as a lamp when it becomes extinguished goes neither hither nor thither, neither to the earth nor to the sky, neither to this direction nor to that, it has been utterly blown out on account of the oil being consumed; similarly a sage obtains *nirvana* when the desires and the passions have been consumed; he goes neither this way nor that, but obtains, utter peace.[9]

Lear experiences the truism of life. He does not suppress his inborn desires, but he blows them out totally for attaining the higher bliss. He restrains his lower impulses and overcomes them. The blowing out of *tama* creates the climax of tragic conflict in the mind of the hero. Lear now yearns to know his real nature. Here is Lear who becomes the best example for tragic elan in him and the play as well :

> Doth any here know me? Why, this is not Lear:
> Doth Lear walk this? Where are his eyes?
> Either his notion weakens or his discernings
> Are lethargied — Ha ! Waking? 'Tis not so,
> Who is that can tell me who I am? (I, iv, 13-16)

As Lear blows out "the wheel of fire", he nears the true essence of life. The dramatist applies his own alchemy to the regeneration of Lear and Gloucester. Both the stories are teamed together for displaying the climax of tragic sufferings and the spiritual attainments. Lear perceives the hollowness of this world just before he goes mad;

> The tempest in my mind
> Doth from my senses take all feeling else,
> Save what beats there. Filial ingratitude!
> ...But I will punish home
> No, I will weep no more. In such a night!
> To shut me out! Pour on, I will endure
> In such a night as this! O, Regan and Goneril
> (III, iv, 13-24)

The repetition of the phrase "In such a night" is linked symbolically with the Goneril and Regan nexus, reminding Lear his karmas; but the verb "endure" fills him with a superhuman strength to expiate his sins and to atone for his past karma. Thus, the account of suffering goes higher than the sins he has committed in his life. The dissociation from his passions and sincere and honest association with the Cordelia element leads him to the way of *nirvana*. As he opens an account of his sufferings, he invites our sympathies as a tragic hero; "I am a man / More sinn'd against than sinning" (III, iii, 55-56).

The storm scene becomes symbolic for the endurance and sufferings of Lear. Gloucester also suffers under two selves : the Edmund self of the baser instincts and the Edgar-self of moral principles. Only the delay of Edgar's identity to his father mars the charm of the parallel-running of the sub-plot. Karma as the nucleus of this tragedy brings into being the obsessive and the guilt-ridden conscience of Gloucester before the readers. Gloucester begets his bastard, Edmund, in the dark and vicious place and the same bastard "cost him his eyes." Lear does not understand the greatness of Cordelia in his sanity, but the realizes her greatness in his insanity. Gloucester with the light of his eyes does not see the higher virtues in Edgar, but he realizes them when he is totally blind. Here is an example of the Edgar-self :

> Men must endure
> Their going hence, even as their coming hither;
> Ripeness is all : come on (V, iii, 9-11).

Gloucester is thus redeemed by his son Edgar and realizes the higher motives of life before his death.

Lear also faces two kinds of storms : the internal and the external. He regards the external storm as the mischievous trick of the "servile ministers." The storm that goes inside his mind shatters him so deep as he undergoes a ceaseless compunction in his body and mind. He thinks of his past karma and links them with the chain of his present ideas — a psychological process which Shakespeare has mastered beautifully in the character of Lear :

> Is man no more than this? Consider him well.
> Thou owest the worm, no silk, the beast no
> Hide, the sheep no wool, the cat not perfume....
> Thou art the thing itself (IV, iii, 15-19)

The moment external storm subsides, the storm in Lear's mind also subsides. This subsidence combines the higher prakriti with human nature. The merger of human and divine nature creates a disinterestedness in Lear's mind — a gradual process of *nirvana* itself. He now longs for his redemption — not a Christian redemption, but a universal regeneration which becomes synonymous to Indian concept of Moksha. Again, there comes the formation of another diagram :

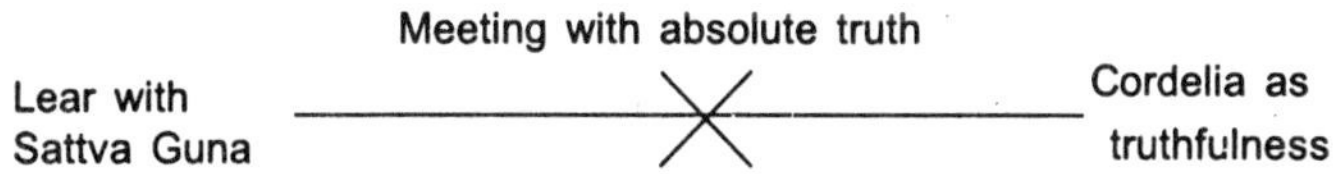

As a metallic gold, he finally associates with the higher principles of the Cordelia-consciousness. Now, he is fully relieved of the violent anger (*krodha*) of his mind and attains the attributes of soul. The doctor attending to the health of Lear also convinces the readers of the quieting wrath (tama) : "the great rage, you see, is kill'd in him" (IV, iii, 79-80). As a soul in bliss, Lear realizes the movement of an eternal wheel of karma and pleads Cordelia thus :

> You do me wrong to take me out O' grave :
> Thou art a soul in bliss; but I am bound
> Upon a Wheel of fire, that mine own tears
> Do scald like molten lead (IV, vii, 45-48)

The death of Goneril, Regan, Gloucester and Edmund stamps the theory of karma. They all meet their retributive justice, as they don't realize the movement of time. As Lear realizes the wheel of time; he kneels down before his daughter, Cordelia, and seeks her forgiveness. He feels abundance of pleasure to accompany Cordelia to prison house for knowing "the mystery of things" as if they were "God spies" (V, iii, 9-10). Lear's meeting with Cordelia symbolizes the moral principles of Fool. He actualizes the Fool-projection of his mind when he addresses Cordelia as a "poor fool." The death of Cordelia once again presents the scenic image in this tragedy. The scene showing the dead Cordelia in Lear's arms defies the range of language. The description of moral height and tragic elan is beyond the purview of the linguistic contents. Here is Lear who has been shown in intoxication with the Cordelia-principles of life :

> Why should a dog, a horse, a rat have a life;
> And thou no breath at all? Thou 'lt come no more,
> Never, never, never, never, never
> Pray you, undo this button....

Look on her, look her lips
Look there, look there ! (V, iii, 6-11)

As a regenerated soul, Lear attains his *nirvana* when he dies with the higher principles of life. He lives in doubt, but dies in faith. Again, Kent confirms the process of *nirvana* in Lear when he informs Albany after the death of Lear :

I have a journey, sir, shortly to go
My master calls me, I must not say no

As a matter of fact, Lear attains that equanimity of human mind which reflects the deactivation of senses, thoughts and desires. It is a stage which relieves Lear from ignorance (*tama*) and the following passions emerging from it : anger (*krodha*), greed (*lobha*), pride (*mada*) and delusion (*maya*). He finally triumphs over these sticky substances of lower life and relieves himself from all karmic particles. This confirms the attainment of his *nirvana*.

REFERENCES

1. Shakespeare, *King Lear : The Complete Works of William Shakespeare* (London : Oxford University Press, Y.N.). All the references are to this book. The references are mentioned inside the paper.
2. Sayed Mehdi Imam, *Mother India*, Vol. XI, No. 5, p. 61. Quoted from K.R.S. Iyengar, *Shakespeare : His World And His Art*. (New Delhi : Sterling Publishers Pvt. Ltd., 1964), p. 550.
3. Gerald S. Blum, *Psychodynamics : The Science of Unconscious Mental Forces*. (Delhi : Prentice-Hall of India Ltd., 1969), p. 57.
4. Jayadayal Goyandka, *Srimad Bhagavadgita* (Gorakhpur : Gita Press, 1976) Ch. 11, 12 & 13.
5. Maynard Mack, *King Lear in Our Time* (Los Angeles : University of California, 1972), pp. 94-95.
6. Gerald S. Blum, *op. cit.*, p. 5.
7. *Ibid.*, p. 42.
8. K.R.S. Iyengar, *op. cit.*, p. 475.
9. Chandradhar Sharma, *A Critical Survey of Indian Philosophy* (Delhi : Motilal Banarasidas Publishers Pvt. Ltd., Rpt. 1994), p. 81.

15

The Spirit of Reconciliation in the Last Plays of Shakespeare

—*Nivedita Mukerjee*

SHAKESPEARE, AFTER sounding the depths of sorrow, suffering and guilt in his tragedies, reached a state of serene self-possession which is the persistent note of the last plays — *Cymbeline*, *The Winter's Tale* and *The Tempest*. Shakespeare still thought of the graver trials and tests which life applies to human character, of the wrongs which man inflicts on man; but his present temper demanded not a tragic issue, — it rather demanded an issue into joy or peace. The dissonance must be resolved into a harmony, clear and rapturous, or solemn and profound. And, accordingly, in each of these plays, *The Winter's Tale*, *Cymbeline*, *The Tempest*, while grievous errors of the heart are shown to us, and wrongs of man to man as cruel as those of the great tragedies, at the end there is a resolution of the dissonance, a reconciliation. The resolution of the discords in these latest plays is not a mere stage necessity, or a necessity of composition, resorted to by the dramatist to effect an ending of his play. Its significance here is ethical and spiritual; it is a moral necessity.

The presence of evil in these plays is not ignored it is only minimized. The dissonances produced by the disturbing presence of evil in these plays have been resolved and the wronged have forgiven the wrongdoer. The protagonists of these plays have experience of evil, but learn to extend 'the quality of mercy' to those who do not deserve it. It is this spirit of reconciliation which makes of the happy ending not a stage device but a moral necessity. There is no cleavage between the tragedies and the romances, but the latter supplements to the former. The latest plays on the other hand have a blending of different planes of reality, of symbolism and the sense of solidity man derives from everyday occupations. The latest plays aim at a complete regeneration; at a melting of the old vessel and a recasting of it into something new.

Cymbeline though not the longest of Shakespeare's dramas, has the largest multiplicity of incidents. The plot is woven of three or four separate strands. There is the wager-story, involving jealousy, conspiracy to murder, repentance and reconciliation. There is the fairy-tale to the wicked step-mother and of the restoration of long-lost children to their father and their heritage. These two stories are wrought into a legendary history of Britain and her struggle with the Rome of Augutus Caesar. The heroine is partly a pagan princess, partly a modern woman with homely common sense, Jupiter and his chariot and the procession of Posthumus's relations belong to the world of the supernatural, Belarius and the two boys are idyllic, and the satirical picture of the court is realistic. The operation of Destiny which is not fettered by Time and Space can be traced in this play. What could be a more appropriate symbol of Destiny than the figure of Jupiter, riding on his eagle and swaying the fortunes of the British as well as the Roman forces? Jupiter controls not only nations but also individuals; Posthumus, Iachimo, the Queen and Pisanio may commit crimes and blunders, but Providence is sure to bring order out of chaos, place the rightful heir in possession of his heritage and then arrange for a final denouement in which the tangled affairs are rearranged, the villain is made to repent, and the inconvenient people alone are stowed away. It is an accident that Imogen meets her brothers before Cloten gets a chance of outraging her, and it is by no carefully laid plot that Posthumus and Belarius with the two Princes help to rescue Cymbeline and his army. Although Cornelius suspects the Queen's intentions, he too does not know the purpose for which he is asked to prepare the poison; his failure to carry out the instruction which saves Imogen is thus part of Jupiter's larger plan to 'cross' those whom he loves best. Posthumus would not have been completely reconciled to Imogen, if Iachimo had not turned up at the right moment to make a clean breast of his perfidy. These coincidences, which, to our limited human insight, seem to have no causal connection, are in fact, part of a cumbrous plan which Jupiter discloses towards the end of the play, and we note with pleasure that the chaotic miscellany is controlled by the king of the gods who has his own way of dealing with human affairs.

The title *The Winter's Tale* suggests a fancy story, an old woman's tale, its very unlikeliness being one of its charms. Probably a merry winter's tale would drive away the time trimly. On this very characteristic of improbability Shakespeare himself insists, beseeching, as it were, future commentators to spare their pains and not to take too seriously what may happen in his kingdoms of dreamland; it is all a tale, a fancy tale, a series of wonders strung together.... The most significant thing in Shakespeare's workmanship is the subtle manner in which he links human character to the workings of the will of Dame Fortune. Not only is she willing to promote human happiness but man's character is great enough to wrest happiness from her. Perdita, the shepherd, the Clown, Mopsa and Dorcas are inhabitants of an idyllic world that is as different from the world of pastoral convention as it is from Shakespeare's England or from any other society of real men and women. The principal feature of this wonderland is its happy innoncence, which can create joy out of anything, which refuses to be put down by continued poverty or sudden calamity. A noteworthy feature of this simple, poetical world is the close connection existing between the creative energy of man and the vitality of nature. It is little wonder that in such a Winter's Tale Destiny should be eager to relieve men and women in times of distress, and that the rogue himself should unwittingly be made an instrument of furthering the happiness of others. When, at the court of Leontes, a Lord enters to announce the arrival of Polixenes and Camillo, Florizel and Perdita are seized with despair, but it is soon revealed that heaven has set spies only to promote their interests, and that what appeared to human eyes as a chapter of accidents is for heaven, a long chain of cause and effect in which not a link has been lost. It is a part of the deep-laid scheme of Providence that, although the adult Antigonus is devoured by a bear and the ship is wrecked, the helpless infant escapes the fangs of the wild animal as well as the ravages of the tempest and is nursed by kindly people until she is suitably married, and restored to her parents.

The Tempest gives the completest expression to the mood of the final period : We must remember that it is Prospero who occupies the central position in it. When the play opens he has achieved complete mastery over the forces governing life. He is a man who is as omniscient and almighty as Destiny. He controls both natural and supernatural forces, the savage as well as the civilized man, external conduct no less than the workings of emotions. The creation of such a character gives us an ideally appropriate point of view for the perception of comedy. The love of Ferdinand and Miranda, the machinations of Antonio and Sebastian, the aspirations of Caliban, the agonies of the shipwrecked crew — these are all real and serious things, but, when we look at them from the vantage-ground which is Prospero's these grave realities appear to be a part of a vast phantasmagoria and drama becomes comedy. The first thing that strikes us in Prospero's magic is that his art is not something superimposed from without; it is a human achievement, the result of years of patient industry. Although he has attained superhuman wisdom and strength, he retains a human father's tenderness and anxiety for his child for whom he secures his lost dukedom and a husband who is heir to the Kingdom of Naples. In Miranda Shakespeare portrays the quintessential innocence of a woman who has been taught by a wise teacher but who has not been sophisticated by experience. For her everything is 'brave' and wonderful, because everything is new. In her passion for Ferdinand, Shakespeare tries to grasp the elemental thrill of a universal passion that has for others been dulled by convention. Ariel, a spirit of the air, is invisible to all except Prospero. He does what Prospero bids him, but makes it clear that he has no personal interest in his contrivances. Only once does he come near the human world, when he is all but touched with pity for human sufferings, but both he and his master are quick to stress the distance separating him from human beings. A thought which seems to run through the whole of *The Tempest*, appearing here and there like a coloured thread in the same web, is that the true freedom of man consists in service. Much more complex than Ariel is caliban, the disinherited savage, the 'servant-monster', 'plain fish', 'the tortoise', 'egged like a man and his fins like arms', with a very ancient and 'fish like smell.' Caliban has the three-fold role of an embodiment of the supernatural, a slave, and a dispossessed Indian. But why is he so incorrigibly hostile to Prospero? Why is he so unresponsive to the 'nurture' he has had from such a great teacher? It will be rash to think that he is by nature dull-witted because we find that even the most civilized person cannot be more sensitive to beauty of sight and sound than is this deformed slave. He has a remarkable personality, strong in will and emotion but singularly poor in intellectual judgement. He thinks that Stephano will be a fitting rival to Prospero, because both are alike in shape, and also because Stephano appeals to his sensuality by plying him with wine (II, ii, 126). It is significant that experience teaches him the difference between Prospero and Stephano, and at the end of the play he sincerely pleads for Prospero's forgiveness (V, i, 294-97).

Thus Shakespeare's final period reveals to us a man longing for spring, in nature and in the hearts of men; cherishing, the reality of the re-birth of nature, and the dream of reborn Man.... Not by any return to the past or the primitive will mankind be renewed, but by Nature's art working upon Nature to transmute it into Human Nature. Prospero is Imagination incarnate, using the animal and the spiritual to do its ministry, making Art subservient to the redemption and transformation of Man. Of Man redeemed and transformed the activity is Love : simple human love. Put to the test of theatrical performance, all three plays appear as plays of reconciliation and forgiveness.

16

Epic Affirmation in *Pericles*

—Basavaraj Naikar

ALTHOUGH CRITICS have doubted the complete authorship of the play by Shakespeare, there is no doubt that it has at least some element of Shakespearean contribution in it. *Pericles* has always been classed with the other last plays as it has many a family resemblance with them. Almost all the major features of the other last plays can be seen in *Pericles* in a miniature form. Hence the justification of the classification of the play as one of the last plays.

Pericles can be easily designated as an epical play because of the ingredient epic vision in it. It is, obviously, not a tragedy because of the presence of the non-tragic feature in it. Nor can it be said to be a successful drama, on account of its violation of many of the requirements of dramatic genre. Many a critic has pointed out the non-dramatic nature of the play and fit it into the pattern of a narrative romance etc. Sir Arthur Quiller-Couch says, "In *Pericles* our workman Shakespeare boldly lays hand on a theme proper to epic or the romantic novel."[1] Even when the play is accepted as belonging to the dramatic genre, it is never designated as a tragedy. On the contrary it is called by different labels. It is variously described as a 'myth of immortality,'[2] 'miracle play,'[3] 'parable of love,'[4] 'dramatic romance,'[5] 'expanded image'[6] of Shakespeare's mature vision and so on. Thus it defies an easy classification on account of its peculiar vision of life. In my view the play can be described as an epical play as it projects an affirmative vision indigenous to the epic form.

The plot of *Pericles,* somehow, does not agree with that of a normal play. Since it is informed by the epic vision of life, the plot, the characters, the events, the language and the style etc., are all affected by it as a result of which drama is compelled to become an instrument of the higher *i.e.*, epic vision. The story itself of the play defies dramatic treatment, as it is too vast and deep to be portrayed within the limits of the dramatic and theatrical form. The play deals with the ups and downs of Pericles' life. It affirms the ultimate ideals of life like truth, beauty and goodness. It does not, however, mean that the play has all the features that are indigenous to the epic form, because Shakespeare was not consciously aiming at the composition of an epic poem. The common description of the play as a tragi-comedy will not really do justice to the underlying vision of the same. Nor is it correct to classify it under the blanket term of "romance." There is no doubt a great deal of romantic element in it, but that does not help the reader to account for the serious view of life, which is not common to the romance form in general. Besides, romance itself can become part of a wider form of literature like epic.

Pericles offers us an epic vision by affirming the transcendental ideals of life like truth, beauty and goodness. Unlike the tragedy which negates the highest ideals of life, *Pericles* offers us an epic interpretation of life and makes the reader participate in life with a greater zest and courage. It is on account of the ingredient epic vision that the play transcends the limitation of the dramatic genre and reaches the epic height. The epic cannot affirm the transcendental ideals until and unless it has taken into account the whole of life either elaborately or briefly. *Pericles,* no doubt, creates an impression of the wholeness of life in an epic fashion. Since Shakespeare had crossed the border of his forties, his tragic imagination had matured into epic imagination. His Dionysiac imagination matured into Apollonian imagination.[7] That is exactly the reason why there is such a remarkable difference between his tragedies and his last plays. As *Pericles* is the earliest of the last plays, it is not as ripe as the last of the last plays, nonetheless it is decidedly different from the preceding plays like *Coriolanus* and *Antony and Cleopatra.* As Shakespeare's tragic vision was ripening into an epic one; he made his own adaptations in the dramatic form. That is the reason why many of the dramatic features were violated and adapted to the expression of his epic vision.

The epic affirmation of the transcendental ideals of Truth, Beauty and Goodness involves the inevitable negation of the negative values like falsehood, ugliness and evil. The epic vision not only includes the tragic vision but other aspects of life as well. Tillyard's description of the last plays of Shakespeare as 'reversal of tragic pattern,'[8] is not satisfactory, as they go beyond the limits of tragic comedies and attain the epical width, depth and resonances in their diverse details. *Pericles* cannot be called a tragedy in spite of the presence of a good deal of tragic element in it. In fact, the first part of *Pericles* can itself become an independent tragedy. But the complete play does not present a tragic vision because of the epic turn it takes in the latter half. Whereas the tragic pattern shows the conflict between Good and Evil resulting in the triumph of Evil over Good, the epic pattern shows the transcendence of the tragic pattern through its reversal. In other words, the epic pattern shows the ultimate triumph of Good over Evil through the transformation of Evil into Good or into an instrument of Good. Although there is a lot of evil in the world of *Pericles,* it is thrown into insignificance by the wider scheme of the universe presented in it. Initially Evil is very powerful and goes to the extent of even overpowering Good. All the events of *Pericles* testify to this phenomenon. When Pericles, for example, discovers the incestuous relationship between King Antiochus and his daughter, evil asserts itself and tries to destroy good. It is expressed in the King's desire to get Pericles murdered. But Pericles instantly escapes from the kingdom, as he is not in a position to fight with the king immediately. Similarly when Pericles learns that his dear wife is dead, he is so helpless that he does not know what to do. But nonetheless he writes a scroll and puts it in the coffin of his wife. Likewise when Pericles leaves his child Marina with Cleon, the Governor of Tharsus and his wife, evil again makes its presence felt. When Marina grows into a pretty young girl, Dionyza grows jealous of her as she (Marina) is far more beautiful than her own daughter *i.e.*, Philoten. She, therefore, tries to get rid of her by getting her murdered. She appoints a man called Leonine to accomplish the evil task. Again evil is seen here trying to destroy good. When Marina is taken to a brothel at Mytilene, she is compelled by the brothel-keepers to sleep with the local officer. In all these instances evil is bent upon humiliating, overpowering and even destroying good. Had it succeeded in doing so, it could have been a very effective tragedy. But Shakespeare's epic imagination could see the whole truth and not the partial one, he, therefore went a step ahead to show the full circle of action.

But tragedy has been given an epic turn in that all the tragic or evil forces are negated by the positive or good forces. In the epic universe of *Pericles* the evil is not only negated but transcended in that it turns out to be an instrument of good. For example good cannot be destroyed by evil so easily in an epic world. In *Pericles* Antiochus does not succeed in having Pericles murdered as Pericles escapes from the kingdom before that happens. Evil is obviously negated by good here. Similarly, when the death of Thaisa is announced to Pericles, he feels extremely sad and wonders at the strange course of life. The illusion of an evil *i.e.* an unexpected and undeserved death of an innocent lady is created in the play. All the subsequent thoughts, feelings and actions of Pericles are affected by the so-called death of his wife. But evil is not going to ruin him. On the contrary it is going to strengthen good in the future. The audience knows that Thaisa is not really dead and that she has become a priestess in Diana's temple. Likewise, when Marina is taken away from home by

Leonine to be killed, evil is thwarted by good in the form of the pirates who snatch away Marina from Leonine. Marina's life is saved by the unexpected arrival of these sailors. But the story does not end there. Although Marina escaped the danger, her virginity is very much in danger. The innocent Marina is taken to a brothel at Mytilene where she is compelled to 'crack the glass of virginity.' But the extraordinary courage and the unshakeable will of Marina enable her to withstand those evil temptations. She is so adherent to her principles that she cannot be overwhelmed by the debauchees of the brothel. Because of her high moral stature and integrity she becomes almost a saint in the eyes of the brothel-keepers. Later on Pericles goes to Mytilene where he is taken by Lysimachus to Marina whom he recognizes to be his own lost daughter. Pericles is, obviously, overjoyed to be united with his daughter. He begins to hear the music of spheres and falls asleep. Directed in his dream by Diana, he goes to the Temple of Diana at Delphi where he is again shocked into ecstasy when he discovers his wife to be alive. The natural evils like the death of Thaisa and the loss of Marina have turned out to be beneficiary and happy events. In all these events the evils like jealousy (of Antiochus for Pericles; of Dionyza for Marina), sensuousness (of the brothel-keepers and the customers), the untimely death (of Thaisa) and the unexpected loss (of Marina) are negated by the higher values like precaution (of Pericles), kindness (of Leontes), the virginity (of Marina), the natural recovery of life (by Thaisa) and the fellow-feeling (of Lychorida) etc. In the conflict between the lower and negative values and the higher and positive values, the former are negated by the latter. In the conflict between good and evil, evil far from thwarting or destroying good, intensifies and contributes to good. Thus although there is a good deal of evil in *Pericles* it never attracts our attention towards itself. It becomes insignificant in the larger scheme of the epic universe. *Pericles* therefore, offers a picture of a balance between the opposite poles of life. Evil occupies its due place in it and remains part of the cosmic harmony.

It may be pointed out here that both good and evil are seen working both within and outside man. These opposites working within man are expressed in his thoughts and feelings, speech and action. His psychology which is revealed in his behaviour is obviously influenced by his ethics. The same ethical principle takes the form of supernatural beings especially gods when it is expressed outside man. Let us take the ethical aspect first. The ethics of the many characters of *Pericles* is epical in that it is quite idealistic. In fact it may be said that they practise what Schopenhauer calls, "sublime ethics."[9] Obviously Pericles, Marina, Lord Cerimon, Lychorida and other characters who exhibit the 'sublime ethics' in that their life is characterized by affirmative thought, feeling, speech, and action. They have an innate sense of the right, the beautiful and the good. It is on account of the immense strength of their idealism that they are able to counteract, thwart and even transform the evils created by the other set of characters that practise hedonistic and materialistic ethics. The encounters between idealism and hedonism are either narrated by Gower, or enacted in the dumb show or presented directly on the stage. When, for example, Pericles reads the riddle and expresses his disapproval of Antiochus' incestuous relation with his own daughter and of the resultant hypocrisy, Antiochus grows afraid of his royal reputation being tarnished. Far from rectifying his behaviour and repenting, he wants to hide the truth and have the truth-speaker *i.e.* Pericles murdered. The principle of selfishness in Antiochus triumphs over the principle of the selfless code of conduct. Not having any scruples, he decides to get Pericles murdered. Antiochus thinks and therefore speaks negatively. He says :

> He has found the meaning,
> For which we mean to have his head. He must
> Live to trumpet forth my infamy,
> Nor tell the world Antiochus doth sin

In such a loathed manner;
And therefore instantly this prince must die;
For by his fall my honor must keep high.

(I, ii, 144-51)

His negative speech, which is the expression of his negative thought, goads him to indulge in negative action. He orders a lord namely Thaliard to murder Pericles. He tells him :

Thaliard, behold here's poison, and here's gold;
We hate the prince of Tyre, and thou must kill him :
It fits thee not to ask the reason why :
Because we bid it. Say, is it done?

(I, i, 156-59)

But this selfish ethics is counteracted by the idealistic ethics as a result of which Pericles has already left the kingdom before Antiochus could do anything to his person. Obviously the evil has defeated its own purpose.

Similarly when Pericles believes the news that Thaisa is dead, he sends away the dead body in a boat along with a scroll requesting the finders of the same to give her a decent burial. Accordingly when Lord Cerimon comes to know the entire affair, he begins to indulge in affirmative action of burying her. But when she recovers her consciousness, he advises her to go to the Temple of Diana at Delphi. Thus the affirmative action of the characters like Cerimon gives an unexpectedly happy turn to the course of events in the play. Likewise when Marina learns that she is going to be murdered, she is really puzzled as to why she, who is so harmless, should be singled out. Her words testify to her affirmative thinking inspired by her 'sublime ethics.' There is no difference whatever between her outlook and a saint's :

I never did hurt in all my life.
I never spake bad word, nor did ill turn
To any living creature; believe me la,
I never kill'd a mouse, nor hurt a fly;

I trod upon a worm against my will,
But I wept for't.

(IV, i, 74-79)

Marina shows the same sterling quality in the brothel when she is made to receive a customer, Lysimachus. Far from being tempted to yield, she preserves her integrity. She faces the ordeal of her life quite heroically. Her words easily testify to her ideals;

For me,
That am a maid, though most ungentle fortune
Have plac'd me in this sty, where, since I came,
Diseases have been sold dearer than physic —
That the gods
Would set me free from this unhallowed place,
Though they did change me to the meanest bird
That files i'th' purer air!

(IV, vi, 94-101)

Her moral is so high that even the customer who has come there to rob her of her virginity realizes her greatness and integrity. He says :

Thou art a piece of virtue, and
I doubt not but thy training hath been noble.

(IV, vi, 111-12)

The sublime ethics which involves the pursuit of the high ideals of life and the practice of affirmative thought, speech and action reveals the epical nature of the behaviour of the characters and testifies to the operation of Good from within man. Commenting on Marina's sterling integrity and essential gracefulness, K.R. Srinivasa Iyengar rightly says that "tempest-born Marina-like 'nectar' in Indian mythology coming out of the churned ocean *i.e.* 'absolute Marina'; she is the grace of Grace, she is the symbol of the Resurrection greater than the life that is dead."[10]

Man's thoughts, feelings and action are symbolized by natural and supernatural element also. The supernatural beings like gods are seen to be directing the behaviour of the characters in *Pericles* in the epic fashion. Like the Greek gods directing the activities of the Homeric heroes, Goddess Diana appears in Pericles' dream and asks him to go to Diana's temple at Delphi. The supernatural beings obviously act as the embodiments of the principles of Good inspiring and directing the human beings along the right path towards the destiny of which human beings themselves are unaware. Gods in *Pericles* therefore, act as the providers not only of the highest ideals of life but also of the sublime ethics required for the achievement of those ideals. As Allardyce Nicolls rightly comments about the last plays, "Often in them we have an impression that we are floating away into a realm of the spirit and we are coming very close to the world of gods."[11] Thus the metaphysical principle of Good expresses itself not only in the sublime ethics but in the supernatural operation also.

The result of the negation of the lower values of life and the affirmation of the higher or transcendental values cannot bring anything other than a sense of fulfilment and supreme happiness. It is on account of the triumph of the transcendental values over the lower ones that *Pericles* is prevented from becoming a tragedy and is made to assume an epical stature. The lost wife and child are recovered; the so-called dead are reborn; the prince who had left the kingdom is returning home. All these events show the transformation of tragedy into epic and of tears into smiles. The play shows the goodness, the meaningfulness and the beauty of life by affirming the higher values like love, sympathy, cooperation, virginity, truthfulness, fraternity, moral heroism etc. When Pericles learns that his so-called dead wife is alive, that his daughter has grown into not only a pretty girl but a paragon of virtue; and that king Antiochus is dead and gone, he is shocked into a happy realization of the moral order of the universe symbolized by the music of the spheres. He almost attains the divine stature in that blissful experience. In fact, he feels the highest joy of his life, which is the result of his adherence to the transcendental principles. As G.A. Baker avers, "The music of the spheres, which appears only in Shakespeare's version, suggests a higher reality, which *Pericles* now apprehends."[12] On recognizing Marina, he bursts out :

O Helicanus, strike me, honour'd sir!
Give me a gash, put me to present pain,
Lest this great sea of joys rushing upon me
O'erbear the shores of my mortality,
And drown me with their sweetness.

(V, i, 190-94)

Pericles' joy at the reunion with his wife and child obviously gives him an ecstatic pleasure, which blurs the demarcation between mortality and immortality. This experience easily resembles the experience of bliss or *brahmananda* of a yogi, which is too sweet to be explicable in words. Pericles realizes the essential and transcendental harmony of the universe in spite of all the apparently disconnected events that have happened in his life. He, therefore, uses the musical analogy to express his awareness of the cosmic harmony.

Per. ...But what music?
Hel. My lord, I hear none.
Per. None?
The music of the spheres! List, my Marina.
Lys. It is not good to cross him; give him way.
Per. Rarest sounds! Do ye not hear?
Per. Most heavenly music!
It nips me into list'ning, and thick slumber
Hangs upon my eyes; let me rest. (sleeps)

(V, i, 225-33)

Overwhelmed by the inexplicable sweetness of the joy, Pericles falls asleep. In this brief, because dramatic scene, Shakespeare has endeavoured to show the transcendental joy of life by affirming the higher values of life. The sense of fulfilment is born out of the awareness of the ultimate beauty, goodness and meaningfulness of his life. Although Pericles' escape from the kingdom of Antioch and his loss of wife and child seem to have created in him a tragic illusion of life, all those seemingly tragic events have gradually and invisibly contributed to the epic harmony and design of life. Pericles' adherence to the affirmative values and hence his idealistic ethics have enabled him to attain the highest 'joy' of life which is equivalent to the *satchidananda* of the Indian concept. Shakespeare's vision is, therefore, affirmative in the sense that it makes the reader participate in life with greater enthusiasm and realize that life is a matter of joy forever. It affirms the validity of human life and the possibility of the elevation of the human life to the divine level. This sense of fulfilment is the special privilege of the epic hero who is an embodiment of the transcendental values of life and whose ultimate success signifies the final victory of good over evil, beauty over ugliness, and truth over falsehood. Pericles resembles the epic heroes like Aeneas and Rama as far as his joy of success and reunion is concerned, although there may be diverse differences with regard to other details. Just as the epic hero is a secular equivalent of the saint or the mystic or the yogi, the epic vision can also be a secular equivalent of the religious or mystic vision. As far as the 'ecstasy' or 'joy' of the epic hero and of the saint is concerned there is not much difference though the ways in which it is attained are slightly different.

The ultimate joy of life attained by Pericles cannot be shown until and unless the entire life span of the hero is depicted elaborately or otherwise. The ultimate concerns of life can become clear to the reader only when life is shown in its entirety or wholeness. *Pericles* thus fulfils the requirements of an epic vision as it deals with the whole truth. In other words, it depicts not the half or one-sided life of Pericles but the complete span of his life. The play assumes the epic wholeness simply because of its concern with the entire cycle of Pericles' life with a concentration on the latter part of his life. It shows not merely the tragic suffering of Pericles on account of his discovery of Antiochus' incestuous love for his own daughter and of the loss of his wife and child, but also the ultimate success and joy of life achieved by Pericles on account of his own sublime behaviour and the supernatural help extended to him. Thus the ultimate picture of Pericles' life is possible only through the depiction of the whole life of his. Since Shakespeare wanted to show the whole truth in his play, he was unconsciously compelled to show the harmony between the human, the natural and the supernatural levels of life. Shakespeare knew that human life couldn't be treated isolatedly because of its inextricable relation with the other levels of existence in the cosmos. Similarly he depicts the entirety of life by dealing not only with the tragic and the comic but also with the satiric, the marvellous, the tranquil etc. His concern with the whole truth can be seen with regard to his characterization also. Many of the characters like Pericles, Thaisa, Marina, Helicanus etc., are the whole beings in that they are the integrated ones in whom there can be seen a harmony between instinct, reason and intuition. It is on account of their integrity or unity of being that they are not frustrated even in the most dire moments of their life. They enjoy a spiritual health, which is so conspicuously missing in a tragic hero. That is exactly the reason why they enjoy a spiritual security of the epic heroes and characters and never go mad like Hamlet or Macbeth etc. Thus *Pericles* obviously testifies to Shakespeare's concern with the whole truth which expresses itself both in plot and in characterization.

Since only depicting the whole of life can show the whole truth, *Pericles* is known for its epic inclusiveness. It refers in brief to everything of life that a man can afford to know. Whereas the tragedies like *Hamlet, Macbeth, Othello* and *King Lear* depict the exclusiveness of the individual principle, *Pericles* like the other last plays, depicts the principles of inclusiveness and interrelatedness and hence the concordance of life according to which the individual is seen in relation to the wider context of the human, the natural and the supernatural life. The epic hero's life is obviously connected with the life of the other characters also. *Pericles,* in its own limited fashion, creates an illusion that everything has a place for it and everything is in its own place. It, for example, depicts not merely the tragic or the comic sentiment but other sentiments as well, like the marvellous (*adbhuta*), the disgusting (*bibhatsa*), the tranquil (*santa*), the amorous (*sringara*), and the heroic (*vira*), etc. Pericles' love for Antiochus' daughter and his later falling in love with Thaisa and the eventual marriage, of course, evoke the amorous atmosphere in the play. When Simonides meets Pericles after sending away all the knights who had aspired for the hand of his daughter in the competition, he tells him about his daughter's fascination for him :

> Sir, my daughter thinks very well of you;
> Ay, so well, that you must be her master,
> And she will be your scholar : therefore look to it.
>
> (II, v, 37-39)

Afterwards Simonides arranges their marriage. All this phenomenon contributes to the amorous element of the play and easily reminds us of the Sanskrit plays. The heroic sentiment also has a place in the play. It can be seen in Pericles' frequent sea-adventures and the consequent suffering in the tempests. Although he does not fight with any enemy physically he has been made to fight with the evil forces. In none of these wars does he get defeated or humiliated on account of his adherence to the affirmative values of life. His heroism is more moral than physical. Pericles' ultimate success and happiness are ascribable to his moral heroism itself. The pathetic (*karuna*) sentiment is evoked in the context in which Marina implores Leonine not to kill her, as she has not harmed anyone in her life. The ferocious (*raudra*) sentiment is evoked in the tempest scenes wherein Pericles' ship is tossed to and fro and causes many a calamity in his family life. The tragic (*karuna*) sentiment is, of course, created in the situations where Antiochus plans the murder of Pericles and appoints a lord to poison him; where Pericles loses his wife and child most unexpectedly; where Dionyza wants to have Marina murdered etc. All these events, no doubt, contribute to the element of sorrow in life. Likewise the comic (*hasya*) sentiment is caused by the situations like the ones in which the lowly characters like Pander, Bawd and Boult discuss among themselves the importance of the feminine flesh in the lust-market. Their lighthearted discussion about the commercial significance of a woman's body, of course, evokes laughter in the spectators. Then the odious (*bibhatsa*) sentiment is evoked in the brothel where the keepers impel her to "crack the glass of her virginity." A highly innocent and integrated soul like Marina being made to be the central figure of the most debaucherous institute creates the odious sentiment. The marvellous (*adbhuta*) sentiment is evoked in the context where Pericles sees and hears the goddess *i.e.* Diana in his dream and is shocked into happiness by the strange course of events. When he goes to the Temple of Diana at Delphi, he is wonderstruck to know that his so-called dead wife is very much alive. At last, there is a place in *Pericles* for the sentiment of tranquillity (*santa*) also. When Pericles recovers his wife and daughter he feels a sense of fulfilment and spiritual quietude. He hears the music of spheres and falls asleep. Thus the play comes to have an epic comprehensiveness by depicting all the nine sentiments as enjoined by the Indian aesthetics. The totality of life suggested however briefly in *Pericles* naturally helps Shakespeare to arrive at the whole truth.

The illusion of the totality of life created by Shakespeare in *Pericles* concomitantly involves the complexity and the multiplicity of life thereby suggesting the underlying metaphysical foundation. *Pericles* suggests the reconciliation of contrarieties[13] or metaphysical poles at the extremes of the hierarchy of life. The unity of life is possible only when the opposite principles of life are reconciled to each other. This epic principle of the reconciliation of contradictions can be seen operative in *Pericles* with regard to plot, characterization and technique. *Pericles* depicts the great and the low; the far and the near; the tragic and the comic; the noble and the profane; the rural and the urban; the real and the fantastic; the demoniac and the angelic etc. The genuine love of Thaisa for Pericles provides a sharp contrast to the debaucherous atmosphere of the brothel where no genuine love is possible. The murderous people like Antiochus and Dionyza are contrasted with the saviours and protectors like Lychorida and others. The princes and dukes like Pericles; Simonides and Helicanus etc. are contrasted with the low ones like Pimp, Pander, Boult etc. The land (*i.e.* Antioch, Pentapolis and Mytilene) is easily contrated with the sea. The court of Antiochus provides a good contrast to the country life (*i.e.* Mytilene). The epic principle of the reconciliation of contradictions can be found with regard to the characterization also. Many of the major characters like Pericles and Antiochus are a combination of the real and the ideal. Although Shakespeare borrowed these characters from the history (*itihasa*) he has infused his own ideals (*purana*) into them. That, in fact, testifies to the epic nature of the play. The supernatural element contributes to the epic atmosphere of the play. The supernatural beings like gods and goddesses play an important role in human life by frequently interfering in the human affairs. The play obviously shows the epic harmony between the human and the supernatural levels of life. Man acts as a member of the cosmic life. This epic pattern has been shown by Shakespeare with a few modifications, which are necessitated by the limitation of the dramatic form. Unlike in epics where gods and goddesses appear on the scene physically, they appear in *Pericles* only metaphorically, symbolically or in dreams etc. Goddesses in *Pericles* guide and direct the human beings along the right lines and therefore act as their moral referees and ideals. Pericles, for example, has a latent faith in the supernatural world, which testifies to his cultivation of the intuitive or supra-rational faculty. Unlike the tragic hero like Hamlet or Macbeth who refuses to believe in anything higher than the egoistic and the irrational, Pericles has a firm belief in the supra-rational attitude to life which enables him to accept the superior order of life. It is only on account of the implicit faith in the higher order of life, which appears like mystery that Pericles does not lose his balance of mind even in the midst of great dangers and calamities. When Pericles is sea-tossed, he, far from cursing the gods, implores them to pacify the sea. His supplication almost has the tone of a prayer :

The god of this great vast, rebuke these surges,
Which wash both heaven and hell; and thou that hast
Upon the wind command, bind them in brass,
Having call'd them from the deep!

(III, i, 1-4)

Similarly, when Pericles loses his wife in the sea-storm, he interrogates the supernatural authorities about the strange and unexpected events happening in human life :

O you gods!
Why do you make us love your godly gifts,
And snatch them straight away? We here below
Recall not what we give and therein may
Use honour with you.

(III, i, 22-26)

When Dionyza refers to the late Thaisa, Pericles reveals his belief in the supernatural guidance of human life :

We cannot but obey
The powers above us. Could I rage and rover
As doth the sea she lies in, yet the end
must be as 'tis.

(III, iii, 9-12)

Although he never ceases to struggle with the evil forces, he believes in the invisible order of the universe and pleads for the concordance of human behaviour with the divine scheme. That is the reason why he allows himself to be directed by the divine orders. When Diana appears to him in a vision, Pericles naturally has no hesitation whatsoever in obeying her. As pointed out by J.F. Danby, "Diana is the tutelary goddess of the last plays."[14] Diana speaks to him in his vision :

> My temple stands in Euphesus; hie thee hither,
> And do upon mine altar sacrifice.
> There, when my maiden priests are met together,
> Before the people all,
> Reveal how thou at sea didst lose thy wife.
> To mourn thy crosses, with thy daughter's call
> And give them repetition to the life.
> Or perform my bidding, or tho liv'st in woe;
> Do't and happy; by my silver bow!
> Awake, and tell thy dream.
>
> (V, i, 238-47)

Pericles feels overwhelmed with the joy of the unexpected turn of events. So he says :

> Celestial Dian, goddess argentine,
> I will obey thee.
>
> (V, i, 248-49)

Pericles realizes that the course of events runs exactly according to the words of Diana. He is shocked into happiness when he recovers his queen and his daughter. Now his belief in the supernatural control of the human life is confirmed. He cannot help but express his thanks to the goddess :

> Pure Dian,
> I bless thee for thy vision, and will offer
> Night oblations to thee.
>
> (V, iii, 68-71)

Like Pericles, Marina also invokes gods and goddesses whenever she is in difficulty. She prays to the gods to release her from the brothel where she is compelled to feast the customers on her body. She says to Lysimachus who wants to rob her of her virginity :

> For me
> That am a maid, though most ungentle fortune
> Have place'd me in this sty, where, since I came,

Diseases have been sold dearer than physic —
That the gods
Would set me free from this unhallowed place,
Though they did change me to the meanest bird
That flies; i'th' purer air!

(IV, vi, 95-101)

Thus the supernatural element plays an important role in the play in that it makes its appearance either in human dreams or as spiritual or moral references. It is precisely because of the harmony between the human and the supernatural world that Pericles enjoys a sort of spiritual security, which is denied to the tragic hero. The line of demarcation between finitude and infinitude is very thin in *Pericles*. Whereas the gods appearing in the human world denotes the infinitude passing into the finitude and the human beings growing into the status of gods denotes the merger of finitude into Infinity. When reunited with his queen and daughter Pericles feels so ecstatic that he feels he transcends the bounds of mortality and reaches the height of immortality. He says to Lysimachus :

Give me a gash, put me to present pain,
Lest this great sea of joys rushing upon me
O'erbear the shores of my mortality,
And drown me with their sweetness.

(V, i, 191, 194)

The joy felt by Pericles is easily comparable to the divine bliss or ecstasy of a saint or a monk. Pericles, therefore, attains the stature of a man-god although a passive one at that. Although Shakespeare has not consciously worked out this pattern, he has hinted at the possibility of the mortal beings achieving immortality within the framework of drama.

Pericles can be accepted as an epic hero on account of his representativeness. "The epic hero is strictly speaking, never an individual. It is traditionally thought that one of the essential characteristics of the epic is in the fact that its theme is not a personal destiny but the destiny of a community."[15] Shakespeare gives him epic stature by not making him a mere individual with his private concerns, but by infusing national qualities in him. Pericles is not a mere man but a representative of a type. Since he is a prince there is not much difference between his personal self and national self. In fact both of these selves affect and are affected by each other. Pericles' dislike of King Antiochus' incest with his daughter is as much personal as national. In other words, King Antiochus' incestuous relationship with his daughter hurts the national sentiments of the people and Pericles obviously symbolizes the national dislike. Later on, after the death of King Antiochus and his daughter, Pericles takes the responsibility of running the kingdom of Antioch. He takes up the reins of administration in his hands and provides peace to his subjects. Pericles thus, ends up as a king of Antioch. He becomes an epic hero as he represents the national sentiments, national ethics and national responsibility, much in the manner of Rama returning to Ayodhya after regaining Sita from the clutches of Ravana by vanquishing him.

Shakespeare wants to deal with the whole truth, which can be shown only through the depiction of life, which happens to be going on at different times and places simultaneously or consecutively. The epic action of *Pericles* cannot be confined to a single day and a single spot. Act I begins with Antioch and goes on shifting from there to Tyre, Tharsus, Pentapolis, Ephesus and Mytilene etc. All these cities are obviously connected with the main events of Pericles' life and testify to the epic largeness of space. Similarly, Shakespeare tries to grapple with the whole truth by capturing the large entities of time. There is nearly sixteen years gap between Act III, scene iv and Act IV, scene i, which shows the growth of Marina from the stage of a baby to that of a young girl. Again there is a gap of a few years between Act IV scene iii and Act IV, scene iv which shows Pericles' return to Tyre as the king and his subsequent search for his daughter. The large units of time such as these are obviously evidence of the epic concept of time. Thus both the spatial and the temporal width enable Shakespeare to show the relatively larger portions of human life thereby suggesting the wholeness of the underlying truth.

It is because of the variety, complexity and depth of the theme that Pericles comes to create an illusion of the wholeness of life and thereby create an awareness of the metaphysical poles like good and evil. The symbolic structure of the play makes the reader aware of the deeper questions of life. It is on account of the profundity of the issue dealt with that the play comes to have the philosophical stature of an epic. Unlike the earlier comedies, *Pericles* disturbs the reader and sets him thinking on the serious moral and metaphysical questions of life. Thus it not only entertains the audience but even instructs him by disturbing him after he leaves the theatre. In this respect it is easily comparable to the epic theatre of Brecht.[16] The play, for example, raises the fundamental questions like — why there is so much evil in life? What is the nature of Evil? What is the role of Good in life? What is the ultimate consequence of the struggle between Good and Evil? Is it possible for man to achieve happiness in this life in spite of a variety of hindrances? Is life worth-living and beautiful? etc. It is such basic questions, which the play raises that give an epic profundity to it. No sensitive reader can help asking these questions : Why should king Antiochus be in incestuous relation with his own daughter? Why should Pericles be the cause of king Antiochus' wrath? Why should Marina be taken to a brothel and made to sacrifice her virginity? Why is it that Pericles is not heartbroken in spite of having lost his wife and child? What are the implicit values that guide him through the ups and downs of life? Does he achieve what he wants? Such basic questions can provide ample food for philosophers, theologists, and metaphysicians.

The play has many major events either shown on the stage or hinted at which assume the archetypal importance thereby contributing to the epic atmosphere of the play. It is on account of the archetypal themes that *Pericles* comes to have a similarity with the major epics of the world. As Stanley Wells says, "The *Odyssey* itself is (like *Pericles*) the story of a voyage and its hero's reunion with his wife."[17] The theme of 'journey' is an archetypal one in the play. Pericles, for example, goes on the sea-journey from Antioch to Tyre, Tharsus, Mytilene etc. The sea and the storm-tossed ship are, obviously, archetypal concomitants of the journey theme. Pericles' sea-journey easily reminds of us the journeys of other epic heroes like Aeneas, Odysseus, Rama and Yudhisthira etc. Pericles' journey is not a merely physical journey but, on the contrary, it comes to have symbolic and hence spiritual significance also. In a way "journey" is to the epic hero what 'pilgrimage' is to the saint. It may even be said that 'journey' and 'pilgrimage' can be used synonymously. As pointed out by M.C. Bradbrook Pericles' journey is "a mixture of an Odyssey and a Pilgrim's Progress...."[18] Pericles' journey from Antioch to Tyre, to Tharsus, Mytilene, Pentapolis and Ephesus etc., shows a certain but gradual maturity of the soul. Pericles achieves at the end of his journey what the saint or the believer achieves at the end of his pilgrimage. Thus the sea-journey of Pericles symbolically suggests the epic truth about the 'process' and the 'becoming' of life through which are suggested the transcendental 'reality' and 'being' of life.

The journey theme in *Pericles* is connected with the theme of exile. Pericles' departure from the home country is equivalent to an exile in that it makes him undergo a great deal of trouble. Pericles naturally has the exile psychology and experiences a temporary crisis. He is alienated from King Antiochus and the kingdom of Antioch. This sort of physical alienation purifies his soul and gives him the strength of soul to face the multiplicity of troubles and hurdles caused by the human evil as well as the natural evil. In this respect he is easily comparable to Aeneas, Odysseus, Rama and Yudhisthira who also go into exile which is real or metaphorical. But the degree of the experience of exile undergone by Pericles is greater than that of Rama and Yudhisthira in that he is separated not only from his kingdom but from his wife and daughter also. He is under the impression that his wife is really dead. Although the death of Thaisa is announced in the fashion of a romance, the effect of this event upon the mind of Pericles is really terrible and shocks him beyond measure. Likewise he is forced to live away from his beloved daughter Marina. Thus the great sense of loss and the resultant feeling of emotional starvation and extra-ordinary loneliness felt by Pericles are suggested if not worked out elaborately by Shakespeare. This exile experience undergone by him assumes epical importance in that it corresponds to the dark night of the soul, which is going to be followed by the ultimate stage of illumination. Pericles' exile is not the exile of the modern existentialistic hero, but the one that has been purifying and strengthening his soul. The exile serves a positive role in the play and prepares the way for the final joy and happiness of life.

The theme of war is very much present in *Pericles,* although the manifestation of the same is not as blatant here as it is in tragedies. Throughout the play the war is operative between Good and Evil. Pericles has to fight the inimical forces symbolized in Antiochus' incest and all his subsequent escapes are impelled by that original problem. In addition to the indulgence in war with human beings, Pericles has to fight the natural forces also like the sea and the storm, which symbolize the element of mystery and unexpectedness of life. It is these natural forces which cause the separation between Pericles and his wife and daughter. Thus although there is no presentation of a physical war taking place on a battlefield, the principle of war is felt throughout the play. But it should be remembered that Shakespeare has not somehow cared to develop this theme systematically or elaborately. Although Pericles does not appear to be as impressive as other epic heroes like Aeneas or Rama or Yudhisthira are, his heroism consists in his opposition of evil and his ingredient adherence to good. The ultimate victory that he wins is mainly due to his potential integrity or wholeness. Many critics have not endeavoured to understand Pericles from this point of view. They have even complained that he is rather a passive hero. There is, of course, no denying that. But the nature and level of his heroism need to be understood properly. He is easily comparable to the other epic heroes like Adam and Faust who are also passive in nature, but ultimately win the war on account of their adherence to the transcendental values of life, and obedience to divine direction. In fact his passivity may be interpreted as an expression of his patience. As J.F. Danby explains, "In *Pericles* it is patience in adversity which is the dominating motif."[19]

The theme of homecoming, which is one of the invariable items of epic literature, could also be found in *Pericles*. The homecoming is suggested through the concomitants of the same. Pericles comes home not merely physically but psychologically and spiritually also. After winning the war with the evil forces, Pericles succeeds in getting back to his kingdom. King Antiochus has died and made things convenient for Pericles who can go and settle in his kingdom now. Thus his homecoming is facilitated by the eventual avoidance of the hindrances. The other concomitants of homecoming like the recovery of the lost ones and the reunion of the separated ones add to the joy of homecoming. Pericles recovers his wife Thaisa who is supposed to be dead. Similarly he recovers his daughter Marina who has grown to be a pretty young girl. Thus Pericles is at last reunited with his wife and daughter and the resultant joy is really beyond description and comparison. The sorrow of having lost the paradise is followed by the joy of having regained the same. Recovery and reunion are part of the homecoming theme, which is itself symbolic of the affirmation of the transcendental values like Truth, Goodness and Beauty involving the negation of Falsity, Evil and Ugliness. With *Pericles* Shakespeare's vision has changed from the tragic to the epical.

Thus the epic themes of journey, exile, war and

homecoming etc., naturally contribute to the epic atmosphere of the play. Although these themes are scattered over in the early plays, they do not appear there in the same sequence and have the same significance.

Pericles captures the ethos of the Elizabethan age by referring to the diversified interests of the said age, in the fashion of an epic. Although Shakespeare does not do this deliberately or consciously, his unconscious but epic genius has observed as much of the life around him as possible. The play, for example, contains a variety of references and allusions to the classical, the Biblical, the Neo-Platonic and the secular customs, beliefs and thoughts which went into the making of Elizabethan ethos. That is the reason why the economics, astrology, social sciences, cosmology, sports and entertainments are all reflected in *Pericles* though in a brief fashion. The references to the classical lore like Hesperides, Venus, Priapus, Neptune's feast, and Neptune's triumph etc., are quite common in the play. Side by side with the classical allusions, there are many an allusion to the Biblical wisdom like light versus evil, burial, (divine) calling etc., which obviously add a Christian tinge to the play. Besides, there are many details of Neo-Platonic beliefs. For example, the thought that virtue was supposed to be greater than richness was popularized by the medieval but neo-Platonic philosopher Boethius (Cerimon's words). Similarly Lysimachus pays compliments to Marina on account of her beauty which is a means of the achievement of goodness. This obviously is a neo-Platonic concept. There are quite a few references to the scientific knowledge also. Shakespeare refers to Ptolemy's concept of the action or movement of 'orbs' or 'spheres.' In addition to these, there are many secular ideas mentioned in *Pericles* which were commonly accepted by all the Elizabethans : the ideas like 'stars as eyes,' 'winged time,' 'heavenly music,' and 'harpies' etc. In addition to these, there are innumerable concepts from the different fields like sports (tennis), animal kingdom (vipers, serpents, sheep, whale); ornithology (meanest bird); science (glass, touchstones); social evils (beggars, selling one's wife, French coins); Nature (storms), etc., represented in *Pericles* and these, no doubt, give an encyclopedic range to the play and reflect the general ethos of the Elizabethan age, in however brief a manner it may be. These diverse strands of the Elizabethan age are part and parcel of the worldview, which was affirmative on the whole. It is on account of this reason that *Pericles* comes to have an epic atmosphere and panorama.

The technique of *Pericles*, obviously, facilitates the expression of the epic vision of life. The details of the technique may be discussed in the following paragraphs in some detail. The epic theme of *Pericles* is so rich and profound that it lends itself to a variety of interpretations. It easily fulfils the medieval concept of an epic, which is supposed to lend itself to the fourfold interpretation. *Pericles* resembles an epic in so far as it allows a variety of interpretations. It can be read not only on literal level but on allegorical, symbolic, anagogical and philosophical levels as well. Not only that, it can be interpreted even from the Marxist, the Freudian, the Japanese and the Indian points of view. On the literal level it can be read as the story of the incestuous relationship between King Antiochus and his daughter which is abhored by young Pericles who marries Thaisa and undergoes a series of great difficulties until he returns to the kingdom after the death of Antiochus and settles down for life. The story of *Pericles* can provide a good deal of wonder and entertainment to children like any other story for that matter. Secondly, it can be interpreted on the allegorical level also. Many ingenious and painstaking critics have put forth their views. For the example, Abbie Findley Potts shows the allegory of the play by pointing out the correspondence between *Pericles* and *The Fairy Queen*. Pericles, according to this interpretation, resembles the Redcrosse Knight whereas Marina and Lysimachus resemble Una and Satyrene respectively. Potts' explanation of the events is worth quoting, "With this 'Mariner' escaping shipwreck Spenser had compared the Redcrosse

Knight escaping from the House of Pride somewhat as Pericles escapes from the plot of Antiochus. Still more to our purpose is the reminder of the canto, which shows Una surprised and carried off by the satyrs, envied by the malicious Naiades, then saved from disaster, first because old Sylvanus took her to be Diana but mainly because she used her lore to teach the animalish creatures who would otherwise abuse her."[20] A little later Potts says, "Finally Marina brings Pericles back to happiness as Una accompanied the Redcrosse Knight through his discipline in the House of Holiness."[21] Such correspondences, obviously, point out the allegorical meaning of the play. Whereas Marina represents innocence, Antiochus stands for malice and wickedness. Similarly Pericles represents adventurousness and moral discipline, whereas Lysimachus stands for lechery. The characters of *Pericles* thus easily lend themselves to the allegorical interpretation and invite comparison with the allegorical works of other writers. Thirdly, the play can be interpreted on the symbolic level also. Pericles, like the other last plays belongs to the symbolic mode of writing rather than to the realistic one. The symbolic nature of the play has been noticed by many a critic. G. Wilson Knight is the chief one among them. He, therefore, says "In choosing the story of *Pericles* Shakespeare is therefore basing his new structure on his own most instinctive symbol. To put it shortly : being at a loss, he chooses a story that gives full rein to his poetic passion for voyages, tempests and wrecks.... He aims to compose a morality play around his own poetic symbolism as dogma."[22] The archetypal symbols in the play are already pointed out in the earlier paragraphs. The characters like Pericles, Marina, Thaisa and Lysimachus come to have symbolic dimensions. Pericles, for example, strikes us a man who has to face the perils of life. Marina is the child born on the sea and symbolizes the positive side of the sea. The sea-journey of Pericles itself becomes a dominant symbol. The plight of Pericles might be the plight of the humanity as well. Fourthly, the play can be interpreted on the anagogical level also. The implicit moral pattern of the play easily gives it the quality of a fable. The critics with a philosophical bent of mind have tried to interpret the play on the anagogical level. G. Wilson Knight's interpretation fulfils the requirements of the anagogical interpretation. He feels that some scenes are openly moralistic in their tone. Referring to Act II, Chorus 14, he says, "The scene, moralistic from the start, has turned into a little morality drama on the theme of good works and indeed recalls the parable of the ungrateful man in the *New Testament;* for, after being let off by Providence functioning through Pericles' charity, Cleon and Dionyza are to prove criminally ungrateful."[23] On the whole the moral of the play seems to be that a goodman (Pericles) will succeed at last in his struggle with the evil forces (Antiochus, the sea, and the storm) if he adheres to the higher principles dictated by his own conscience or by his god or goddess (Diana). Thus *Pericles* comes to resemble the other regular morality plays of England. All these kinds of interpretations are not to be taken as the only ones or the final ones. In fact, the play can be interpreted from the Freudian, the Marxist and the Indian points of view also. Even then, none of these interpretations can be the final one. But nevertheless they testify to the rich potentiality of the theme and are an evidence of the epical nature of the same. *Pericles,* no doubt, exhibits the epic stature on account of its multiple layers of meaning.

The technique of the play supports the communication of the epic vision of life. For example, Diana's appearance in Pericles' dream (V, i) and her guidance to him about the course of action he should choose in future are facilitated by the dramatic devices such as *deus ex machina* which itself facilitates the presentation of the supernatural element in the world of *Pericles*. The dreams and visions which are so common in the last plays act as the reminders of ideals which are momentarily neglected or forgotten. The dreams and visions, therefore, become the means of the epic affirmation of the transcendental order of human life. In *Pericles*, we have evidence of drama becoming a vehicle of the higher *i.e.*, epic vision of life. As far as the dream element is concerned, *Pericles* is easily comparable to the Noh Drama of Japan wherein drama is employed as an instrument of higher *i.e.*, religious or philosophical instruction.

The presence of Gower in *Pericles* is one of the very striking features of the play. Gower is considered as one man chorus. He invariably appears at the beginning of every act and narrates certain things and events and establishes the link between the preceding and the following acts. In my view, Shakespeare was subconsciously compelled to employ this device in order to express his epic vision through the medium of drama. The employment of the characters, *i.e.*, Gower enables Shakespeare to compensate for the limitations of the dramatic form. What cannot be actually presented on the stage has been narrated by Gower. Thus Gower offers continuity and unity to the theme of *Pericles*. In a way he can be taken to be an embodiment of epic imagination itself as he performs what he preaches about Shakespeare's imagination. Gower acts as a means through which Shakespeare offers a vision of the whole truth, which is the special concern of epic literature. Gower narrates the events which take place at different places at different times or simultaneously. He thus covers the large measures of time, space and captures the diverse aspects of life in order to offer the whole perspective of the issue. He, for example, narrates the action that has taken place before the play starts *i.e.*, about Antiochus, his daughter and his incestuous relation with her etc. (I, i). He then describes how Pericles flees Tharsus in order to escape murder at Thaliard's hands and journeys on the sea and is sea-tossed (II). He links up the events between Act II and Act III by providing a historical picture of events which have taken place. He describes how after the death of Antiochus and his daughter, there was a disturbance in the kingdom of Antioch about the heirship of the crown and how Pericles' arrival is awaited etc. (III). Then he narrates Pericles' arrival at his home kingdom and the germination of jealousy in Dionyza regarding

Marina (IV). Gower further describes Pericles' travel from Tharsus to Mytilene and his deep sorrow at the sight of the epitaph on the grave of the dead Marina (IV, iv). In Act V, he mentions Marina's escape from the brothel. In act V, scene ii, he refers to the regent's desire to marry Marina and Diana's postponement of the same for some time. In the epilogue, Gower mentions the ultimate reward received from life by Pericles, his wife and his daughter and his loyal courtier Helicanus; the punishment extended to Cleon and his wife for their evil thoughts and actions. The character of Gower helps Shakespeare to show what is happening at different places like Antioch, Tharsus, Pentapolis and Mytilene etc., simultaneously or chronologically. This technical devices enables Shakespeare to show the large canvas of his subject, which cannot be presented within the traditional limits of the dramatic form. Gower's narrations are preceded and followed by the usual dramatic scenes. This arrangement in fact corresponds to the epic technique where the narration is preceded and followed by representation. On many an occasion Gower makes philosophical observations about the characters and events of the play, which express the general truths of human life. Such statements, therefore, come to have the choric quality about them because they express not merely Shakespeare's personal thoughts and feelings but those of his age and country. In short, it may be said that the use of the character of Gower in *Pericles* enables Shakespeare to give an epic dimension to his play. The role of "Gower" is easily comparable to that of Sutradhara in Sanskrit plays which are epical in nature.

The use of the dumb show in *Pericles* is one of the technical peculiarities of the play. Dumb show was quite common in the medieval drama (*i.e.*, *Moralities* and *Mysteries*) as well as in the Elizabethan drama. The dumb shows in *Pericles* play an important role in that they give a symbolic dimension to the action by not restricting the meaning by articulating it but by suggesting the same through symbolic gestures. In the first dumb-show (Act II, Chorus) a messenger comes and delivers a letter to Pericles who knights him by offering him a reward. The meaning of this symbolic action is clarified by Gower's speech that follows the dumb show. In the second dumb-show (Act III, Chorus) a messenger comes and delivers a letter reading which Pericles and Thaisa grow extremely happy. The chorus that follows clarifies the meaning by stating that the letter carries the news of the demise of King Antiochus and his daughter. In the third dumb-show (Act IV, scene iv) Cleon and Dionyza show Pericles the tomb at the sight of which he begins to lament. All these dumb-shows, obviously, compress the action into the shortest possible span of time and place and give a continuity and unity to the theme of the play. These dumb-shows in *Pericles* are easily comparable to those of the Noh Drama of Japan. They not only provide the technical variety to the play but also help the dramatist to present in the form of drama what defies the dramatic treatment and achieve a panoramic completeness of theme.

The play contains a few homeric or extended similes which contribute to the epic nature of the play. Although there are a number of similes and metaphors, which are short as well as interesting, I am going to touch upon only the extended similes. Pericles' description of Antiochus is an extended simile :

> You are a fair viol, and your sense the strings,
> Who, finger'd to make man his lawful music,
> Would draw heaven down and all the gods to hearken;
> But being play'd upon before your time,
> Hell only danceth at so harsh a chime.
>
> (I, i, 82-86)

Similarly his description of the effect of vice on man is also an extended image. He says :

> For vice repeated is like the wand'ring wind,
> Blows dust in others' eyes, to spread itself;
> And yet the end of all is bought thus dear,

> The breath is gone, and the sore eyes see clear
> To stop the air would hurt them.
>
> (I, i, 97-101)

On another occasion Pericles describes his ships in a homeric fashion :

> And these our ships, you happily may think
> Are like the Trojan horses was stuff'd within
> With bloody veins expecting overthrow,
> Are stor'd with corn to make your needy bread,
> And give them life whom hunger starv'd half dead.
>
> (I, iv, 92-96)

All these similes can be designated as extended or homeric similes as they describe the things or events concerned in a complete fashion. The effect of premature action, the consequences of evil and the deceptive appearance of the ships are all described in a comprehensive, though brief fashion. These extended similes, obviously, give an epic dimension to the play.

The didactic element, which is so indigenous to epic literature, can be seen in *Pericles* also. Like the epics, *Pericles* teaches a lesson not only through its total structure of symbols but through the individual lines, which contain epigrammatic or otherwise generalizations about the truth of life. Such generalizations, obviously, give an epic reflectiveness and a philosophical profundity to the play. King Simonides generalizes about the special liking of women : "Loud music is too harsh for ladies / Since they love men in arms as well as beds" (II, iii, 96-97). Helicanus points out the great advantages of unity among the courtiers : "When peers thus knit, a kingdom ever stands" (II, iv, 58). Cleon observes about the unexpected but continual rush of troubles in life : "One sorrow never comes but brings an heir / That may succeed as his inheritor" (I, iv, 63-64). Helicanus points out the evil of flattery : "They do abuse the king that flatter him / For flattery is the bellows blows up sin" (I, iv, 49-50). Pericles refers to the instruments of sin when he says : "Poison and treason are the hands of sin" (I, i, 140). He also points out how death reminds us of the ephemerality of life : "For death remembered should be like a mirror, / Who tells us life's but breath, to trust is error" (I, i, 46-47). Such generalizations describe the eternal truths of life and add to the epic profundity of the play. G. Wilson Knight designates it as the 'gnomic'[24] element in the play.

Certain simplicity, ease and profundity as against that of the great tragedies which is marked by turbulence and torrentiality by and large characterize the language of *Pericles*. The language of *Pericles,* on the whole, exhibits the equanimity and quietude which is so indigenous to the epics. The success of the language of *Pericles* lies in the fact that it does not attract the attention of the reader to itself but directs it towards the symbolic structure of the play thereby facilitating the communication of the profound acts as instruments of the transcendental vision of life.

REFERENCES

1. Sir Arthur Quiller-Couch, *Shakespeare's Workmanship* (London : T. Fisher Unwin Ltd., 1923), p. 244.
2. Kenneth Muir, *The Sources of Shakespeare's Plays* (London : Methuen & Co., 1977), p. 345.
3. F.D. Hoeniger, "*Pericles* and the Miracle Play," in *Shakespeare's Later Comedies,* ed. D.J. Palmer, (Harmondsworth : Penguin Books Ltd., 1971), p. 216.
4. G. Wilson Knight, *Shakespeare and Religion* (London : Routledge & Kegan Paul, 1969), pp. 29-30.
5. Frederick S. Boas, *Shakespeare and His Predecessors* (Calcutta : Rupa & Co., 1963), p. 425.
6. Derek Traversi, *Shakespeare : The Last Phase* (London : Hollis & Carter, 1969), p. vii.
7. Frederick Nietzsche, *The Birth of Tragedy.* Trans. Francis Golfing (New York : Doubleday & Company Inc., 1967), p. 59.
8. Dewitt H. Parker, *Schopenhauer Selections* (New York : Charles Scribner's Sons, 1928), p. 134.
9. E.M.W. Tillyard, *Shakespeare's Last Plays* (London : Chatto & Windus, 1964), p. 26.

10. K.R. Srinivasa Iyengar, "Beyond Tragedy," in *Shakespeare : His World and His Art* (New Delhi : Sterling Publishers Pvt. Ltd., 1986), p. 573.
11. Allardyce Nicolls, "Shakespeare and the Court Masque," in *Shakespeare's Later Comedies,* ed. D.J. Palmer, p. 169.
12. G.A. Baker, "Themes and Variations in *Pericles,*" in *Shakespeare's Later Comedies,* ed. D.J. Palmer, p. 212.
13. John Steinfort Kedney, *Hegel's Aesthetics : A Critical Exposition* (Chicago : Scott, Foresman & Company, 1897), p. 298.
14. J.F. Danby, "*Pericles, Arcadia*, and the Scheme of Romance," in *Shakespeare's Later Comedies,* ed. D.J. Palmer, p. 191.
15. Georg Lukaks, *The Theory of the Novel* (London : Merlin Press, 1978), p. 66.
16. John Willet ed. & tr. *Brecht on Theatre* (New York : Hill and Wang, 1977), pp. 22-38.
17. Stanley Wells, "Shakespeare and Romance," in *Shakespeare's Later Comedies,* ed. D.J. Palmer, p. 118.
18. M.C. Bradbrook, *The Growth and Structure of Elizabethan Comedy,* (Cambridge : Cambridge University Press, 1973), p. 199.
19. J.F. Danby, "*Pericles,* Arcadia, and the Scheme of Romance." In *Shakespeare's Later Comedies,* ed. D.J. Palmer, p. 193.
20. Abbie Findley Potts, *Shakespeare and the Farie Queen* (New York : Cornell University Press, 1958), pp. 220-22.
21. *Ibidem.,* pp. 223-24.
22. G. Wilson Knight, *The Crown of Life* (London : Oxford University Press, 1947), p. 70.
23. *Ibidem,* p. 70.
24. *Ibidem*, p. 48.

LIST OF CONTRIBUTORS

R.S. Pathak, Professor and Head, Department of English and other European Languages, Dr. Harisingh Gour University, Sagar, Madhya Pradesh.

Shabiba Khan (Mrs.), Assistant Professor of English, Saifia PG College, Bhopal, Madhya Pradesh.

Mohit K. Ray, Professor of English, Burdwan University, Burdwan, West Bengal.

Basavaraj Naikar, Professor and Chairman, Department of Studies in English, Karnataka University, Pavate Nagar, Dharwad, Karnataka.

N. Narasimha Ramayya, 4-44, Buddanagar Colony, Near Sri Sai Model School, Peerzadiguda, Uppal, Hyderabad, Andhra Pradesh.

Shweta Khanna, Institute of Technology, Banaras Hindu University, Varanasi, Uttar Pradesh.

Sudhir Dixit, Department of English, Government Narmada P.G. College, Hoshangabad, Madhya Pradesh.

B.G. Tandon, 232, Mahashwetanagar, Ujjain, Madhya Pradesh.

Rama Kundu, Professor of English, Burdwan University, Burdwan, West Bengal.

Sahadeo A. Chougule, Reader in English, Night College Kolhapur, Maharashtra.

O.P. Budholia, Department of English, K.R.G. Government (Autonomous) College, Gwalior, Madhya Pradesh.

Nivedita Mukerjee, Department of English, Government P.G. College, BHEL, Bhopal, Madhya Pradesh.